Domain-Driven Design in PHP

A Highly Practical Guide

Carlos Buenosvinos
Christian Soronellas
Keyvan Akbary

BIRMINGHAM - MUMBAI

Domain-Driven Design in PHP

First published: June 2017

Production reference: 1090617

Published by Packt Publishing Ltd.
Livery Place
35 Livery Street
Birmingham
B3 2PB, UK.

ISBN 978-1-78728-494-4

www.packtpub.com

Credits

Authors

Carlos Buenosvinos
Christian Soronellas
Keyvan Akbary

Acquisition Editor

Frank Pohlmann

Indexer

Pratik Shirodkar

Technical Editor

Joel Wilfred D'souza

Layout co-ordinator

Aparna Bhagat

Foreword

I must admit that when I first heard of the *Domain-Driven Design in PHP* initiative, I was a bit worried. The danger was twofold: first of all, when glancing over the table of contents, the subject matter looked like it was a rehash of content that was already available in several other Domain-Driven Design books. Second, writing a book on Domain-Driven Design targeted specifically toward the PHP community seemed needlessly narrowing, particularly as Domain-Driven Design itself is not language specific. As such, this might inhibit PHP developers from looking past the boundaries of their own community, especially when considering that there's a lot going on beyond the scope of PHP. In fact, even Domain-Driven Design is one of those things, as it didn't originate in the PHP community.

After reading the book, I'm happy to inform you that my worries have been invalidated!

With regard to my first concern: of course there is some overlap with previously published Domain-Driven Design books. Yet the authors have restrained themselves. The theoretical parts are exactly what you need to be able to understand what's going on in the code samples. Besides, if you never read another Domain-Driven Design book, this one gives you what you need to start applying some Domain-Driven Design principles and patterns in your code, as it's practical by nature.

My second concern — about the PHP aspect of this book — has been addressed very well. It turns out there are a lot of things to say about Domain-Driven Design *in a PHP world*. This book is specifically targeted at an audience consisting of PHP developers. The code samples resemble real-world PHP projects, and the authors use a programming style we know from projects using Symfony or Silex. For persisting Domain objects, Doctrine ORM — which is the *de facto* standard data mapper for PHP — is used.

This book also fulfills a need I've often seen in the PHP community: the need for concrete examples. It's not always easy for authors to come up with proper illustrations of how to apply certain ideas that have a low risk of being misinterpreted or abused in real-world projects. And in Domain-Driven Design, which is philosophical by nature, this is even more challenging.

In the case of this book, the authors haven't been afraid to show many useful examples, along with some interesting alternative solutions. They aren't just handwaving at solutions either; they take the time to provide detailed explanations — such as when they talk about saving snapshots for Aggregates with a large number of Domain Events, or when they discuss integrating Bounded Contexts using RabbitMQ. I can't recall having previously seen an implementation of these things in a book or article on Domain-Driven Design.

For me personally, Domain-Driven Design is one the most interesting subjects in software development today. There is so much to discover, and there are many subjects related to it: Agile software development, TDD, and BDD, but also living documentation, visualization, and knowledge crunching techniques. Once you start looking into all of this, you'll realize that Domain-Driven Design is an area of expertise worth investigating, as it enables you to add much more to your own worth as a software developer.

So, I guess what I want to say is this: dive into this book, learn from it, and then pick up another book (see the list of references at the end of this book for suggestions of future reading). Continuous learning is a fundamental part of keeping up to date in the software industry, so don't stop here.

Oh, and by the way: if you get a chance to go to Barcelona, make sure you take part in one of the many PHP or Symfony events. The community is big, friendly, and full of interesting ideas. You'll find the authors of this book there too. They are all invested in the local PHP community and are happy to share their insights and experiences with you!

Matthias Noback
Author of `A Year with Symfony`

About the Authors

Carlos Buenosvinos is a PHP Extreme Programmer with more than 15 years of experience developing web applications and more than 10 years experience as a Tech Lead and CTO leading teams of between 20 and 100 people. He is a Certified ScrumMaster (CSM) and has coached and trained close to two dozen different companies in Agile practices, both as an employee and as a consultant. On the technical side, he is a Zend PHP Engineer, a Zend Framework Engineer, and MySQL certified. He is also a board member of the PHP Barcelona User Group. He has worked with e-commerce (Atrapalo and eBay), payment processing (Vendo), classifieds (Emagister), and B2B recruiting tools (XING). He is interested in JavaScript, DevOps, and Scala. He likes developing for mobile, Raspberry Pi, and games.

- Twitter: `@buenosvinos`
- Web: `https://carlosbuenosvinos.com`
- GitHub: `https://github.com/carlosbuenosvinos`

Christian Soronellas is a passionate Software Developer, Software Journeyman, and Craftsman Apprentice. He's an Extreme Programmer soul with more than 10 years of experience in web development. He's also a Zend PHP 5.3 Certified Engineer, a Zend Framework Certified Engineer, and a SensioLabs Certified Symfony Developer. He has worked as a freelancer, as well as at Privalia, Emagister, Atrapalo, and Enalquiler as a Software Architect.

- Twitter: `@theUniC`
- GitHub: `https://github.com/theUniC`

Keyvan Akbary is a polyglot Software Developer who loves Software fundamentals, the Craftsmanship movement, Extreme Programming, SOLID principles, Clean Code, Design Patterns, and Testing. He's also a sporadic Functional Programmer. He understands technology as a medium for providing value. He has worked on countless projects as a freelancer, on video streaming (Youzee), and on an online marketplace (MyBuilder) — all in addition to founding a crowdfunding company (Funddy). Currently, Keyvan is working in FinTech as a Lead Developer at TransferWise London.

- Twitter: `@keyvanakbary`
- Web: `http://keyvanakbary.com`
- GitHub: `https://github.com/keyvanakbary`

Acknowledgments

First of all, we would like to thank all our friends and family. Without their support, writing this book would have been an even more difficult task. Thanks for accommodating our schedules and taking care of our children in order to free up time for us to focus on writing. You're wonderful, and part of this book is also yours.

We are three Spaniards who wrote a book in English, so if you'd guess our English is far from perfect, you'd be correct. Luckily for us, `Edd Mann` has supported us with the language since the beginning. He's not just a great collaborator but also a great friend, and we owe him a huge thanks. The final review was done by the professional copy editor `Natalye Childress`. She has done a great work rewriting our words to make them understandable. Thank you so much. Our book is easier and more enjoyable to read.

A group of PHP developers in Barcelona defends what we call *el camino del rigor*, or *the path of rigor*. It existed before the *craftsmanship* movement, and it means to struggle with everything stacked against us in order to build exceptional things in an exceptional way. Two particular developers and friends from that group are `Albert Casademont` and `Ricard Clau`, both of whom are extraordinary people committed to the community. Thank you so much for helping with the revision process. Your contributions have been incredibly valuable.

We would like to thank every developer who has worked with us in the companies where we've applied Domain-Driven Design. We know you've been struggling when learning and applying these concepts. Some of you weren't so open-minded at the beginning, but after using the basic building blocks for a while, you became evangelists. Thanks for your faith.

Our book was for sale from the moment we put the first chapters on `Leanpub`. Early adopters who bought the book in its beginning stages gave us the much needed love and support to get this done. Thanks for the motivation to keep going.

Thanks also to `Matthias Noback` for his foreword and feedback on the book. The end result is better because of his contributions.

A special mention to `Vaughn Vernon` — not just because his work was an incredible source of information and inspiration for us, but also because he helped us find a good publisher, gave us valuable advice, and shared ideas with us. Thanks so much for your help.

Last but not least, we'd like to express our gratitude to all the people who have reported issues, made suggestions, and otherwise contributed to our `GitHub repository`. To all of you, thank you. You've helped us make this book better. More importantly, you've helped the community grow and helped other developers be better developers. As `Robert C. Martin` wrote in his book, `Clean Code: A Handbook of Agile Software Craftsmanship`, "You are reading this book for two reasons. First, you are a programmer. Second, you want to be a better programmer. Good. We need better programmers." So thanks to Jordi Abad, Jonathan Wondrusch, César Rodríguez, Yannick Voyer, Victor Guardiola, Oriol González, Henry Snoek, Tom Jowitt, Sascha Schimke, Sven Herrmann, Daniel Abad, Luis Rovirosa, Luis Cordova, Raúl Ramos, Juan Maturana, Nil Portugués, Nikolai Zujev, Fernando Pradas, Raúl Araya, Neal Brooks, Hubert Béague, Aleksander Rekść, Sebastian Machuca, Nicolas Oelgart, Sebastiaan Stok, Vladimir Hraban, Vladas Dirzys, and Marc Aube.

www.PacktPub.com

For support files and downloads related to your book, please visit www.PacktPub.com.

Did you know that Packt offers eBook versions of every book published, with PDF and ePub files available? You can upgrade to the eBook version at www.PacktPub.com and as a print book customer, you are entitled to a discount on the eBook copy. Get in touch with us at service@packtpub.com for more details.

At www.PacktPub.com, you can also read a collection of free technical articles, sign up for a range of free newsletters and receive exclusive discounts and offers on Packt books and eBooks.

https://www.packtpub.com/mapt

Get the most in-demand software skills with Mapt. Mapt gives you full access to all Packt books and video courses, as well as industry-leading tools to help you plan your personal development and advance your career.

Why subscribe?

- Fully searchable across every book published by Packt
- Copy and paste, print, and bookmark content
- On demand and accessible via a web browser

Customer Feedback

Thanks for purchasing this Packt book. At Packt, quality is at the heart of our editorial process.

If you'd like to join our team of regular reviewers, you can e-mail us at customerreviews@packtpub.com. We award our regular reviewers with free eBooks and videos in exchange for their valuable feedback. Help us be relentless in improving our products!

This book is dedicated to my dearest Vanessa, and to Valentina and Gabriela. Thanks for your love, your support, and your patience.

– Carlos

To my dear Elena. Without your encouragement, your love, and your patience, this book would not have been possible.

– Christian

To my parents, John and Mercedes, who raised me free of constraints. This will be the first book of many. To my love, Clara, for your unconditional support and infinite patience.

– Keyvan

Table of Contents

Preface

In 2014, after two years of reading about and working with Domain-Driven Design, Carlos and Christian, friends and workmates, traveled to Berlin to participate in Vaughn Vernon's `Implementing Domain-Driven Design Workshop`. The training was fantastic, and all the concepts that were swirling around in their minds prior to the trip suddenly became very real. However, they were the only two PHP developers in a room full of Java and .NET developers.

Around the same time, `php[tek]`, an annual PHP conference, opened its call for papers, and Carlos sent one about Hexagonal Architecture. His talk was rejected, but Eli White — of `musketeers.me` and `php[architect]` fame — got in touch with him a month later wondering if he was interested in writing an article about Hexagonal Architecture for the magazine php[architect]. So in June 2014, *Hexagonal Architecture with PHP* was published. That article, which you'll find in the `Appendix`, was the origin of this book.

In late 2014, Carlos and Christian talked about extending the article and sharing all their knowledge of and experience in applying Domain-Driven Design in production. They were very excited about the idea behind the book: helping the PHP community delve into Domain-Driven Design from a practical approach. At that time, concepts such as Rich Domain Models and framework-agnostic applications weren't so common in the PHP community. So in December 2014, the first commit to the GitHub book repository was pushed.

Around the same time, in a parallel universe, Keyvan co-founded Funddy, a crowdfunding platform for the masses built on top of the concepts and building blocks of Domain-Driven Design. Domain-Driven Design proved itself effective in the exploratory process and modeling of building an early-stage startup like Funddy. It also helped handle the complexity of the company, with its constantly changing environment and requirements. And after connecting with Carlos and Christian and discussing the book, Keyvan proudly signed on as the third writer.

Together, we've written the book we wanted to have when we started with Domain-Driven Design. It's full of examples, production-ready code, shortcuts, and our recommendations based on our experiences of what worked and what didn't for our respective teams. We arrived at Domain-Driven Design via its building blocks — Tactical Patterns — which is why this book is mainly about them. Reading it will help you learn them, write them, and implement them. You'll also discover how to integrate Bounded Contexts using synchronous and asynchronous approaches, which will open your world to strategic design — though the latter is a road you'll have to discover on your own.

This book is heavily inspired by `Implementing Domain-Driven Design` by Vaughn Vernon (aka *the Red Book*), and `Domain-Driven Design: Tackling Complexity in the Heart of Software` by Eric Evans (aka *the Blue Book*). You should buy both books. You should read them carefully. You should love them.

Who Should Read This Book

If you're a PHP Developer, Architect, or Tech Lead, we highly recommend this book. It will help you become a better professional. It will give you a new overview of and approach to the applications you're developing. If you're a Junior profile, getting into Value Objects, Entities, Repositories, and Domain Events is important in order to model any Domain you'll face in the future. For an average profile, understanding the benefits of Hexagonal Architecture and the boundaries between your framework and your Application is key for writing code that's easier to maintain in the real world (framework migrations, testing, etc.). More advanced readers will have fun both exploring how to use Domain Events in order to integrate Applications and delving deeper into Aggregate design.

Although Domain-Driven Design is not about technology, you still need it to make HTTP requests to access your Domain. Throughout the book, we recommend using specific PHP frameworks and libraries, such as Symfony, Silex, and Doctrine. For some examples, we also use specific technologies, such as MySQL, RabbitMQ, Redis, and Elasticsearch. However, most important are the behind-the-scenes concepts — concepts that are applicable regardless of the technology used to implement them.

Additionally, the book is loaded with tons of details and examples, such as how to properly design and implement all the building blocks of Domain-Driven Design — including Value Objects, Entities, Services, Domain Events, Aggregates, Factories, Repositories, and Application Services — with PHP. It explains what the role of the main PHP libraries and frameworks used in Domain-Driven Design are. The book also teaches how to apply Hexagonal Architecture within your application, regardless of whether you use an open source framework or your own one. Finally, it shows how to integrate Bounded Contexts using REST frameworks and messaging mechanisms. If you're interested in any of these subjects, this book is for you.

DDD and PHP Community

In 2016, Carlos and Christian went to the first official Domain-Driven Design conference, `DDD Europe`. They were really happy to see some PHP open source leaders, such as Marco Pivetta (Doctrine) and Sebastian Bergmann (PHPUnit), attending the conference.

Domain-Driven Design arrived in the PHP community two years prior to that conference. However, there's still a lack of documentation and real code examples. Why? We think not many people have worked with this kind of approach in production yet — even people in other more established communities such as Java. Maybe this is because their project complexity is low, or maybe it's because they don't know how to do it. Whatever the reason, this book is written for the community. One of our goals is to teach you how you can write an application that solves your Domain issues without being coupled to specific frameworks or technologies.

Summary of Chapters

The book is arranged with each chapter exploring a separate tactical building block of Domain-Driven Design. It also includes an introduction to Domain-Driven Design, information on how to integrate different Bounded Contexts or applications, and an appendix.

Chapter 1: Getting Started with Domain-Driven Design

What is Domain-Driven Design about? What role does it play in complex systems? Is it worth learning about and exploring? What are the main concepts a developer needs to know when jumping into it?

Chapter 2: Architectural Styles

Bounded Contexts can be implemented in different ways and using different approaches. However, two styles are getting more popular, and they are Hexagonal Architecture and CQRS + ES. In this chapter, we'll see these two main Architectural Styles, understand what their main strengths are, and discover when to use them.

Chapter 3: Value Objects

Value Objects are the basic pieces for rich modeling. We'll learn what their properties are and what makes them so important. We'll figure out how to persist them using Doctrine and custom ORMs. We'll show how to properly validate and unit test them. And finally, we'll see what a test case of testing immutability looks like.

Chapter 4: Entities

Entities are Domain-Driven Design building blocks that are uniquely identified and mutable. We'll see how to create and validate them and how to properly map them using a custom ORM and Doctrine. We'll also assess whether or not annotations are the best mapping approach for Entities and look at the different strategies for generating an Identity.

Chapter 5: Domain Services

In this chapter, you'll learn about what a Domain Service is and when to use it. We'll review what Anemic Domain Models and Rich Domain Models are. Lastly, we'll deal with Infrastructure issues when writing Domain Services.

Chapter 6: Domain-Events

Domain Events are a great Inversion of Control (IoC) mechanism. In Domain-Driven Design, they're important for communicating different Bounded Contexts asynchronously, improving your Application performance using eventual consistency, and decoupling your Application from its Infrastructure.

Chapter 7: Modules

With so many tactical building blocks, it's a bit difficult to know where to place them in code, especially if you're dealing with a framework like Symfony. We'll review how PHP namespaces can be used for implementing Modules. We'll also discover different hierarchies of folders for organizing Domain Model code, Application Code, and Infrastructure Code.

Chapter 8: Aggregates

Aggregates are probably the most difficult part of tactical Domain-Driven Design. We'll look at the key concepts when dealing with them and discover how to design them. We'll also propose a practical scenario where two Aggregates become one when adding a business rule, and we'll demonstrate how the rest of the objects must be refactored.

Chapter 9: Factories

Factory Methods and objects help us keep business invariants, which is why they're so important in Domain-Driven Design. Here, we'll also explore the relationship between Factories and Aggregates.

Chapter 10: Repositories

Repositories are key for retrieving and adding Entities and Aggregates to collections. We'll review the different types of Repositories and learn how to implement them using Doctrine, custom ORMs, and Redis.

Chapter 11: Application

An Application is the thin layer that connects outside clients to your Domain. In this chapter, we'll show you how to write your Application Services so that they're easy to test and keep thin. We'll also review how to prepare request objects, define dependencies, and return results.

Chapter 12: Integrating Bounded Contexts

We'll explore the different tactical approaches to communicate Bounded Contexts and see real implementations. REST is our suggestion for synchronous communication, and messaging with RabbitMQ is our suggestion for asynchronous communication.

Appendix: Hexagonal Architecture with PHP

Here is where you'll find the original article written by Carlos and published by php[architect] in June 2014.

Code and Examples

The authors have created an organization at GitHub called `Domain-Driven Design in PHP`, which is where all the code examples from this book, additional snippets, and some complete sample projects are available. For example, you can find `Last Wishes`, a simple Domain-Driven Design-style application showing different examples explained in this book. Additionally, you'll find our *CQRS Blog*, along with `Gamify`, a Bounded Context that adds gamification capabilities to *Last Wishes*.

Finally, if you find any issue or fix or have a suggestion or comment while reading this book, you can create an issue in the `DDD in PHP Book Issues` repository. We fix them as they come in. If you're interested, we also urge you to watch our projects and provide feedback.

1
Getting Started with Domain-Driven Design

So what is all the fuss about? If you've already read books on this topic by Vaughn Vernon and Eric Evans, you're probably familiar with what we're about to say, as we borrow heavily from their definitions and explanations. **Domain-Driven Design** (DDD), is an approach that helps us succeed in understanding and building software model designs. It provides us with *strategic* and *tactical* modeling tools to aid designing high-quality software that meets our business goals.

 The main goal of this book is to show you PHP code examples of the Domain-Driven Design tactical patterns. If you want to learn more about the strategic patterns and the main Domain-Driven Design, you should read `Domain Driven Design Distilled` by *Vaughn Vernon* or `Domain-Driven Design Reference: Definitions and Pattern Summaries` by *Eric Evans*.

More importantly, *Domain-Driven Design is not about technology*. Instead, it's about developing knowledge around business and using technology to provide value. Only once you're capable of understanding the business your company works within will you be able to participate in the software model discovery process to produce a Ubiquitous Language.

Why Domain-Driven Design Matters

Software is not just about code. If you think about it, code is rarely the end goal of our profession. Code is just the medium to solve business problems. So why does it have to talk a different language? Domain-Driven Design emphasizes making sure businesses and software speak the same language. Once broken the barrier, there is no need for translations or tedious syncing, information doesn't get lost. Everyone contributes to discovering the Business Domain, not just coders. The resulting software is the only truth for the common language.

Domain-Driven Design it also provides a framework for strategic and tactical design — strategic to pinpoint the most important areas to develop based on business value, and tactical to build a working Domain Model of battle-tested building blocks and patterns.

The Three Pillars of Domain-Driven Design

Domain-Driven Design is an approach for delivering software, and it's focused on three pillars:

1. **Ubiquitous Language**: Domain Experts and software developers work together to build a common language for the business areas being developed. There's no *us versus them*; it's always *us*. Developing software is a business investment and not just a cost. The effort involved in building the Ubiquitous Language helps spread deep Domain insight among all team members.
2. **Strategic Design**: Domain-Driven Design addresses the strategy behind the direction of the business and not just the technical aspects. It helps define the internal relationships and early warning feedback systems. On the technical side, strategic design protects each business service by providing the motivation for how an service-oriented architecture should be achieved.
3. **Tactical Design**: Domain-Driven Design provides the tools and the building blocks for iterative software deliverable. Tactical design tools produce software that is not only correct, but that is also testable and less error prone.

Ubiquitous Language

Along with `Chapter 12`, *Integrating Bounded Contexts*, Ubiquitous Language is one of the main strengths of Domain-Driven Design.

 In Terms of Context
For now, consider that a Bounded Context is a conceptual boundary around a system. The Ubiquitous Language inside a boundary has a specific contextual meaning. Concepts outside of this context can have different meanings.

So, how to find, explore and capture this very special language, the following pointers would highlight the same:

- Identify key business processes, their inputs, and their outputs
- Create a glossary of terms and definitions
- Capture important software concepts with some kind of documentation
- Share and expand upon the collected knowledge with the rest of the team (Developers and Domain Experts)

Since Domain-Driven Design was born, new techniques for improving the process of building the Ubiquitous Language have emerged. The most important one, which is used regularly now, is Event Storming.

Event Storming

Alberto Brandolini explains Event Storming and its advantages in a `blog post`, and he does it far more succinctly than we could.Event Storming is a workshop format for quickly exploring complex business domains:

- It is **powerful**: It has allowed me and many practitioners to come up with a comprehensive model of a complete business flow in hours instead of weeks.
- It is **engaging**: The whole idea is to bring people with the questions and people who know the answer in the same room and to build a model together.
- It is **efficient**: The resulting model is perfectly aligned with a Domain-Driven Design implementation style (particularly fitting an Event Sourcing approach), and allows for a quick determination of Context and Aggregate boundaries.

- It is **easy**: The notation is ultra-simple. No complex UML that might cut off participants from the heart of the discussion.
- It is **fun**: I always had a great time leading the workshops, people are energized and deliver more than they expected. The right questions arise, and the atmosphere is the right one.

If you want to know more about Event Storming, check out Brandolini's book, `Introducing EventStorming`.

Considering Domain-Driven Design

Domain-Driven Design is not a silver bullet; as with everything in software, it depends on the context. As a rule of thumb, use it to simplify your Domain, but never to add more complexity.

If your application is data-centric and your use cases mainly manipulate rows in a database and perform CRUD operations — that is, Create, Read, Update, and Delete — you don't need Domain-Driven Design. Instead, the only thing your company needs is a fancy face in front of your database.

If your application has less than 30 use cases, it might be simpler to use a framework like Symfony or Laravel to handle your business logic.

However, if your application has more than 30 use cases, your system may be moving toward the dreaded `Big Ball of Mud`. If you know for sure your system will grow in complexity, you should consider using Domain-Driven Design to fight that complexity.

If you know your application is going to grow and is likely to change often, Domain-Driven Design will definitely help in managing the complexity and refactoring your model over time.

If you don't understand the Domain you're working on because it's new and nobody has invested in a solution before, this might mean it's complex enough for you to start applying Domain-Driven Design. In this case, you'll need to work closely with Domain Experts to get the models right.

The Tricky Parts

Applying Domain-Driven Design is not easy. It requires time and effort to get around the Business Domain, terminology, research, and collaboration with Domain Experts rather than coding jargon. You'll need to have the commitment of Domain Experts for getting involved in the process too. This will requires an open and healthy continuous conversation to model their spoken language into software. On top of that, we'll have to make an effort to avoid thinking technically, to think seriously about the behavior of objects and the Ubiquitous Language first.

Strategical Overview

In order to provide a general overview of the strategical side of Domain-Driven Design, we'll use an approach from *Jimmy Nilsson's* book, `Applying Domain-Driven Design and Patterns`. Consider two different spaces: the problem space and the solution space.

In the problem space, Domain-Driven Design uses Domains and Subdomains to group and organize what companies want to solve. In the case of an **Online Travel Agency (OTA)**, the problem is about dealing with things like flight tickets and booking hotels. Such a Domain can be organized into different Subdomains such as Pricing, Inventory, User Management, and so on.

In the solution space, Domain-Driven Design provides two patterns: Bounded Contexts and Context Maps. The goal is to define how to provide an implementation to all the identified Subdomains by defining their interactions and the details of those interactions. Continuing with the OTA example, each of the Subdomains will be solved with a Bounded Context implementation — for example, consider a custom Web Application developed by a team for the Pricing Management Subdomain, and an off-the-shelf solution for the User Management Subdomain. The Context Map will show how each Bounded Context is related to the rest. Inside the Context Map, we can see what type of relation two Bounded Contexts have (example: customer-supplier, partners). The ideal approach is to have each Subdomain implemented by one Bounded Context, but that's not always possible. In terms of implementation, when following Domain-Driven Design, you'll end up with distributed architectures. As you may already know, distributed architectures are more complex than monolithic ones, so why is this approach interesting, especially for big and complex companies? Is it really worth it? Well, it is.

Distributed architectures are proven to increase overall company productivity because they define boundaries for your product that can be developed by focused teams.

If your Domain — the problem you need to solve — is not complex, applying the strategical part of Domain-Driven Design can add unnecessary overhead and slow down your development speed.

If you want to know more about the strategical part of Domain-Driven Design, you should take a look at the first three chapters of *Vaughn Vernon's* book, `Implementing Domain-Driven Design`, or the book `Domain-Driven Design: Tackling Complexity in the Heart of Software` by *Eric Evans*, both of which specifically focus on this aspect.

Related Movements: Microservices and Self-Contained Systems

There are other movements promoting architectures that follow the same principles Domain-Driven Design is promoting. Microservices and Self-Contained Systems are good examples of this. *James Lewis* and *Martin Fowler* define Microservices in the `Microservices Resource Guide`:

> The Microservice architectural style is an approach to developing a single application as a suite of small services, each running in its own process and communicating with lightweight mechanisms, often an HTTP resource API. These services are built around business capabilities and are also independently deployable using fully automated machinery. There is a bare minimum of centralized management of these services, which may be written in different programming languages and also use different data storage technologies.

If you want to know more about Microservices, their guide is a good place to start.How is this related to Domain-Driven Design? As explained in *Sam Newman's* book, `Building Microservices`, Microservices are implementations of Domain-Driven Design Bounded Contexts.

In addition to Microservices, another related movement is **Self-Contained Systems** (**SCS**). According to the `Self-Contained Systems` website:

> The Self-contained System approach is an architecture that focuses on a separation of the functionality into many independent systems, making the complete logical system a collaboration of many smaller software systems. This avoids the problem of large monoliths that grow constantly and eventually become unmaintainable. Over the past few years, we have seen its benefits in many mid-sized and large-scale projects. The idea is to break a large system apart into several smaller self-contained system, or SCSs, that follow certain rules.

The website also spells out seven characteristics of SCS:

> Each SCS is an autonomous web application. For the SCS's domain all data, the logic to process that data and all code to render the web interface is contained within the SCS. An SCS can fulfill its primary use cases on its own, without having to rely on other systems being available.

> Each SCS is owned by one team. This does not necessarily mean that only one team might change the code, but the owning team has the final say on what goes into the code base, for example by merging pull-requests.

> Communication with other SCSs or 3rd party systems is asynchronous wherever possible. Specifically, other SCSs or external systems should not be accessed synchronously within the SCS's own request/response cycle. This decouples the systems, reduces the effects of failure, and thus supports autonomy. The goal is decoupling concerning time: An SCS should work even if other SCSs are temporarily offline. This can be achieved even if the communication on the technical level is synchronous, example by replicating data or buffering requests.

> An SCS can have an optional service API. Because the SCS has its own web UI it can interact with the user — without going through a UI service. However, an API for mobile clients or for other SCSs might still be useful.

> Each SCS must include data and logic. To really implement any meaningful features both are needed. An SCS should implement features by itself and must therefore include both.

> An SCS should make its features usable to end-users by its own UI. Therefore the SCS should have no shared UI with other SCSs. SCSs might still have links to each other. However, asynchronous integration means that the SCS should still work even if the UI of another SCS is not available. To avoid tight coupling an SCS should share no business code with other SCSs. It might be fine to create a pull-request for an SCS or use common libraries, example: database drivers or oAuth clients.

Exercise
Discuss the pros and cons of such distributed architectures with your workmates. Think about using different languages, deployment processes, infrastructure responsibilities, and so on.

Wrap-Up

During this chapter you've learned:

- Domain-Driven Design is not about technology; it's actually about providing value in the field you're working in by focusing on the model. Everyone takes part in the process of discovering the Domain, and developers and Domain Experts team up to build the knowledge base by sharing the same language, the Ubiquitous Language.
- Domain-Driven Design provides tactical and strategic modeling tools to design high-quality software. Strategic design targets the business direction, helps in defining the internal relationships, and technically protects each business service by defining strong boundaries. Tactical design provides useful building blocks for iterative design.
- Domain-Driven Design only makes sense in certain contexts. It's not a silver bullet for every problem in software, so whether or not you use it highly depends on the amount of complexity you're dealing with.
- Domain-Driven Design is a long-term investment; it requires active effort. Domain Experts will be required to collaborate closely with developers, and developers will have to think in terms of the business. In the end, the business customer is the one who has to be pleased.

Implementing Domain-Driven Design requires effort. If it were easy, everybody would be writing high-quality code. Get ready, because you'll soon learn how to write code that, when read, will perfectly describe the business your company operates on. Enjoy this journey!

2
Architectural Styles

In order to be able to build complex applications, one of the key requirements is having an architectural design that fits the application's needs. One advantage of Domain-Driven Design is that it's not tied to any particular architecture style. Instead, we're free to choose the architecture that best fits the needs of every Bounded Context inside the Core Domain, which offers a diverse set of architectural choices for every specific Domain problem.

For example, an Order Processing System can use Event Sourcing to track all the different order operations; a Product Catalog can use CQRS to expose the product details to the different clients; and a Content Management System can use plain Hexagonal Architecture to expose requirements such as blogs, static pages, and so on.

This chapter presents an introduction to every relevant architecture style in the land of PHP, following the evolution from traditional old school PHP code to a more sophisticated architecture. Please note that although there are many other existing architecture styles, such as Data Fabric or SOA, we found some of them a bit too complex to introduce from the PHP perspective.

The Good Old Days

Before the release of PHP 4, the language didn't embrace the Object-Oriented paradigm. Back then, the usual way of writing applications was by using procedures and global state. Concepts like **Separation of Concerns (SoC)** and **Model-View-Controller (MVC)** were alien among the PHP community.

The example below is an application written in this traditional way, where applications were composed of many front controllers mixed with HTML code. During this time, Infrastructure-, Presentation-, UI-, and Domain-layer code were all tangled together:

```php
include __DIR__ . '/bootstrap.php';

$link = mysql_connect('localhost', 'a_username', '4_p4ssw0rd');

if (!$link) {
    die('Could not connect: ' . mysql_error());
}

mysql_set_charset('utf8', $link);
mysql_select_db('my_database', $link);

$errormsg = null ;
if (isset($_POST['submit'] && isValid($_POST['post']))) {
    $post = getFrom($_POST['post']);
    mysql_query('START TRANSACTION', $link);
    $sql = sprintf(
        "INSERT INTO posts (title, content) VALUES ('%s','%s')",
        mysql_real_escape_string($post['title']),
        mysql_real_escape_string($post['content']
    ));

    $result = mysql_query($sql, $link);
    if ($result) {
        mysql_query('COMMIT', $link);
    } else {
        mysql_query('ROLLBACK', $link);
        $errormsg = 'Post could not be created! :(';
    }
}

$result = mysql_query('SELECT id, title, content FROM posts', $link);
?>
<html>
    <head></head>
    <body>
        <?php if (null !== $errormsg) : ?>
            <div class="alert error"><?php echo $errormsg; ?></div>
        <?php else: ?>
            <div class="alert success">
                Bravo! Post was created successfully!
            </div>
        <?php endif; ?>
        <table>
            <thead><tr><th>ID</th><th>TITLE</th>
```

```
            <th>ACTIONS</th></tr></thead>
            <tbody>
            <?php while($post = mysql_fetch_assoc($result)) : ?>
                <tr>
                    <td><?php echo $post['id']; ?></td>
                    <td><?php echo $post['title']; ?></td>
                    <td><?php editPostUrl($post['id']); ?></td>
                </tr>
            <?php endwhile; ?>
            </tbody>
        </table>
    </body>
</html>
<?php mysql_close($link); ?>
```

This style of coding is often referred to as the *Big Ball of Mud* we mentioned in the first chapter. An improvement seen in this style, however, was to encapsulate the header and the footer of the webpage in their own separate files, which were included in the header and footer files. This avoided duplication and favored reuse:

```
include __DIR__ . '/bootstrap.php';

$link = mysql_connect('localhost', 'a_username', '4_p4ssw0rd');

if (!$link) {
    die('Could not connect: ' . mysql_error());
}

mysql_set_charset('utf8', $link);
mysql_select_db('my_database', $link);

$errormsg = null;

if (isset($_POST['submit'] && isValid($_POST['post'])) {
    $post = getFrom($_POST['post']);
    mysql_query('START TRANSACTION', $link);
    $sql = sprintf(
        "INSERT INTO posts(title, content) VALUES('%s','%s')",
        mysql_real_escape_string($post['title']),
        mysql_real_escape_string($post['content'])
    );

    $result = mysql_query($sql, $link);
    if ($result) {
        mysql_query('COMMIT', $link);
    } else {
        mysql_query('ROLLBACK', $link);
        $errormsg = 'Post could not be created! :(';
```

```
        }
    }

    $result = mysql_query('SELECT id, title, content FROM posts', $link);
    ?>
    <?php include __DIR__ . '/header.php'; ?>
    <?php if (null !== $errormsg) : ?>
        <div class="alert error"><?php echo $errormsg; ?></div>
    <?php else: ?>
        <div class="alert success">
            Bravo! Post was created successfully!
        </div>
    <?php endif; ?>
    <table>
        <thead>
            <tr>
                <th>ID</th>
                <th>TITLE</th>
                <th>ACTIONS</th>
            </tr>
        </thead>
        <tbody>
        <?php while($post = mysql_fetch_assoc($result)): ?>
            <tr>
                <td><?php echo $post['id']; ?></td>
                <td><?php echo $post['title']; ?></td>
                <td><?php editPostUrl($post['id']); ?></td>
            </tr>
        <?php endwhile; ?>
        </tbody>
    </table>
    <?php include __DIR__ . '/footer.php'; ?>
```

Nowadays, and although it is highly discouraged, there are still applications that use this procedural way of coding. The main disadvantage of this style of architecture is that there's no real Separation of Concerns — the maintenance and cost of evolving an application being developed this way increases drastically in relation to other well-known and proven architectures.

Layered Architecture

From the code maintainability and reuse perspectives, the best way to make this code a bit easier to maintain would be by splitting up concepts, that is creating layers for each different concern. In our previous example, it's easy to shape different layers: one to encapsulate the data access and manipulation, another one to handle infrastructure concerns, and a final one for encapsulating the orchestration of the previous two. An essential rule of Layered Architecture — is that each layer must be tightly coupled with the layers beneath it, as shown in the following picture:

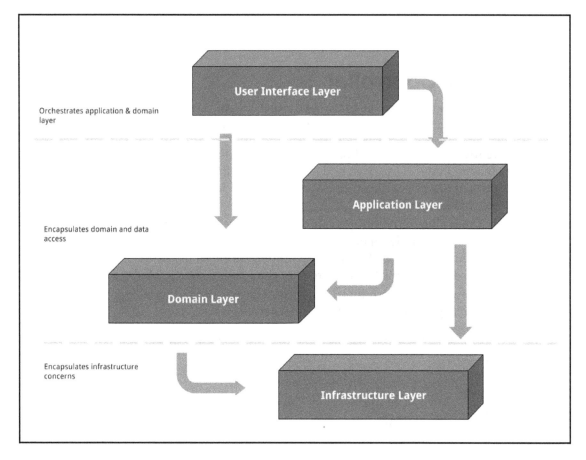

Layered Architecture for SoC

What Layered Architecture really seeks is the separation of the different components of an application. For instance, in terms of the previous example, a blog post representation must be completely independent of a blog post as a conceptual entity. A blog post as a conceptual entity can instead be associated with one or more representations, as opposed to being tightly coupled to a specific representation. This is commonly referred to as Separation of Concerns.

Another architecture paradigm and pattern that seeks the same purpose is the Model-View-Controller pattern. It was initially thought of and widely used for building desktop GUI applications, and now it's mainly used in web applications, thanks to popular web frameworks like Symfony, Zend Framework, and CodeIgniter.

Model-View-Controller

Model-View-Controller is an architectural pattern and paradigm that divides the application into three main layers, described in the following points:

- **The Model**: Captures and centralizes all the Domain Model behavior. This layer manages all the data, logic, and business rules independently of the data representation. It has been said that **the Model layer is the heart and soul of every MVC application**.
- **The Controller**: Orchestrates interactions between the other layers, triggers actions on the Model in order to update its state, and refreshes the representations associated with the Model. Additionally, the Controller can send messages to the View layer in order to change the specific Model representation.
- **The View**: Exposes the differing representations of the Model layer and provides a way to trigger changes on the Model's state.

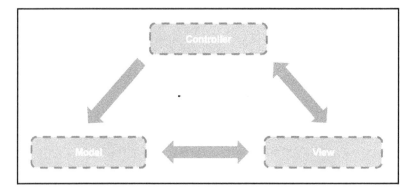

The MVC pattern

Example of Layered Architecture

The Model

Continuing with the previous example, we mentioned that different concerns should be split up. In order to do so, all layers should be identified in our original tangled code. Throughout this process, we need to pay special attention to the code conforming to the Model layer, which will be the beating heart of the application:

```
class Post
{
    private $title;
    private $content;

    public static function writeNewFrom($title, $content)
    {
        return new static($title, $content);
    }

    private function __construct($title, $content)
    {
        $this->setTitle($title);
        $this->setContent($content);
    }

    private function setTitle($title)
    {
        if (empty($title)) {
            throw new RuntimeException('Title cannot be empty');
        }

        $this->title = $title;
    }

    private function setContent($content)
    {
        if (empty($content)) {
            throw new RuntimeException('Content cannot be empty');
        }

        $this->content = $content;
    }
}

class PostRepository
{
```

```php
    private $db;

    public function __construct()
    {
        $this->db = new PDO(
            'mysql:host=localhost;dbname=my_database',
            'a_username',
            '4_p4ssw0rd',
            [
                PDO::MYSQL_ATTR_INIT_COMMAND => 'SET NAMES utf8mb4',
            ]
        );
    }

    public function add(Post $post)
    {
        $this->db->beginTransaction();

        try {
            $stm = $this->db->prepare(
                'INSERT INTO posts (title, content) VALUES (?, ?)'
            );

            $stm->execute([
                $post->title(),
                $post->content(),
            ]);

            $this->db->commit();
        } catch (Exception $e) {
            $this->db->rollback();
            throw new UnableToCreatePostException($e);
        }
    }
}
```

The Model layer is now defined by a `Post` class and a `PostRepository` class. The `Post` class represents a blog post, and the `PostRepository` class represents the whole collection of blog posts available. Additionally, another layer — one that coordinates and orchestrates the Domain Model behavior — is needed inside the Model. Enter the Application layer:

```
class PostService
{
    public function createPost($title, $content)
    {
        $post = Post::writeNewFrom($title, $content);

        (new PostRepository())->add($post);

        return $post;
    }
}
```

The `PostService` class is what is known as an Application Service, and its purpose is to orchestrate and organize the Domain behavior. In other words, the Application services are the ones that make things happen, and they're the direct clients of a Domain Model. No other type of object should be able to directly talk to the internal layers of the Model layer.

The View

The View is a layer that can both send and receive messages from the Model layer and/or from the Controller layer. Its main purpose is to represent the Model to the user at the UI level, as well as to refresh the representation in the UI each time the Model is updated. Generally speaking, the View layer receives an object — often a **Data Transfer Object (DTO)** instead of instances of the Model layer — thereby gathering all the needed information to be successfully represented. For PHP, there are several template engines that can help a great deal in separating the Model representation from the Model itself and from the Controller. The most popular one by far is called `Twig`. Let's see how the View layer would look with Twig.

DTOs Instead of Model Instances?
This is an old and active topic. Why create a DTO instead of giving an instance of the Model to the View layer? The main reason and the short answer is, again, Separation of Concerns. Letting the View inspect and use a Model instance leads to tight coupling between the View layer and the Model layer. In fact, a change in the Model layer can potentially break all the views that make use of the changed Model instances.

```
{% extends "base.html.twig" %}

{% block content %}
    {% if errormsg is defined %}
        <div class="alert error">{{ errormsg }}</div>
    {% else %}
        <div class="alert success">
            Bravo! Post was created successfully!
        </div>
    {% endif %}
    <table>
        <thead>
            <tr>
                <th>ID</th>
                <th>TITLE</th>
                <th>ACTIONS</th>
            </tr>
        </thead>
        <tbody>
        {% for post in posts %}
            <tr>
                <td>{{ post.id }}</td>
                <td>{{ post.title }}</td>
                <td><a href="{{ editPostUrl(post.id) }}">Edit Post</a></td>
            </tr>
        {% endfor %}
        </tbody>
    </table>
{% endblock %}
```

Most of the time, when the Model triggers a state change, it also notifies the related Views so that the UI is refreshed. In a typical web scenario, the synchronization between the Model and its representations can be a bit tricky because of the client-server nature. In these kind of environments, some JavaScript-defined interactions are usually needed to maintain that synchronization. For this reason, JavaScript MVC frameworks like the ones below have become widely popular in recent years:

- AngularJS
- Ember.js
- Marionette.js
- React

The Controller

The Controller layer is responsible for organizing and orchestrating the View and the Model. It receives messages from the View layer and triggers Model behavior in order to perform the desired action. Furthermore, it sends messages to the View in order to display Model representations. Both operations are performed thanks to the Application layer, which is responsible for orchestrating, organizing, and encapsulating Domain behavior.

In terms of a web application in PHP, the Controller usually comprehends a set of classes, which, in order to fulfill their purpose, "speak HTTP." In other words, they receive an HTTP request and return an HTTP response:

```php
class PostsController
{
    public function updateAction(Request $request)
    {
        if (
            $request->request->has('submit') &&
            Validator::validate($request->request->post)
        ) {
            $postService = new PostService();

            try {
                $postService->createPost(
                    $request->request->get('title'),
                    $request->request->get('content')
                );

                $this->addFlash(
                    'notice',
                    'Post has been created successfully!'
                );
            } catch (Exception $e) {
                $this->addFlash(
                    'error',
                    'Unable to create the post!'
                );
            }
        }

        return $this->render('posts/update-result.html.twig');
    }
}
```

Inverting Dependencies: Hexagonal Architecture

Following the essential rule of Layered Architecture, there's a risk when implementing Domain interfaces that contain infrastructural concerns.

As an example, with MVC, the `PostRepository` class from the previous example should be placed in the Domain Model. However, placing infrastructural details right in the middle of our Domain violates Separation of Concerns. This can be problematic; it's difficult to avoid violating the essential rules of Layered Architecture, which leads to a style of code that can become hard to test if the Domain layer is aware of technical implementations.

The Dependency Inversion Principle (DIP)

How can we fix this? As the Domain Model layer depends on concrete infrastructure implementations, the `Dependency Inversion Principle`, or DIP, could be applied by relocating the Infrastructure layer on top of the other three layers.

The Dependency Inversion Principle
High-level modules should not depend on low-level modules. Both should depend on abstractions.
Abstractions should not depend on details. Details should depend on abstractions. *Robert C. Martin*

By using the Dependency Inversion Principle, the architecture schema changes, and the Infrastructure layer — which can be referred to as the low-level module — now depends on the UI, the Application layer, and the Domain layer, which are the high-level modules. The dependency has been inverted.

But what is Hexagonal Architecture, and how does it fit within all of this? Hexagonal Architecture (also known as Ports and Adapters) was defined by Alistair Cockburn in his book, `Hexagonal Architecture`. It depicts the application as a hexagon, where each side represents a Port with one or more Adapters. A Port is a connector with a pluggable Adapter that transforms an outside input to something the inside application can understand. In terms of the DIP, a Port would be a high-level module, and an Adapter would be a low-level module. Furthermore, if the application needs to emit a message to the outside, it will also use a Port with an Adapter to send it and transform it into something that the outside can understand. For this reason, Hexagonal Architecture brings up the concept of symmetry in the application, and it's also the main reason why the schema of the architecture changes. It's often represented as a hexagon because it no longer makes sense to talk about a top layer or a bottom layer. Instead, Hexagonal Architecture talks mainly in terms of the outside and the inside.

There are great videos on YouTube by *Matthias Noback* where he talks about Hexagonal Architecture. You may want to take a look at one of those for more `detailed information`.

Applying Hexagonal Architecture

Continuing with the blog example application, the first concept we need is a Port where the outside world can talk to the application. For this case, we'll use an HTTP Port and its corresponding Adapter. The outside will use the Port to send messages to the application. The blog example was using a database to store the whole collection of blog posts, so in order to allow the application to retrieve blog posts from the database, a Port is needed:

```
interface PostRepository
{
    public function byId(PostId $id);
    public function add(Post $post);
}
```

This interface exposes the Port that the application will retrieve information about blog posts through, and it'll be located in the Domain Layer. Now an Adapter for this Port is needed. The Adapter is in charge of defining the way in which the blog posts will be retrieved using a specific technology:

```
class PDOPostRepository implements PostRepository
{
    private $db;

    public function __construct(PDO $db)
    {
        $this->db = $db;
    }

    public function byId(PostId $id)
    {
        $stm = $this->db->prepare(
            'SELECT * FROM posts WHERE id = ?'
        );

        $stm->execute([$id->id()]);

        return recreateFrom($stm->fetch());
    }

    public function add(Post $post)
```

```
        {
            $stm = $this->db->prepare(
                'INSERT INTO posts (title, content) VALUES (?, ?)'
            );

            $stm->execute([
                $post->title(),
                $post->content(),
            ]);
        }
    }
```

Once we have the Port and its Adapter defined, the last step is to refactor the `PostService` class so that it uses them. This can be easily achieved by using `Dependency Injection`:

```
class PostService
{
    private $postRepository;

    public function __construct(PostRepositor $postRepository)
    {
        $this->postRepository = $postRepository;
    }

    public function createPost($title, $content)
    {
        $post = Post::writeNewFrom($title, $content);

        $this->postRepository->add($post);

        return $post;
    }
}
```

This is just a simple example of Hexagonal Architecture. It's a flexible architecture that promotes Separation of Concerns, like Layered Architecture. It also promotes symmetry, due to having an inside application that communicates with the outside via ports. From now on, this will be the foundational architecture used to build and explain CQRS and Event Sourcing.

For more examples about this architecture, you can check out the `Appendix`, *Hexagonal Architecture with PHP*. For a more detailed example, you should jump to the `Chapter 11`, *Application*, which explains advanced topics like transactionality and other cross-cutting concerns.

Command Query Responsibility Segregation (CQRS)

Hexagonal Architecture is a good foundational architecture, but it has some limitations. For example, complex UIs can require Aggregate information displayed in diverse forms (Chapter 8, *Aggregates*), or they can require data obtained from multiple Aggregates. And in this scenario, we could end up with a lot of finder methods inside the Repositories (maybe as many as the UI views which exist within the application). Or, maybe we can decide to move this complexity to the Application Services, using complex structures to accumulate data from multiple Aggregates. Here's an example:

```
interface PostRepository
{
    public function save(Post $post);
    public function byId(PostId $id);
    public function all();
    public function byCategory(CategoryId $categoryId);
    public function byTag(TagId $tagId);
    public function withComments(PostId $id);
    public function groupedByMonth();
    // ...
}
```

When these techniques are abused, the construction of the UI views can become really painful. We should evaluate the tradeoff between making Application Services return Domain Model instances and returning some kind of DTOs. With the latter option, we avoid tight coupling between the Domain Model and Infrastructure code (web controllers, CLI controllers, and so on).

Luckily, there's another approach. If the problem is having multiple and disparate views, we can exclude them from the Domain Model and start treating them as a purely infrastructural concern. This option is based on a design principle, the **Command Query Separation** (**CQS**). This principle was defined by Bertrand Meyer, and, in turn, it gave birth to a new architectural pattern named **Command Query Responsibility Segregation** (**CQRS**), as defined by Greg Young.

Command Query Separation (CQS)
Asking a question should not change the answer - Bertrand Meyer
This design principle states that every method should be either a command that performs an action, or a query that returns data to the caller, but not both, Wikipedia

CQRS seeks an even more aggressive Separation of Concerns, splitting the Model in two:

- The **Write Model**: Also known as the **Command Model**, it performs the writes and takes responsibility for the true Domain behavior.
- The **Read Model**: It takes responsibility of the reads within the application and treats them as something that should be out of the Domain Model.

Every time someone triggers a command to the Write Model, this performs the write to the desired data store. Additionally, it triggers the Read Model update, in order to display the latest changes on the Read Model.

This strict separation causes another problem: Eventual Consistency. The consistency of the Read Model is now subject to the commands performed by the Write Model. In other words, the Read Model is eventually consistent. That is, every time the Write Model performs a command, it will pull up a process that will be responsible for updating the Read Model according to the last updates on the Write Model. There's a window of time where the UI may present stale information to the user. In the web scenario, this happens often, as we're somewhat limited by the current technologies.

Think about a caching system in front of a web application. Every time the database is updated with new information, the data on the cache layer may potentially be stale, so every time it gets updated, there should be a process that updates the cache system. Cache systems are eventually consistent.

These kinds of processes, speaking in CQRS terminology, are called Write Model Projections, or just Projections. We project the Write Model onto the Read Model. This process can be synchronous or asynchronous, depending on your needs, and it can be done thanks to another useful tactical design pattern — Chapter Domain Events — which will be explained in detail later on in the book. The basis of the Write Model projections is to gather all the published Domain Events and update the Read Model with all the information coming from the events.

The Write Model

This is the true holder of Domain behavior. Continuing with our example, the Repository interface would be simplified to the following:

```
interface PostRepository
{
    public function save(Post $post);
    public function byId(PostId $id);
}
```

Now the `PostRepository` has been freed from all the read concerns except one: The `byId` function which is responsible for loading the Aggregate by its ID so that we can operate on it. And once this is done, all the query methods are also stripped down from the Post model, leaving it only with command methods. This means we'll effectively get rid of all the getter methods and any other methods exposing information about the Post Aggregate. Instead, Domain Events will be published in order to be able to trigger Write Model projections by subscribing to them:

```
class AggregateRoot
{
    private $recordedEvents = [];

    protected function recordApplyAndPublishThat(
        DomainEvent $domainEvent
    ) {
        $this->recordThat($domainEvent);
        $this->applyThat($domainEvent);
        $this->publishThat($domainEvent);
    }

    protected function recordThat(DomainEvent $domainEvent)
    {
        $this->recordedEvents[] = $domainEvent;
    }

    protected function applyThat(DomainEvent $domainEvent)
    {
        $modifier = 'apply' . get_class($domainEvent);

        $this->$modifier($domainEvent);
    }

    protected function publishThat(DomainEvent $domainEvent)
    {
        DomainEventPublisher::getInstance()->publish($domainEvent);
    }
```

```php
        public function recordedEvents()
        {
            return $this->recordedEvents;
        }

        public function clearEvents()
        {
            $this->recordedEvents = [];
        }
    }

    class Post extends AggregateRoot
    {
        private $id;
        private $title;
        private $content;
        private $published = false;
        private $categories;

        private function __construct(PostId $id)
        {
            $this->id = $id;
            $this->categories = new Collection();
        }

        public static function writeNewFrom($title, $content)
        {
            $postId = PostId::create();

            $post = new static($postId);

            $post->recordApplyAndPublishThat(
                new PostWasCreated($postId, $title, $content)
            );
        }

        public function publish()
        {
            $this->recordApplyAndPublishThat(
                new PostWasPublished($this->id)
            );
        }

        public function categorizeIn(CategoryId $categoryId)
        {
            $this->recordApplyAndPublishThat(
                new PostWasCategorized($this->id, $categoryId)
            );
```

```
    }

    public function changeContentFor($newContent)
    {
        $this->recordApplyAndPublishThat(
            new PostContentWasChanged($this->id, $newContent)
        );
    }

    public function changeTitleFor($newTitle)
    {
        $this->recordApplyAndPublishThat(
            new PostTitleWasChanged($this->id, $newTitle)
        );
    }
}
```

All actions that trigger a state change are implemented via Domain Events. For each Domain Event published, there's an apply method responsible for reflecting the state change:

```
class Post extends AggregateRoot
{
    // ...

    protected function applyPostWasCreated(
        PostWasCreated $event
    ) {
        $this->id = $event->id();
        $this->title = $event->title();
        $this->content = $event->content();
    }

    protected function applyPostWasPublished(
        PostWasPublished $event
    ) {
        $this->published = true;
    }

    protected function applyPostWasCategorized(
        PostWasCategorized $event
    ) {
        $this->categories->add($event->categoryId());
    }

    protected function applyPostContentWasChanged(
        PostContentWasChanged $event
    ) {
```

```
        $this->content = $event->content();
    }

    protected function applyPostTitleWasChanged(
        PostTitleWasChanged $event
    ) {
        $this->title = $event->title();
    }
}
```

The Read Model

The Read Model, also known as the Query Model, is a pure denormalized data model lifted from Domain concerns. In fact, with CQRS, all the read concerns are treated as reporting processes, an infrastructure concern. In general, when using CQRS, the Read Model is subject to the needs of the UI and how complex the views compounding the UI are. In a situation where the Read Model is defined in terms of relational databases, the simplest approach would be to set one-to-one relationships between database tables and UI views. These database tables and UI views will be updated using Write Model projections triggered from the Domain Events published by the write side:

```sql
-- Definition of a UI view of a single post with its comments
CREATE TABLE single_post_with_comments (
    id INTEGER NOT NULL,
    post_id INTEGER NOT NULL,
    post_title VARCHAR(100) NOT NULL,
    post_content TEXT NOT NULL,
    post_created_at DATETIME NOT NULL,
    comment_content TEXT NOT NULL
) ENGINE=InnoDB DEFAULT CHARSET=utf8mb4 COLLATE=utf8mb4_unicode_ci;

-- Set up some data
INSERT INTO single_post_with_comments VALUES
    (1, 1, "Layered" , "Some content", NOW(), "A comment"),
    (2, 1, "Layered" , "Some content", NOW(), "The comment"),
    (3, 2, "Hexagonal" , "Some content", NOW(), "No comment"),
    (4, 2, "Hexagonal", "Some content", NOW(), "All comments"),
    (5, 3, "CQRS", "Some content", NOW(), "This comment"),
    (6, 3, "CQRS", "Some content", NOW(), "That comment");

-- Query it
SELECT * FROM single_post_with_comments WHERE post_id = 1;
```

An important feature of this architectural style is that the Read Model should be completely disposable, since the true state of the application is handled by the Write Model. This means the Read Model can be removed and recreated when needed, using Write Model projections.

Here we can see some examples of possible views within a blog application:

```
SELECT * FROM
    posts_grouped_by_month_and_year
ORDER BY month DESC,year ASC;

SELECT * FROM
    posts_by_tags
WHERE tag = "ddd";

SELECT * FROM
    posts_by_author
WHERE author_id = 1;
```

It's important to point out that CQRS doesn't constrain the definition and implementation of the Read Model to a relational database. It depends exclusively on the needs of the application being built. It could be a relational database, a document-oriented database, a key-value store, or whatever best suits the needs of your application. Following the blog post application, we'll use `Elasticsearch` — a document-oriented database — to implement a Read Model:

```
class PostsController
{
    public function listAction()
    {
        $client = new ElasticsearchClientBuilder::create()->build();

        $response = $client-> search([
            'index' => 'blog-engine',
            'type' => 'posts',
            'body' => [
                'sort' => [
                    'created_at' => ['order' => 'desc']
                ]
            ]
        ]);

        return [
            'posts' => $response
        ];
    }
}
```

The Read Model code has been drastically simplified to a single query against an Elasticsearch index.

This reveals that the Read Model doesn't really need an object-relational mapper, as this might be overkill. However, the Write Model might benefit from the use of an object-relational mapper, as this would allow you to organize and structure the Read Model according to the needs of the application.

Synchronizing the Write Model with the Read Model

Here comes the tricky part. How do we synchronize the Read Model with the Write Model? We already said we would do it by using Domain Events captured in a Write Model transaction. For each type of Domain Event captured, a specific projection will be executed. So a one-to-one relationship between Domain Events and projections will be set.

Let's have a look at an example of configuring projections so that we can get a better idea. First of all, we need to define a skeleton for the projections:

```
interface Projection
{
    public function listensTo();
    public function project($event);
}
```

So defining an `Elasticsearch` projection for a `PostWasCreated` event would be as simple as this:

```
namespace Infrastructure\Projection\Elasticsearch;

use Elasticsearch\Client;
use PostWasCreated;

class PostWasCreatedProjection implements Projection
{
    private $client;

    public function __construct(Client $client)
    {
        $this->client = $client;
    }

    public function listensTo()
    {
        return PostWasCreated::class;
    }
```

```php
    public function project($event)
    {
        $this->client->index([
            'index' => 'posts',
            'type' => 'post',
            'id' => $event->getPostId(),
            'body' => [
                'content' => $event->getPostContent(),
                // ...
            ]
        ]);
    }
}
```

The Projector implementation is a kind of specialized Domain Event listener. The main difference between that and the default Domain Event listener is that the Projector reacts to a group of Domain Events instead of only one:

```php
namespace Infrastructure\Projection;

class Projector
{
    private $projections = [];

    public function register(array $projections)
    {
        foreach ($projections as $projection) {
            $this->projections[$projection->eventType()] = $projection;
        }
    }

    public function project( array $events)
    {
        foreach ($events as $event) {
            if (isset($this->projections[get_class($event)])) {
                $this->projections[get_class($event)]
                    ->project($event);
            }
        }
    }
}
```

The following code shows how the flow between the projector and the events would appear:

```
$client = new ElasticsearchClientBuilder::create()->build();

$projector = new Projector();
$projector->register([
    new Infrastructure\Projection\Elasticsearch\
        PostWasCreatedProjection($client),
    new Infrastructure\Projection\Elasticsearch\
        PostWasPublishedProjection($client),
    new Infrastructure\Projection\Elasticsearch\
        PostWasCategorizedProjection($client),
    new Infrastructure\Projection\Elasticsearch\
        PostContentWasChangedProjection($client),
    new Infrastructure\Projection\Elasticsearch\
        PostTitleWasChangedProjection($client),
]);

$events = [
    new PostWasCreated(/* ... */),
    new PostWasPublished(/* ... */),
    new PostWasCategorized(/* ... */),
    new PostContentWasChanged(/* ... */),
    new PostTitleWasChanged(/* ... */),
];

$projector->project($event);
```

This code is kind of synchronous, but the process can be asynchronous if needed. And you could make your customers aware of this out-of-sync data by placing some alerts in the view layer.

For the next example, we'll use the amqplib PHP extension in combination with ReactPHP:

```
// Connect to an AMQP broker
$cnn = new AMQPConnection();
$cnn->connect();

// Create a channel
$ch = new AMQPChannel($cnn);

// Declare a new exchange
$ex = new AMQPExchange($ch);
$ex->setName('events');

$ex->declare();
```

```
// Create an event loop
$loop = ReactEventLoopFactory::create();

// Create a producer that will send any waiting messages every half a
second
$producer = new Gos\Component\React\AMQPProducer($ex, $loop, 0.5);

$serializer = JMS\Serializer\SerializerBuilder::create()->build();

$projector = new AsyncProjector($producer, $serializer);

$events = [
    new PostWasCreated(/* ... */),
    new PostWasPublished(/* ... */),
    new PostWasCategorized(/* ... */),
    new PostContentWasChanged(/* ... */),
    new PostTitleWasChanged(/* ... */),
];

$projector->project($event);
```

For this to work, we need an asynchronous projector. Here's a naive implementation of that:

```
namespace Infrastructure\Projection;

use Gos\Component\React\AMQPProducer;
use JMS\Serializer\Serializer;

class AsyncProjector
{
    private $producer;
    private $serializer;

    public function __construct(
        Producer $producer,
        Serializer $serializer
    ) {
        $this->producer = $producer;
        $this->serializer = $serializer;
    }

    public function project(array $events)
    {
        foreach ($events as $event) {
            $this->producer->publish(
                $this->serializer->serialize(
                    $event, 'json'
                )
            )
```

```
                );
            }
        }
    }
```

And the event consumer on the RabbitMQ exchange would look something like this:

```
// Connect to an AMQP broker
$cnn = new AMQPConnection();
$cnn-> connect();

// Create a channel
$ch = new AMQPChannel($cnn);

// Create a new queue
$queue = new AMQPQueue($ch);
$queue->setName('events');
$queue->declare();

// Create an event loop
$loop = React\EventLoop\Factory::create();

$serializer = JMS\Serializer\SerializerBuilder::create()->build();

$client = new Elasticsearch\ClientBuilder::create()->build();

$projector = new Projector();
$projector->register([
    new Infrastructure\Projection\Elasticsearch\
        PostWasCreatedProjection($client),
    new Infrastructure\Projection\Elasticsearch\
        PostWasPublishedProjection($client),
    new Infrastructure\Projection\Elasticsearch\
        PostWasCategorizedProjection($client),
    new Infrastructure\Projection\Elasticsearch\
        PostContentWasChangedProjection($client),
    new Infrastructure\Projection\Elasticsearch\
        PostTitleWasChangedProjection($client),
]);

// Create a consumer
$consumer = new Gos\Component\ReactAMQP\Consumer($queue, $loop, 0.5, 10);

// Check for messages every half a second and consume up to 10 at a time.
$consumer->on(
    'consume',
    function ($envelope, $queue) use ($projector, $serializer) {
        $event = $serializer->unserialize($envelope->getBody(), 'json');
```

```
        $projector->project($event);
    }
);

$loop->run();
```

From now on, it could be as simple as making all the needed Repositories consume an instance of the projector and then making them invoke the projection process:

```
class DoctrinePostRepository implements PostRepository
{
    private $em;
    private $projector;

    public function __construct(EntityManager $em, Projector $projector)
    {
        $this->em = $em;
        $this->projector = $projector;
    }

    public function save(Post $post)
    {
        $this->em->transactional(
            function (EntityManager $em) use ($post)
            {
                $em->persist($post);

                foreach ($post->recordedEvents() as $event) {
                    $em->persist($event);
                }
            }
        );

        $this->projector->project($post->recordedEvents());
    }

    public function byId(PostId $id)
    {
        return $this->em->find($id);
    }
}
```

The `Post` instance and the recorded events are triggered and persisted in the same transaction. This ensures that no events are lost, as we'll project them to the Read Model if the transaction is successful. As a result, no inconsistencies will exist between the Write Model and the Read Model.

To ORM or Not To ORM

One of the most common questions when implementing CQRS is if an **Object-Relational Mapper (ORM)** is really needed. We strongly believe that using an ORM for the Write Model is perfectly fine and has all of the advantages of using a tool, which will help us save a lot of work in case we use a relational database. But we shouldn't forget that we still need to persist and retrieve the Write Model's state in a relational database.

Event Sourcing

CQRS is a powerful and flexible architecture. There's an added benefit to it in regard to gathering and saving the Domain Events (which occurred during an Aggregate operation), giving you a high-level degree of detail of what's going on within your Domain. Domain Events are one of the key tactical patterns because of their significance within the Domain, as they describe past occurrences.

Be careful with recording too many events

An ever-growing number of events is a smell. It might reveal an addiction to event recording at the Domain, most likely incentivized by the business. As a rule of thumb, remember to keep it simple.

By using CQRS, we've been able to record all the relevant events that occurred in the Domain Layer. The state of the Domain Model can be represented by reproducing the Domain Events we previously recorded. We just need a tool for storing all those events in a consistent way. We need an event store.

The fundamental idea behind Event Sourcing is to express the state of Aggregates as a linear sequence of events

With CQRS, we partially achieved the following: The Post entity alters its state by using Domain Events, but it's persisted, as explained already, thereby mapping the object to a database table.

Event Sourcing takes this a step further. If we were using a database table to store the state of all the blog posts, another to store the state of all the blog post comments, and so on, using Event Sourcing would allow us to use a single database table: A single append — only database table that would store all the Domain Events published by all the Aggregates within the Domain Model. Yes, you read that correctly. A **single** database table.

With this model in mind, tools like object-relational mappers are no longer needed. The only tool needed would be a simple database abstraction layer by which events can be appended:

```
interface EventSourcedAggregateRoot
{
    public static function reconstitute(EventStream $events);
}

class Post extends AggregateRoot implements EventSourcedAggregateRoot
{
    public static function reconstitute(EventStream $history)
    {
        $post = new static($history->getAggregateId());

        foreach ($events as $event) {
            $post->applyThat($event);
        }

        return $post;
    }
}
```

Now the `Post` Aggregate has a method which, when given a set of events (or, in other words, an event stream), is able to replay the state step by step until it reaches the current state, all before saving. The next step would be building an adapter of the `PostRepository` port that will fetch all the published events from the `Post` Aggregate and append them to the data store where all the events are appended. This is what we call an event store:

```
class EventStorePostRepository implements PostRepository
{
    private $eventStore;
    private $projector;

    public function __construct($eventStore, $projector)
    {
        $this->eventStore = $eventStore;
        $this->projector = $projector;
    }

    public function save(Post $post)
    {
        $events = $post->recordedEvents();

        $this->eventStore->append(new EventStream(
            $post->id(),
            $events)
        );
        $post->clearEvents();

        $this->projector->project($events);
    }
}
```

This is how the implementation of the `PostRepository` looks when we use an event store to save all the events published by the `Post` Aggregate. Now we need a way to restore an Aggregate from its events history. A `reconstitute` method implemented by the `Post` Aggregate and used to rebuild a blog post state from triggered events comes in handy:

```
class EventStorePostRepository implements PostRepository
{
    public function byId(PostId $id)
    {
        return Post::reconstitute(
            $this->eventStore->getEventsFor($id)
        );
    }
}
```

The event store is the workhorse that carries out all the responsibility in regard to saving and restoring event streams. Its public API is composed of two simple methods: They are append and getEventsFrom. The former appends an event stream to the event store, and the latter loads event streams to allow Aggregate rebuilding.

We could use a key-value implementation to store all events:

```
class EventStore
{
    private $redis;
    private $serializer;

    public function __construct($redis, $serializer)
    {
        $this->redis = $redis;
        $this->serializer = $serializer;
    }

    public function append(EventStream $eventstream)
    {
        foreach ($eventstream as $event) {
            $data = $this->serializer->serialize(
                $event, 'json'
            );

            $date = (new DateTimeImmutable())->format('YmdHis');

            $this->redis->rpush(
                'events:' . $event->getAggregateId(),
                $this->serializer->serialize([
                    'type' => get_class($event),
                    'created_on' => $date,
                    'data' => $data
                ],'json')
            );
        }
    }

    public function getEventsFor($id)
    {
        $serializedEvents = $this->redis->lrange('events:' . $id, 0, -1);

        $eventStream = [];
        foreach($serializedEvents as $serializedEvent){
            $eventData = $this->serializerdeserialize(
                $serializedEvent,
                'array',
```

```
                    'json'
            );

            $eventStream[] = $this->serializer->deserialize(
                $eventData['data'],
                $eventData['type'],
                'json'
            );
        }

        return new EventStream($id, $eventStream);
    }
}
```

This event store implementation is built upon `Redis`, a widely used key-value store. The events are appended in a list using the prefix events: In addition, before persisting the events, we extract some metadata like the event class or the creation date, as it will come in handy later.

Obviously, in terms of performance, it's expensive for an Aggregate to go over its full event history to reach its final state all of the time. This is especially the case when an event stream has hundreds or even thousands of events. The best way to overcome this situation is to take a snapshot from the Aggregate and replay only the events in the event stream that occurred after the snapshot was taken. A snapshot is just a simple serialized version of the Aggregate state at any given moment. It can be based on the number of events of the Aggregate's event stream, or it can be time based. With the first approach, a snapshot will be taken every n triggered events (every 50, 100, or 200 events, for example). With the second approach, a snapshot will be taken every n seconds.

To follow the example, we'll use the first way of snapshotting. In the event's metadata, we store an additional field, the version, from which we'll start replaying the Aggregate history:

```
class SnapshotRepository
{
    public function byId($id)
    {
        $key = 'snapshots:' . $id;
        $metadata = $this->serializer->unserialize(
            $this->redis->get($key)
        );

        if (null === $metadata) {
            return;
        }
```

```
            return new Snapshot(
                $metadata['version'],
                $this->serializer->unserialize(
                    $metadata['snapshot']['data'],
                    $metadata['snapshot']['type'],
                    'json'
                )
            );
    }

    public function save($id, Snapshot $snapshot)
    {
        $key = 'snapshots:' . $id;
        $aggregate = $snapshot->aggregate();

        $snapshot = [
            'version' => $snapshot->version(),
            'snapshot' => [
                'type' => get_class($aggregate),
                'data' => $this->serializer->serialize(
                    $aggregate, 'json'
                )
            ]
        ];

        $this->redis->set($key, $snapshot);
    }
}
```

And now we need to refactor the EventStore class so that it starts using the SnapshotRepository to load the Aggregate with acceptable performance times:

```
class EventStorePostRepository implements PostRepository
{
    public function byId(PostId $id)
    {
        $snapshot = $this->snapshotRepository->byId($id);

        if (null === $snapshot) {
            return Post::reconstitute(
                $this->eventStore->getEventsFrom($id)
            );
        }

        $post = $snapshot->aggregate();

        $post->replay(
            $this->eventStore->fromVersion($id, $snapshot->version())
```

```
        );

        return $post;
    }
}
```

We just need to take Aggregate snapshots periodically. We could do this synchronously or asynchronously by a process responsible for monitoring the event store. The following code is a simple example demonstrating the implementation of Aggregate snapshotting:

```
class EventStorePostRepository implements PostRepository
{
    public function save(Post $post)
    {
        $id = $post->id();
        $events = $post->recordedEvents();
        $post->clearEvents();
        $this->eventStore->append(new EventStream($id, $events));
        $countOfEvents =$this->eventStore->countEventsFor($id);
        $version = $countOfEvents / 100;

        if (!$this->snapshotRepository->has($post->id(), $version)) {
            $this->snapshotRepository->save(
                $id,
                new Snapshot(
                    $post, $version
                )
            );
        }

        $this->projector->project($events);
    }
}
```

To ORM or Not To ORM

It's clear from the use case of this architectural style that using an ORM just to persist / fetch events would be overkill. Even if we use a relational database for storing them, we only need to persist / fetch events from the data store.

Wrap-Up

As there are plenty of options for architectural styles, you may have gotten a bit confused in this chapter. You'll have to consider the tradeoffs for each one of them in order to choose wisely. One thing is clear: the Big Ball of Mud approach is not an option, as the code will rot pretty fast. Layered Architecture is a better option, but it presents some disadvantages, like tight coupling between layers. Arguably, the most balanced option would be Hexagonal Architecture, as it can be used as a foundational base architecture, and it promotes a high-level degree of decoupling and symmetry between the inside and outside of the application. This is what we recommend for most scenarios.

We've also seen CQRS and Event Sourcing as relatively flexible architectures that will help you in fighting serious complexity. CQRS and Event Sourcing both have their places, but don't let the *coolness factor* distract you from the value they provide. As they both come with some overhead, you should have a technical reason for justifying their use. These architectural styles are indeed really useful, and the heuristics to start using them can be discovered in the number of finders on the Repositories for CQRS and the volume of triggered events for Event Sourcing. If the number of finder methods starts growing and Repositories become difficult to maintain, then it's time to consider the use of CQRS, in order to split read and write concerns. And after that, if the volume of events on each Aggregate operation tends to grow and the business is interested in more granular information, then an option to consider is whether a move toward Event Sourcing might pay off.

Extracted from a paper by Brian Foote and Joseph Yoder:
A BIG BALL OF MUD is haphazardly structured, sprawling, sloppy, duct-tape and bailing wire, `spaghetti code jungle`.

3

Value Objects

By using the `self` keyword, we don't The Value Objects are a fundamental building block of Domain-Driven Design, and they're used to model concepts of your Ubiquitous Language in code. A Value Object is not just a thing in your Domain — it measures, quantifies, or describes something. Value Objects can be seen as small, simple objects — such as money or a date range — whose equality is not based on identity, but instead on the content held.

For example, a product price could be modeled using a Value Object. In this case, it's not representing a thing, but rather a value that allows us to measure how much Money a product is worth. The memory footprint for these objects is trivial to determine (calculated by their constituent parts) and there's very little overhead. As a result, new instance creation is favored over reference reuse, even when being used to represent the same value. Equality is then checked based on the comparability of the fields of both instances.

Definition

Ward Cunningham `defines` a Value Object as:

> A measure or description of something. Examples of Value Objects are things like numbers, dates, monies and strings. Usually, they are small Objects which are used quite widely. Their identity is based on their state rather than on their Object identity. This way, you can have multiple copies of the same conceptual Value Object. Every $5 note has its own identity (thanks to its serial number), but the cash economy relies on every $5 note having the same Value as every other $5 note.

Martin Fowler `defines` a Value Object as:

> A small Object such as a Money or the date range object. Their key property is that they follow value semantics rather than reference semantics. You can usually tell them because their notion of equality isn't based on identity, instead two Value Objects are equal if all their fields are equal. Although all fields are equal, you don't need to compare all fields if a subset is unique — for example currency codes for currency objects are enough to test equality. A general heuristic is that Value Objects should be entirely immutable. If you want to change a Value Object you should replace the object with a new one and not be allowed to update the values of the value object itself — updatable value objects lead to aliasing problems.

Examples of Value Objects are numbers, text strings, dates, times, a person's full name (composed of first name, middle name, last name, and title), currencies, colors, phone numbers, and postal addresses.

Exercise
Try to locate more examples of potential Value Objects in your current Domain.

Value Object vs. Entity

Consider the following examples from `Wikipedia`, in order to better understand the difference between Value Objects and Entities:

- **Value Object**: When people exchange dollar bills, they generally do not distinguish between each unique bill; they only are concerned about the face value of the dollar bill. In this context, dollar bills are Value Objects. However, the Federal Reserve may be concerned about each unique bill; in this context each bill would be an entity.
- **Entity**: Most airlines distinguish each seat uniquely on every flight. Each seat is an entity in this context. However, Southwest Airlines, EasyJet and Ryanair do not distinguish between every seat; all seats are the same. In this context, a seat is actually a Value Object.

Exercise
Think about the concept of an address (street, number, zip code, and so on). What is a possible context where an address could be modeled as an Entity and not as a Value Object? Discuss your findings with a peer.

Currency and Money Example

The `Currency` and `Money` Value Objects are probably the most used examples for explaining Value Objects, thanks to the `Money pattern`. This design pattern provides a solution for modeling a problem that avoids a floating-point rounding issue, which in turn allows for deterministic calculations to be performed.

In the real world, a currency describes monetary units in the same way that meters and yards describe distance units. Each currency is represented with a three-letter uppercase ISO code:

```
class Currency
{
    private $isoCode;

    public function __construct($anIsoCode)
    {
        $this->setIsoCode($anIsoCode);
    }

    private function setIsoCode($anIsoCode)
    {
        if (!preg_match('/^[A-Z]{3}$/', $anIsoCode)) {
            throw new InvalidArgumentException();
        }

        $this->isoCode = $anIsoCode;
    }

    public function isoCode()
    {
        return $this->isoCode;
    }
}
```

One of the main goals of Value Objects is also the holy grail of Object-Oriented design: encapsulation. By following this pattern, you'll end up with a dedicated location to put all the validation, comparison logic, and behavior for a given concept.

Extra Validations for Currency

In the previous code example, we can build a Currency with an AAA Currency ISO code. That isn't valid at all. Write a more specific rule that will check if the ISO Code is valid. A full list of valid currency ISO codes can be found here. If you need help, take a look at the Money packagist library.

Money is used to measure a specific amount of currency. It's modeled using an amount and a currency. Amount, in the case of the Money pattern, is implemented using an integer representation of the Currency's least-valuable fraction — For example in the case of USD or EUR, cents.

As a bonus, you might also notice that we're using self encapsulation to set the ISO code, which centralizes changes in the Value Object itself:

```php
class Money
{
    private $amount;
    private $currency;

    public function __construct($anAmount, Currency $aCurrency)
    {
        $this->setAmount($anAmount);
        $this->setCurrency($aCurrency);
    }

    private function setAmount($anAmount)
    {
        $this->amount = (int) $anAmount;
    }

    private function setCurrency(Currency $aCurrency)
    {
        $this->currency = $aCurrency;
    }

    public function amount()
    {
        return $this->amount;
    }

    public function currency()
    {
        return $this->currency;
    }
}
```

Now that you know the formal definition of Value Objects, let's dive deeper into some of the powerful features they offer.

Characteristics

While modeling an Ubiquitous Language concept in code, you should always favor Value Objects over Entities. Value Objects are easier to create, test, use, and maintain.

Keeping this in mind, you can determine whether the concept in question can be modeled as a Value Object if:

- It measures, quantifies, or describes a thing in the Domain
- It can be kept immutable
- It models a conceptual whole by composing related attributes as an integral unit
- It can be compared with others through value equality
- It is completely replaceable when the measurement or description changes
- It supplies its collaborators with side-effect-free behavior

Measures, Quantifies, or Describes

As discussed before, a Value Object should not be considered just a *thing* in your Domain. As a value, it measures, quantifies, or describes a concept in the Domain.

In our example, the `Currency` object describes what type of Money it is. The `Money` object measures or quantifies units of a given currency.

Immutability

This is one of the most important aspects to grasp. Object values shouldn't be able to be altered over their lifetime. Because of this immutability, Value Objects are easy to reason and test and are free of undesired/unexpected side effects. As such, Value Objects should be created through their constructors. In order to build one, you usually pass the required primitive types or other Value Objects through this constructor.

Value Objects are always in a valid state; that's why we create them in a single atomic step. Empty constructors with multiple setters and getters move the creation responsibility to the client, resulting in the `Anemic Domain Model`, which is considered an anti-pattern.

It's also good to point out that it's not recommended to hold references to Entities in your Value Objects. Entities are mutable, and holding references to them could lead to undesirable side effects occurring in the Value Object.

In languages with method overloading, such as Java, you can create multiple constructors with the same name. Each of these constructors are provided with different options to build the same type of resulting object. In PHP, we're able to provide a similar capability by way of factory methods. These specific factory methods are also known as semantic constructors. The main goal of fromMoney is to provide more contextual meaning than the plain constructor. More radical approaches propose to make the __construct method private and build every instance using a semantic constructor.

In our Money object, we could add some useful factory methods like the following:

```
class Money
{
    // ...
    public static function fromMoney(Money $aMoney)
    {
        return new self(
            $aMoney->amount(),
            $aMoney->currency()
        );
    }

    public static function ofCurrency(Currency $aCurrency)
    {
        return new self(0, $aCurrency);
    }
}
```

By using the self keyword, we don't couple the code with the class name. As such, a change to the class name or namespace won't affect these factory methods. This small implementation detail helps when refactoring the code at a later date.

static vs. self
Using static over self can result in undesirable issues when a Value Object inherits from another Value Object.

Due to this immutability, we must consider how to handle mutable actions that are common place in a stateful context. If we require a state change, we now have to return a brand new Value Object representation with this change. If we want to increase the amount of, for example, a Money Value Object, we're required to instead return a new Money instance with the desired modifications.

Fortunately, it's relatively simple to abide by this rule, as shown in the example below:

```
class Money
{
    // ...
    public function increaseAmountBy($anAmount)
    {
        return new self(
            $this->amount() + $anAmount,
            $this->currency()
        );
    }
}
```

The `Money` object returned by `increaseAmountBy` is different from the `Money` client object that received the method call. This can be observed in the example comparability checks below:

```
$aMoney = new Money(100, new Currency('USD'));
$otherMoney = $aMoney->increaseAmountBy(100);

var_dump($aMoney === otherMoney); // bool(false)

$aMoney = $aMoney->increaseAmountBy(100);
var_dump($aMoney === $otherMoney); // bool(false)
```

Conceptual Whole

So why not just implement something similar to the following example, avoiding the need for a new Value Object class altogether?

```
class Product
{
    private id;
    private name;
    /**
     * @var int
     */
    private $amount;
    /**
     * @var string
     */
    private $currency;

    // ...
}
```

This approach has some noticeable flaws, if say, for example, you want to validate the ISO. It doesn't really make sense for the Product to be responsible for the Currency's ISO validation (thus violating the Single Responsibility Principle). This is highlighted even more so if you want to reuse the accompanying logic in other parts of your Domain (to abide by the DRY principle).

With these factors in mind, this use case is a perfect candidate for being abstracted out into a Value Object. Using this abstraction not only gives you the opportunity to group related properties together, but it also allows you to create higher-order concepts and a more concrete Ubiquitous Language.

Exercise
Discuss with a peer whether or not an email could be considered a Value Object. Does the context it's used in matter?

Value Equality

As discussed at the beginning of the chapter, two Value Objects are equal if the content they measure, quantify, or describe is the same.

For example, imagine two `Money` objects representing 1 USD. Can we consider them equal? In the *real world*, are two bills of 1 USD valued the same? Of course they are. Directing our attention back to the code, the Value Objects in question refer to separate instances of `Money`. However, they both represent the same value, which makes them equal.

In regards to PHP, it's commonplace to compare two Value Objects using the == operator. Examining the `PHP Documentation` definition of the operator highlights an interesting behavior:

> When using the comparison operator ==, object variables are compared in a simple manner, namely: Two object instances are equal if they have the same attributes and values, and are instances of the same class.

This behavior works in agreement with our formal definition of a Value Object. However, as an exact class match predicate is present, you should be wary when handling subtyped Value Objects.

Keeping this in mind, the even stricter === operator doesn't help us, unfortunately:

> When using the identity operator ===, object variables are identical if and only if they refer to the same instance of the same class.

The following example should help confirm these subtle differences:

```
$a = new Currency('USD');
$b = new Currency('USD');

var_dump($a == $b); // bool(true)
var_dump($a === $b); // bool(false)

$c = new Currency('EUR');

var_dump($a == $c); // bool(false)
var_dump($a === $c); // bool(false)
```

A solution is to implement a conventional equals method in each Value Object. This method is tasked with checking the type and equality of its composite attributes. Abstract data type comparability is easy to implement using the built-in type hinting in PHP. You can also use the get_class() function to aid in the comparability check if necessary.

The language, however, is unable to decipher what equality truly means in your Domain concept, meaning it's your responsibility to provide the answer. In order to compare the Currency objects, we just need to confirm that both their associated ISO codes are the same. The === operator does the job pretty well in this case:

```
class Currency
{
    // ...
    public function equals(Currency $currency)
    {
        return $currency->isoCode() === $this->isoCode();
    }
}
```

Because Money objects use Currency objects, the equals method needs to perform this comparability check, along with comparing the amounts:

```
class Money
{
    // ...
    public function equals(Money $money)
    {
        return
            $money->currency()->equals($this->currency()) &&
            $money->amount() === $this->amount();
    }
}
```

Replaceability

Consider a `Product` Entity that contains a `Money` Value Object used to quantify its price. Additionally, consider two `Product` Entities with an identical price — for example 100 USD. This scenario could be modeled using the two individual `Money` objects or two references pointing to a single Value Object.

Sharing the same Value Object can be risky; if one is altered, both will reflect the change. This behavior can be considered an unexpected side effect. For example, if Carlos was hired on February 20, and we know that Christian was also hired on the same day, we may set Christian's hire date to be the same instance as Carlos's. If Carlos then changes the month of his hire date to May, Christian's hire date changes too. Whether it's correct or not, it's not what people expect.

Due to the problems highlighted in this example, when holding a reference to a Value Object, it's recommended to replace the object as a whole rather than modifying its value:

```
$this->price = new Money(100, new Currency('USD'));
//...
$this->price = $this->price->increaseAmountBy(200);
```

This kind of behavior is similar to how basic types such as strings work in PHP. Consider the function `strtolower`. It returns a new string rather than modifying the original one. No reference is used; instead, a new value is returned.

Side-Effect-Free Behavior

If we want to include some additional behavior — like an `add` method — in our `Money` class, it feels natural to check that the input fits any preconditions and maintains any invariance. In our case, we only wish to add monies with the same currency:

```
class Money
{
    // ...
    public function add(Money $money)
    {
        if ($money->currency() !== $this->currency()) {
            throw new InvalidArgumentException();
        }

        $this->amount += $money->amount();
    }
}
```

If the two currencies don't match, an exception is raised. Otherwise, the amounts are added. However, this code has some undesirable pitfalls. Now imagine we have a mysterious method call to `otherMethod` in our code:

```
class Banking
{
    public function doSomething()
    {
        $aMoney = new Money(100, new Currency('USD'));

        $this->otherMethod($aMoney);//mysterious call
        // ...
    }
}
```

Everything is fine until, for some reason, we start seeing unexpected results when we're returning or finished with `otherMethod`. Suddenly, `$aMoney` no longer contains 100 USD. What happened? And what happens if `otherMethod` internally uses our previously defined `add` method? Maybe you're unaware that add mutates the state of the `Money` instance. This is what we call a side effect. You must avoid generating side effects. You must not mutate your arguments. If you do, the developer using your objects may experience strange behaviors. They'll complain, and they'll be correct.

So how can we fix this? Simple — by making sure that the Value Object remains immutable, we avoid this kind of unexpected problem. An easy solution could be returning a new instance for every potentially mutable operation, which the `add` method does:

```
class Money
{
    // ...
    public function add(Money $money)
    {
        if (!$money->currency()->equals($this->currency())) {
            throw new \InvalidArgumentException();
        }

        return new self(
            $money->amount() + $this->amount(),
            $this->currency()
        );
    }
}
```

With this simple change, immutability is guaranteed. Each time two instances of `Money` are added together, a new resulting instance is returned. Other classes can perform any number of changes without affecting the original copy. Code free of side effects is easy to understand, easy to test, and less error prone.

Basic Types

Consider the following code snippet:

```
$a = 10;
$b = 10;
var_dump($a == $b);
// bool(true)
var_dump($a === $b);
// bool(true)
$a = 20;
var_dump($a);
// integer(20)
$a = $a + 30;
var_dump($a);
// integer(50);
```

Although `$a` and `$b` are different variables stored in different memory locations, when compared, they're the same. They hold the same value, so we consider them equal. You can change the value of `$a` from `10` to `20` at any time that you want, making the new value `20` and eliminating the `10`. You can replace integer values as much as you want without consideration of the previous value because you're not modifying it; you're just replacing it. If you apply any operation — such as addition (That is. `$a + $b`) — to these variables, you get another new value that can be assigned to another variable or a previously defined one. When you pass `$a` to another function, except when explicitly passed by reference, you're passing a value. It doesn't matter if `$a` gets modified within that function, because in your current code, you'll still have the original copy. Value Objects behave as basic types.

Testing Value Objects

Value Objects are tested in the same way normal objects are. However, the immutability and side-effect-free behavior must be tested too. A solution is to create a copy of the Value Object you're testing before performing any modifications. Assert both are equal using the implemented equality check. Perform the actions you want to test and assert the results. Finally, assert that the original object and copy are still equal.

Let's put this into practice and test the side-effect-free implementation of our add method in the Money class:

```
class MoneyTest extends FrameworkTestCase
{
    /**
     * @test
     */
    public function copiedMoneyShouldRepresentSameValue()
    {
        $aMoney = new Money(100, new Currency('USD'));

        $copiedMoney = Money::fromMoney($aMoney);

        $this->assertTrue($aMoney->equals($copiedMoney));
    }

    /**
     * @test
     */
    public function originalMoneyShouldNotBeModifiedOnAddition()
    {
        $aMoney = new Money(100, new Currency('USD'));

        $aMoney->add(new Money(20, new Currency('USD')));

        $this->assertEquals(100, $aMoney->amount());
    }

    /**
     * @test
     */
    public function moniesShouldBeAdded()
    {
        $aMoney = new Money(100, new Currency('USD'));

        $newMoney = $aMoney->add(new Money(20, new Currency('USD')));

        $this->assertEquals(120, $newMoney->amount());
    }

    // ...
}
```

Persisting Value Objects

Value Objects are not persisted on their own; they're typically persisted within an Aggregate. Value Objects shouldn't be persisted as complete records, though that's an option in some cases. Instead, it's best to use Embedded Value or Serialize LOB patterns. Both patterns can be used when persisting your objects with an open source ORM such as Doctrine, or with a bespoke ORM. As Value Objects are small, Embedded Value is usually the best choice because it provides an easy way to query Entities by any of the attributes the Value Object has. However, if querying by those fields isn't important to you, serialize strategies can be very easy to implement.

Consider the following `Product` Entity with string id, `name`, and `price` (`Money` Value Objects) attributes. We've intentionally decided to simplify this example, with the id being a string and not a Value Object:

```
class Product
{
    private $productId;
    private $name;
    private $price;

    public function __construct(
        $aProductId,
        $aName,
        Money $aPrice
    ) {
        $this->setProductId($aProductId);
        $this->setName($aName);
        $this->setPrice($aPrice);
    }

    // ...
}
```

Assuming you have a `Chapter 10`, *Repositories* for persisting `Product` Entities, an implementation to create and persist a new `Product` could look like this:

```
$product = new Product(
    $productRepository->nextIdentity(),
    'Domain-Driven Design in PHP',
    new Money(999, new Currency('USD'))
);
$productRepository->persist(product);
```

Now let's look at both the ad hoc ORM and the Doctrine implementations that could be used to persist a `Product` Entity containing Value Objects. We'll highlight the application of the Embedded Value and Serialized LOB patterns, along with the differences between persisting a single Value Object and a collection of them.

Why Doctrine?

The `Doctrine` is a great ORM. It solves 80 percent of the requirements a PHP application faces. It has a great community. With a correctly tuned setup, it can perform the same or even better than a bespoke ORM (without losing maintainability). We recommend using Doctrine in most cases when dealing with Entities and business logic. It will save you a lot of time and headaches.

Persisting Single Value Objects

Many different options are available for persisting a single Value Object. These range from using Serialize LOB or Embedded Value as mapping strategies, to using an Ad Hoc ORM or an open source alternative, such as Doctrine. We consider an Ad Hoc ORM to be a custom-built ORM that your company may have developed in order to persist Entities in a database. In our scenario, the Ad Hoc ORM code is going to be implemented using the DBAL library. According to the `official documentation`, The **Doctrine Database Abstraction & Access Layer** (**DBAL**) offers a lightweight and thin runtime layer around a PDO-like API and a lot of additional, horizontal features like database schema introspection and manipulation through an OO API.

Embedded Value with an Ad Hoc ORM

If we're dealing with an Ad Hoc ORM using the Embedded Value pattern, we need to create a field in the Entity table for each attribute in the Value Object. In this case, two extra columns are needed when persisting a `Product` Entity — one for the amount of the Value Object, and one for its currency ISO code:

```
CREATE TABLE `products` (
    id INT NOT NULL,
    name VARCHAR( 255) NOT NULL,
    price_amount INT NOT NULL,
    price_currency VARCHAR( 3) NOT NULL
) ENGINE=InnoDB DEFAULT CHARSET=utf8mb4 COLLATE=utf8mb4_unicode_ci;
```

For persisting the Entity in the database, our `Chapter 10`, *Repositories* has to map each of the fields of the Entity and the ones from the `Money` Value Object.

If you're using an `Ad hoc ORM` Repository based on DBAL—let's call it `DbalProductRepository`—you must take care of creating the `INSERT` statement, binding the parameters, and executing the statement:

```
class DbalProductRepository
    extends DbalRepository
    implements ProductRepository
{
    public function add(Product $aProduct)
    {
        $sql = 'INSERT INTO products VALUES (?, ?, ?, ?)' ;
        $stmt = $this->connection()->prepare($sql);
        $stmt->bindValue(1, $aProduct->id());
        $stmt->bindValue(2, $aProduct->name());
        $stmt->bindValue(3, $aProduct->price()->amount());
        $stmt->bindValue(4, $aProduct
            ->price()->currency()->isoCode());
        $stmt->execute();

        // ...
    }
}
```

After executing this snippet of code to create a `Products` Entity and persist it into the database, each column is filled with the desired information:

```
mysql> select * from products \G
*************************** 1. row ***************************
id: 1
name: Domain-Driven Design in PHP
price_amount: 999
price_currency: USD
1 row in set (0.00 sec)
```

As you can see, you can map your Value Objects and query parameters in an `Ad hoc` manner in order to persist your Value Objects. However, everything is not as easy as it seems. Let's try to fetch the persisted Product with its associated `Money` Value Object. A common approach would be to execute a `SELECT` statement and return a new Entity:

```
class DbalProductRepository
    extends DbalRepository
    implements ProductRepository
{
    public function productOfId($anId)
```

```
    {
        $sql = 'SELECT * FROM products WHERE id = ?';
        $stmt = $this->connection()->prepare($sql);
        $stmt->bindValue(1, $anId);
        $res = $stmt->execute();
        // ...

        return new Product(
            $row['id'],
            $row['name'],
            new Money(
                $row['price_amount'],
                new Currency($row['price_currency'])
            )
        );
    }
}
```

There are some benefits to this approach. First, you can easily read, step by step, how the persistence and subsequent creations occur. Second, you can perform queries based on any of the attributes of the Value Object. Finally, the space required to persist the Entity is just what is required — no more and no less.

However, using the ad hoc ORM approach has its drawbacks. As explained in the Chapter 6, *Domain-Events*, Entities (in Aggregate form) should fire an Event in the constructor if your Domain is interested in the Aggregate's creation. If you use the new operator, you'll be firing the Event as many times as the Aggregate is fetched from the database.

This is one of the reasons why Doctrine uses internal proxies and serialize and unserialize methods to reconstitute an object with its attributes in a specific state without using its constructor. An Entity should only be created with the new operator once in its lifetime:

Constructors

Constructors don't need to include a parameter for each attribute in the object. Think about a blog post. A constructor may need an id and a title; however, internally it can also be setting its status attribute to draft. When publishing the post, a publish method should be called in order to alter its status accordingly and set a published date.

If your intention is still to roll out your own ORM, be ready to solve some fundamental problems such as Events, different constructors, Value Objects, lazy load relations, and so on. That's why we recommend giving Doctrine a try for Domain-Driven Design applications.

Besides, in this instance, you need to create a `DbalProduct` Entity that extends from the `Product` Entity and is able to reconstitute the Entity from the database without using the new operator, instead using a static factory method.

Embedded Value (Embeddables) with Doctrine >= 2.5.*

The latest stable Doctrine release is currently *version 2.5* and it comes with support for mapping Value Objects, thereby removing the need to do this yourself as in *Doctrine 2.4*. Since December 2015, Doctrine also has support for nested embeddables. The support is not 100 percent, but it's high enough to give it a try. In case it doesn't work for your scenario, take a look at the next section. For official documentation, check the Doctrine `Embeddables` `reference`. This option, if implemented correctly, is definitely the one we recommend most. It would be the simplest, most elegant solution, that also provides search support in your *DQL* queries.

Because the `Product`, `Money`, and `Currency` classes have already been shown, the only thing remaining is to show the Doctrine mapping files:

```
<?xml version="1.0" encoding="utf-8"?>
<doctrine-mapping
    xmlns="http://doctrine-project.org/schemas/orm/doctrine-mapping"
    xmlns:xsi="http://www.w3.org/2001/XMLSchema-instance"
    xsi:schemaLocation="
        http://doctrine-project.org/schemas/orm/doctrine-mapping
    https://raw.github.com/doctrine/doctrine2/master/doctrine-mapping.xsd">

    <entity
        name="Product"
        table="product">
        <id
            name="id"
            column="id"
            type="string"
            length="255">
            <generator strategy="NONE">
            </generator>
        </id>

        <field
            name="name"
            type="string"
            length="255"
        />

        <embedded
```

```
            name="price"
            class="Ddd\Domain\Model\Money"
        />
    </entity>
</doctrine-mapping>
```

In the product mapping, we're defining `price` as an instance variable that will hold a `Money` instance. At the same time, `Money` is designed with an amount and a `Currency` instance:

```xml
<?xml version="1.0" encoding="utf-8"?>
<doctrine-mapping
    xmlns="http://doctrine-project.org/schemas/orm/doctrine-mapping"
    xmlns:xsi="http://www.w3.org/2001/XMLSchema-instance"
    xsi:schemaLocation="
        http://doctrine-project.org/schemas/orm/doctrine-mapping
    https://raw.github.com/doctrine/doctrine2/master/doctrine-mapping.xsd">

    <embeddable
        name="Ddd\Domain\Model\Money">

        <field
            name="amount"
            type="integer"
        />
        <embedded
            name="currency"
            class="Ddd\Domain\Model\Currency"
        />
    </embeddable>
</doctrine-mapping>
```

Finally, it's time to show the Doctrine mapping for our `Currency` Value Object:

```xml
<?xml version="1.0" encoding="utf-8"?>
<doctrine-mapping
    xmlns="http://doctrine-project.org/schemas/orm/doctrine-mapping"
    xmlns:xsi="http://www.w3.org/2001/XMLSchema-instance"
    xsi:schemaLocation="
        http://doctrine-project.org/schemas/orm/doctrine-mapping
    https://raw.github.com/doctrine/doctrine2/master/doctrine-mapping.xsd">

    <embeddable
        name="Ddd\Domain\Model\Currency">

        <field
            name="iso"
            type="string"
```

```
            length="3"
        />
    </embeddable>
</doctrine-mapping>
```

As you can see, the above code has a standard embeddable definition with just one string field that holds the ISO code. This approach is the easiest way to use embeddables and is much more effective. By default, Doctrine names your columns by prefixing them using the Value Object name. You can change this behavior to meet your needs by changing the column-prefix attribute in the XML notation.

Embedded Value with Doctrine <= 2.4.*

If you're still stuck in *Doctrine 2.4*, you may wonder what an acceptable solution for using Embedded Values with *Doctrine < 2.5* is. We need to now surrogate all the Value Object attributes in the `Product` Entity, which means creating new artificial attributes that will hold the information of the Value Object. With this in place, we can map all those new attributes using Doctrine. Let's see what impact this has on the `Product` Entity:

```
class Product
{
    private $productId;
    private $name;
    private $price;
    private $surrogateCurrencyIsoCode;
    private $surrogateAmount;

    public function __construct($aProductId, $aName, Money $aPrice)
    {
        $this->setProductId($aProductId);
        $this->setName($aName);
        $this->setPrice($aPrice);
    }

    private function setPrice(Money $aMoney)
    {
        $this->price = $aMoney;
        $this->surrogateAmount = $aMoney->amount();
        $this->surrogateCurrencyIsoCode =
            $aMoney->currency()->isoCode();
    }

    private function price()
    {
        if (null === $this->price) {
```

```php
        $this->price = new Money(
            $this->surrogateAmount,
            new Currency($this->surrogateCurrency)
        );
    }
    return $this->price;
}

// ...
}
```

As you can see, there are two new attributes: one for the amount, and another for the ISO code of the currency. We've also updated the setPrice method in order to keep attribute consistency when setting it. On top of this, we updated the price getter in order to return the Money Value Object built from the new fields. Let's see how the corresponding XML Doctrine mapping should be changed:

```xml
<?xml version="1.0" encoding="utf-8"?>
<doctrine-mapping
    xmlns="http://doctrine-project.org/schemas/orm/doctrine-mapping"
    xmlns:xsi="http://www.w3.org/2001/XMLSchema-instance"
    xsi:schemaLocation="
        http://doctrine-project.org/schemas/orm/doctrine-mapping
    https://raw.github.com/doctrine/doctrine2/master/doctrine-mapping.xsd">

    <entity
        name="Product"
        table="product">

        <id
            name="id"
            column="id"
            type="string"
            length="255" >
            <generator strategy="NONE">
            </generator>
        </id>

        <field
            name="name"
            type="string"
            length="255"
        />

        <field
            name="surrogateAmount"
            type="integer"
```

```
            column="price_amount"
        />
        <field
            name="surrogateCurrencyIsoCode"
            type="string"
            column="price_currency"
        />
    </entity>
</doctrine-mapping>
```

Surrogate Attributes

These two new fields don't strictly belong to the Domain, as they don't refer to Infrastructure details. Rather, they're a necessity due to the lack of embeddable support in Doctrine. There are alternatives that can push these two attributes outside the pure Domain; however, this approach is simpler, easier, and, as a tradeoff, acceptable. There's another use of surrogate attributes in this book; you can find it in the sub-section *Surrogate Identity* of the section *Identity Operation* of Chapter 4, *Entities*.

If we wanted to push these two attributes outside of the Domain, this could be achieved through the use of an Abstract Factory. First, we need to create a new Entity, DoctrineProduct, in our Infrastructure folder. This Entity will extend from Product Entity. All surrogate fields will be placed in the new class, and methods such as price or setPrice should be reimplemented. We'll map Doctrine to use the new DoctrineProduct as opposed to the Product Entity.

Now we're able to fetch Entities from the database, but what about creating a new Product? At some point, we're required to call new Product, but because we need to deal with DoctrineProduct and we don't want our Application Services to know about Infrastructure details, we'll need to use Factories to create Product Entities. So, in every instance where Entity creation occurs with new, you'll instead call createProduct on ProductFactory.

There could be many additional classes required to avoid placing the surrogate attributes in the original Entity. As such, it's our recommendation to surrogate all the Value Objects to the same Entity, though this admittedly leads to a less pure solution.

Serialized LOB and Ad Hoc ORM

If the addition of searching capabilities to the Value Objects attributes is not important, there's another pattern that can be considered: the Serialized LOB. This pattern works by serializing the whole Value Object into a string format that can easily be persisted and fetched. The most significant difference between this solution and the embedded alternative is that in the latter option, the persistence footprint requirements are reduced to a single column:

```
CREATE TABLE `products` (
    id INT NOT NULL,
    name VARCHAR( 255) NOT NULL,
    price TEXT NOT NULL
) ENGINE=InnoDB DEFAULT CHARSET=utf8mb4 COLLATE=utf8mb4_unicode_ci;
```

In order to persist the `Product` Entities using this approach, a change in the `DbalProductRepository` is required. The `Money` Value Object must be serialized into a string before persisting the `final` Entity:

```
class DbalProductRepository extends DbalRepository implements
ProductRepository
{
    public function add(Product $aProduct)
    {
        $sql = 'INSERT INTO products VALUES (?, ?, ?)';
        $stmt = this->connection()->prepare(sql);
        $stmt->bindValue(1, aProduct->id());
        $stmt->bindValue(2, aProduct->name());
        $stmt->bindValue(3, $this->serialize($aProduct->price()));

        // ...
    }

    private function serialize($object)
    {
        return serialize($object);
    }
}
```

Let's see how our Product is now represented in the database. The table column `price` is a `TEXT` type column that contains a serialization of a `Money` object representing 9.99 USD:

```
mysql > select * from products \G
*************************** 1.row***************************
id   : 1
name : Domain-Driven Design in PHP
```

```
price : O:22:"Ddd\Domain\Model\Money":2:{s:30:"Ddd\Domain\Model\\
Money amount";i :
999;s:32:"Ddd\Domain\Model\Money currency";O : 25:"Ddd\Domain\Model\\
Currency":1:{\
s:34:" Ddd\Domain\Model\Currency isoCode";s:3:"USD";}}1 row in set(\ 0.00
sec)
```

This approach does the job. However, it's not recommended due to problems occurring when refactoring classes in your code. Could you imagine the problems if we decided to rename our Money class? Could you imagine the changes that would be required in our database representation when moving the Money class from one namespace to another? Another tradeoff, as explained before, is the lack of querying capabilities. It doesn't matter whether you use Doctrine or not; writing a query to get the products cheaper than, say, 200 USD is almost impossible while using a serialization strategy.

The querying issue can only be solved by using Embedded Values. However, the serialization refactoring problems can be fixed using a specialized library for handling serialization processes.

Improved Serialization with JMS Serializer

The serialize/unserialize native PHP strategies have a problem when dealing with class and namespace refactoring. One alternative is to use your own serialization mechanism — for example, concatenating the amount, a one character separator such as |, and the currency ISO code. However, there's another favored approach: using an open source serializer library such as JMS Serializer. Let's see an example of applying it when serializing a Money object:

```
$myMoney = new Money(999, new Currency('USD'));

$serializer = JMS\Serializer\SerializerBuilder::create()->build();
$jsonData = $serializer->serialize(myMoney, 'json');
```

In order to unserialize the object, the process is straightforward:

```
$serializer = JMS\Serializer\SerializerBuilder::create()->build();
// ...
$myMoney = $serializer->deserialize(jsonData, 'Ddd', 'json');
```

With this example, you can refactor your Money class without having to update your database. JMS Serializer can be used in many different scenarios — for example, when working with REST APIs. An important feature is the ability to specify which attributes of an object should be omitted in the serialization process — for example, a password.

Check out the Mapping Reference and the Cookbook for more information. JMS Serializer is a must in any Domain-Driven Design project.

Serialized LOB with Doctrine

In Doctrine, there are different ways of serializing objects in order to eventually persist them.

Doctrine Object Mapping Type

Doctrine has support for the Serialize LOB pattern. There are plenty of predefined mapping types you can use in order to match Entity attributes with database columns or even tables. One of those mappings is the object type, which maps an SQL CLOB to a PHP object using serialize() and unserialize().

According to the Doctrine DBAL 2 Documentation, object type:

> Maps and converts object data based on PHP serialization. If you need to store an exact representation of your object data, you should consider using this type as it uses serialization to represent an exact copy of your object as string in the database. Values retrieved from the database are always converted to PHP's object type using unserialization or null if no data is present.

> This type will always be mapped to the database vendor's text type internally as there is no way of storing a PHP object representation natively in the database. Furthermore this type requires a SQL column comment hint so that it can be reverse engineered from the database. Doctrine cannot correctly map back this type correctly using vendors that do not support column comments, and will instead fall back to the text type instead.

> Because the built-in text type of PostgreSQL does not support NULL bytes, the object type will result in unserialization errors. A workaround to this problem is to serialize()/unserialize() and base64_encode()/base64_decode() PHP objects and store them into a text field manually.

Let's look at a possible XML mapping for the Product Entity by using the object type:

```xml
<?xml version="1.0" encoding="utf-8"?>
<doctrine-mapping
    xmlns="http://doctrine-project.org/schemas/orm/doctrine-mapping"
    xmlns:xsi="http://www.w3.org/2001/XMLSchema-instance"
    xsi:schemaLocation="
        http://doctrine-project.org/schemas/orm/doctrine-mapping
    https://raw.github.com/doctrine/doctrine2/master/doctrine-mapping.xsd">

    <entity
        name="Product"
        table="products">

        <id
            name="id"
            column="id"
            type="string"
            length="255">
            <generator strategy="NONE">
            </generator>
        </id>
        <field
            name="name"
            type="string"
            length="255"
        />
        <field
            name="price"
            type="object"
        />
    </entity>
</doctrine-mapping>
```

The key addition is `type="object"`, which tells Doctrine that we're going to be using an object mapping. Let's see how we could create and persist a `Product` Entity using Doctrine:

```php
// ...
$em->persist($product);
$em->flush($product);
```

Let's check that if we now fetch our `Product` Entity from the database, it's returned in an expected state:

```php
// ...
$repository = $em->getRepository('Ddd\\Domain\\Model\\Product');
$item = $repository->find(1);
var_dump($item);
```

```
/*
class Ddd\Domain\Model\Product#177 (3) {
    private $productId => int(1)
    private $name => string(41) "Domain-Driven Design in PHP"
    private $money => class Ddd\Domain\Model\Money#174 (2) {
        private $amount => string(3) "100"
        private $currency => class Ddd\Domain\Model\Currency#175 (1){
            private $isoCode => string(3) "USD"
        }
    }
}
*/
```

Last but not least, the `Doctrine DBAL 2 Documentation` states that:

> Object types are compared by reference, not by value. Doctrine updates this value if the reference changes and therefore behaves as if these objects are immutable value objects.

This approach suffers from the same refactoring issues as the Ad hoc ORM did. The object mapping type is internally using `serialize/unserialize`. What about instead using our own serialization?

Doctrine Custom Types

Another option is to handle the Value Object persistence using a Doctrine Custom Type. A Custom Type adds a new mapping type to Doctrine — one that describes a custom transformation between an Entity field and the database representation, in order to persist the former.

As the `Doctrine DBAL 2 Documentation` explains:

> Just redefining how database types are mapped to all the existing Doctrine types is not at all that useful. You can define your own Doctrine Mapping Types by extending `Doctrine\DBAL\Types\Type`. You are required to implement 4 different methods to get this working.

With the object type, the serialization step includes information, such as the class, that makes it quite difficult to safely refactor our code.

Let's try to improve on this solution. Think about a custom serialization process that could solve the problem.

One such way could be to persist the Money Value Object as a string in the database encoded in amount|isoCode format:

```php
use Ddd\Domain\Model\Currency;
use Ddd\Domain\Model\Money;
use Doctrine\DBAL\Types\TextType;
use Doctrine\DBAL\Platforms\AbstractPlatform;

class MoneyType extends TextType
{
    const MONEY = 'money';

    public function convertToPHPValue(
        $value,
        AbstractPlatform $platform
    ) {
        $value = parent::convertToPHPValue($value, $platform);
        $value = explode('|', $value);
        return new Money(
            $value[0],
            new Currency($value[1])
        );
    }

    public function convertToDatabaseValue(
        $value,
        AbstractPlatform $platform
    ) {
        return implode(
            '|',
            [
                $value->amount(),
                $value->currency()->isoCode()
            ]
        );
    }

    public function getName()
    {
        return self::MONEY;
    }
}
```

Using Doctrine, you're required to register all Custom Types. It's common to use an EntityManagerFactory that centralizes this EntityManager creation.

Alternatively, you could perform this step by bootstrapping your application:

```php
use Doctrine\DBAL\Types\Type;
use Doctrine\ORM\EntityManager;
use Doctrine\ORM\Tools\Setup;

class EntityManagerFactory
{
    public function build()
    {
        Type::addType(
            'money',
            'Ddd\Infrastructure\Persistence\Doctrine\Type\MoneyType'
        );
        return EntityManager::create(
            [
                'driver' => 'pdo_mysql',
                'user' => 'root',
                'password' => '',
                'dbname' => 'ddd',
            ],
            Setup::createXMLMetadataConfiguration(
                [__DIR__.'/config'],
                true
            )
        );
    }
}
```

Now we need to specify in the mapping that we want to use our Custom Type:

```xml
<?xml version = "1.0" encoding = "utf-8"?>
<doctrine-mapping>
    <entity
        name = "Product"
        table = "product">

        <!-- ... -->
        <field
            name = "price"
            type = "money"
        />
    </entity>
</doctrine-mapping>
```

Why Use XML Mapping?

Thanks to the XSD schema validation in the headers of the XML mapping file, many **Integrated Development Environment** (**IDEs**) setups provide auto-complete functionality for all the elements and attributes present in the mapping definition. However, in other parts of the book, we use YAML to show a different syntax.

Let's check the database to see how the price was persisted using this approach:

```
mysql> select * from products \G
*************************** 1. row***************************
id: 1
name: Domain-Driven Design in PHP
price: 999|USD
1 row in set (0.00 sec)
```

This approach is an improvement on the one before in terms of future refactoring. However, searching capabilities remain limited due to the format of the column. With the Doctrine Custom types, you can improve the situation a little, but it's still not the best option for building your DQL queries. See `Doctrine Custom Mapping Types` for more information.

Time to Discuss

Think about and discuss with a peer how would you create a Doctrine Custom Type using JMS to `serialize` and `unserialize` a Value Object.

Persisting a Collection of Value Objects

Imagine that we'd now like to add a collection of prices to be persisted to our `Product` Entity. These prices could represent the different prices the product has borne throughout its lifetime or the product price in different currencies. This could be named `HistoricalPrice`, as shown below:

```
class HistoricalProduct extends Product
{
    /**
     * @var Money[]
     */
    protected $prices;

    public function __construct(
        $aProductId,
        $aName,
```

```
        Money $aPrice,
        array $somePrices
    ) {
        parent::__construct($aProductId, $aName, $aPrice);
        $this->setPrices($somePrices);
    }

    private function setPrices(array $somePrices)
    {
        $this->prices = $somePrices;
    }

    public function prices()
    {
        return $this->prices;
    }
}
```

`HistoricalProduct` extends from `Product`, so it inherits the same behavior, plus the price collection functionality.

As in the previous sections, serialization is a plausible approach if you don't care about querying capabilities. However, Embedded Values are a possibility if we know exactly how many prices we want to persist. But what happens if we want to persist an undetermined collection of historical prices?

Collection Serialized into a Single Column

Serializing a collection of Value Objects into a single column is most likely the easiest solution. Everything that was previously explained in the section about persisting a single Value Object applies in this situation. With Doctrine, you can use an Object or Custom Type — with some additional considerations to bear in mind: Value Objects should be small in size, but if you wish to persist a large collection, be sure to consider the maximum column length and the maximum row width that your database engine can handle.

Exercise
Come up with both `Doctrine` Object Type and `Doctrine Custom` Type implementation strategies for persisting a Product with different prices.

Collection Backed by a Join Table

In case you want to persist and query an Entity by its related Value Objects, you have the choice to persist the Value Objects as Entities. In terms of the Domain, those objects would still be Value Objects, but we'll need to give them an id and set them up with a one-to-many/one-to-one relation with the owner, a real Entity. To summarize, your ORM handles the collection of Value Objects as Entities, but in your Domain, they're still treated as Value Objects.

The main idea behind the Join Table strategy is to create a table that connects the owner Entity and its Value Objects. Let's see a database representation:

```
CREATE TABLE ` historical_products` (
    `id` char( 36) COLLATE utf8mb4_unicode_ci NOT NULL,
    `name` varchar( 255) COLLATE utf8mb4_unicode_ci NOT NULL,
    `price_amount` int( 11 ) NOT NULL,
    `price_currency` char( 3) COLLATE utf8mb4_unicode_ci NOT NULL,
    PRIMARY KEY (`id`)
) ENGINE=InnoDB DEFAULT CHARSET=utf8mb4 COLLATE=utf8mb4_unicode_ci;
```

The `historical_products` table will look the same as products. Remember that `HistoricalProduct` extends `Product` Entity in order to easily show how to deal with persisting a collection. A new prices table is now required in order to persist all the different `Money` Value Objects that a `Product` Entity can handle:

```
CREATE TABLE `prices`(
    `id` int(11) NOT NULL AUTO_INCREMENT,
    `amount` int(11) NOT NULL,
    `currency` char(3) COLLATE utf8mb4_unicode_ci NOT NULL,
    PRIMARY KEY (`id`)
) ENGINE=InnoDB DEFAULT CHARSET=utf8mb4 COLLATE=utf8mb4_unicode_ci;
```

Finally, a table that relates products and prices is needed:

```
CREATE TABLE `products_prices` (
    `product_id` char( 36) COLLATE utf8mb4_unicode_ci NOT NULL,
    `price_id` int( 11 ) NOT NULL,
    PRIMARY KEY (`product_id`, `price_id`),
    UNIQUE KEY `UNIQ_62F8E673D614C7E7` (`price_id`),
    KEY `IDX_62F8E6734584665A` (`product_id`),
    CONSTRAINT `FK_62F8E6734584665A` FOREIGN KEY (`product_id`)
        REFERENCES `historical_products` (`id`),
    CONSTRAINT `FK_62F8E673D614C7E7` FOREIGN KEY (`price_id`)
        REFERENCES `prices`(`id`)
) ENGINE=InnoDB DEFAULT CHARSET=utf8mb4 COLLATE=utf8mb4_unicode_ci;
```

Collection Backed by a Join Table with Doctrine

Doctrine requires that all database Entities have a unique identity. Because we want to persist Money Value Objects, we need to then add an artificial identity so Doctrine can handle its persistence. There are two options: including the surrogate identity in the Money Value Object, or placing it in an extended class.

The issue with the first option is that the new identity is only required due to the Database persistence layer. This identity is not part of the Domain.

An issue with the second option is the amount of alterations required in order to avoid this so-called boundary leak. With a class extension, creating new instances of the Money Value Object class from any Domain Object isn't recommended, as it would break the Inversion Principle. The solution is to again create a Money Factory that would need to be passed into Application Services and any other Domain Objects.

In this scenario, we recommend using the first option. Let's review the changes required to implement it in the Money Value Object:

```
class Money
{
    private $amount;
    private $currency;
    private $surrogateId;
    private $surrogateCurrencyIsoCode;

    public function __construct($amount, Currency $currency)
    {
        $this->setAmount($amount);
        $this->setCurrency($currency);
    }

    private function setAmount($amount)
    {
        $this->amount = $amount;
    }

    private function setCurrency(Currency $currency)
    {
        $this->currency = $currency;
        $this->surrogateCurrencyIsoCode =
            $currency->isoCode();
    }
```

```php
    public function currency()
    {
        if (null === $this->currency) {
            $this->currency = new Currency(
                $this->surrogateCurrencyIsoCode
            );
        }
        return $this->currency;
    }

    public function amount()
    {
        return $this->amount;
    }

    public function equals(Money $aMoney)
    {
        return
            $this->amount() === $aMoney->amount() &&
            $this->currency()->equals($this->currency());
    }
}
```

As seen above, two new attributes have been added. The first one, `surrogateId`, is not used by our Domain, but it's required for the persistence Infrastructure to persist this Value Object as an Entity in our Database. The second one, `surrogateCurrencyIsoCode`, holds the ISO code for the currency. Using these new attributes, it's really easy to map our Value Object with Doctrine.

The `Money` mapping is quite straightforward:

```xml
<?xml version = "1.0" encoding = "utf-8"?>
<doctrine-mapping
    xmlns="http://doctrine-project.org/schemas/orm/doctrine-mapping"
    xmlns:xsi="http://www.w3.org/2001/XMLSchema-instance"
    xsi:schemaLocation="
        http://doctrine-project.org/schemas/orm/doctrine-mapping
    https://raw.github.com/doctrine/doctrine2/master/doctrine-mapping.xsd">

    <entity
        name="Ddd\Domain\Model\Money"
        table="prices">

        <id
            name="surrogateId"
            type="integer"
```

```
            column="id">
            <generator
                strategy="AUTO">
            </generator>

        </id>
        <field
            name="amount"
            type="integer"
            column="amount"
        />
        <field
            name="surrogateCurrencyIsoCode"
            type="string"
            column="currency"
        />
    </entity>
</doctrine-mapping>
```

Using Doctrine, the `HistoricalProduct` Entity would have following mapping:

```
<?xml version="1.0" encoding="utf-8"?>
<doctrine-mapping
    xmlns="http://doctrine-project.org/schemas/orm/doctrine-mapping"
    xmlns:xsi="http://www.w3.org/2001/XMLSchema-instance"
    xsi:schemaLocation="
        http://doctrine-project.org/schemas/orm/doctrine-mapping
    https://raw.github.com/doctrine/doctrine2/master/doctrine-mapping.xsd">

    <entity
        name="Ddd\Domain\Model\HistoricalProduct"
        table="historical_products"
        repository-class="
Ddd\Infrastructure\Domain\Model\DoctrineHistoricalProductRepository
        ">
        <many-to-many
            field="prices"
            target-entity="Ddd\Domain\Model\Money">

            <cascade>
                <cascade-all/>
            </cascade>

            <join-table
                name="products_prices">
                <join-columns>
                    <join-column
                        name="product_id"
```

```
                        referenced-column-name="id"
                    />
                </join-columns>
                <inverse-join-columns>
                    <join-column
                        name="price_id"
                        referenced-column-name="id"
                        unique="true"
                    />
                </inverse-join-columns>
            </join-table>
        </many-to-many>
    </entity>
</doctrine-mapping>
```

Collection Backed by a Join Table with an Ad Hoc ORM

It's possible to do the same with an Ad hoc ORM, where Cascade `INSERTS` and `JOIN`
queries are required. It's important to be careful about how the removal of Value Objects is
handled, in order to not leave orphan the `Money` Value Objects.

Exercise

Think up a solution for `DbalHistoricalRepository` that would handle
the persist method.

Collection Backed by a Database Entity

Database Entity is the same solution as Join Table, with the addition of the Value Object
that's only managed by the owner Entity. In the current scenario, consider that the `Money`
Value Object is only used by the `HistoricalProduct` Entity; a Join Table would be overly
complex. So the same result could be achieved using a one-to-many database relation.

Exercise

Think of the mapping required between `HistoricalProduct` and `Money`
if a Database Entity approach is used.

NoSQL

What about NoSQL mechanisms such as *Redis*, *MongoDB*, or *CouchDB*? Unfortunately, you can't escape these problems. In order to persist an Aggregate using *Redis*, you need to serialize it into a string before setting the value. If you use PHP `serialize/unserialize` methods, you'll face namespace or class name refactoring issues again. If you choose to serialize in a custom way (JSON, custom string, and so on.), you'll be required to again rebuild the Value Object during *Redis* retrieval.

PostgreSQL JSONB and MySQL JSON Type

If our database engine would allow us to not only use the Serialized LOB strategy but also search based on its value, we would have the best of both approaches. Well, good news: now you *can* do this. As of *PostgreSQL version 9.4*, support for `JSONB` has been added. Value Objects can be persisted as JSON serializations and subsequently queried within this JSON serialization.

MySQL has done the same. As of *MySQL 5.7.8*, MySQL supports a native JSON data type that enables efficient access to data in **JSON (JavaScript Object Notation)** documents. According to the `MySQL 5.7 Reference Manual`, the JSON data type provides these advantages over storing JSON-format strings in a string column:

- Automatic validation of JSON documents stored in JSON columns. Invalid documents produce an error.
- Optimized storage format. JSON documents stored in JSON columns are converted to an internal format that permits quick read access to document elements. When the server later must read a JSON value stored in this binary format, the value need not be parsed from a text representation. The binary format is structured to enable the server to look up subobjects or nested values directly by key or array index without reading all values before or after them in the document.

If Relational Databases add support for document and nested document searches with high performance and with all the benefits of an **Atomicity**, **Consistency**, **Isolation**, **Durability(ACID)** philosophy, it could save a lot of complexity in many projects.

Security

Another interesting detail of modeling your Domain concepts using Value Objects is regarding its security benefits. Consider an application within the context of selling flight tickets. If you deal with International Air Transport Association airport codes, also known as `IATA codes`, you can decide to use a string or model the concept using a Value Object. If you choose to go with the string, think about all the places where you'll be checking that the string is a valid IATA code. What's the chance you forget somewhere important? On the other hand, think about trying to instantiate new `IATA("BCN'; DROP TABLE users;--")`. If you centralize the *guards* in the constructor and then pass an IATA Value Object into your model, avoiding SQL Injections or similar attacks gets easier.

If you want to know more about the security side of Domain-Driven Design, you can follow `Dan Bergh Johnsson` or read his `blog`.

Wrap-Up

Using Value Objects for modeling concepts in your Domain that measure, quantify, or describe is highly recommended. As shown, Value Objects are easy to create, maintain, and test. In order to handle persistence within a Domain-Driven Design application, using an ORM is a must. However, in order to persist Value Objects using Doctrine, the preferred way is using embeddables. In case you're stuck in *version 2.4*, there are two options: adding the Value Object fields directly into your Entity and mapping them (less elegant, but easier), or extending your Entities (far more elegant, but more complex).

4
Entities

We've talked about the benefits of trying to first model everything in the Domain as a Value Object. But when modeling the Domain, there will probably be situations where you'll find that some concept in the Ubiquitous Language demands a thread of Identity.

Introduction

Clear examples of objects requiring an Identity include:

- A **person**. A person always has an Identity and it's always the same in terms of their name or identification card.
- An **order** in an e-commerce system. In such a context, every new order created has its own Identity and it's the same over time.

These concepts have an Identity that endures over time. No matter how many times data in the concepts changes, their Identities remain the same. That's what makes them Entities and not Value Objects. In terms of PHP implementation, they would be plain old classes. For example, consider the following in the case of a person:

```php
namespace Ddd\Identity\Domain\Model;

class Person
{
    private $identificationNumber;
    private $firstName;
    private $lastName;

    public function __construct(
        $anIdentificationNumber, $aFirstName, $aLastName
    ) {
        $this->identificationNumber = $anIdentificationNumber;
```

```
        $this->firstName = $aFirstName;
        $this->lastName  = $aLastName;
    }

    public function identificationNumber()
    {
        return $this->identificationNumber;
    }

    public function firstName()
    {
        return $this->firstName;
    }

    public function lastName()
    {
        return $this->lastName;
    }
}
```

Or, consider the following in the case of an order:

```
namespace Ddd\Billing\Domain\Model\Order;

class Order
{
    private $id;
    private $amount;
    private $firstName;
    private $lastName;

    public function __construct(
        $anId, Amount $amount, $aFirstName, $aLastName
    ) {
        $this->id = $anId;
        $this->amount = $amount;
        $this->firstName = $aFirstName;
        $this->lastName = $aLastName;
    }

    public function id()
    {
        return $this->id;
    }

    public function firstName()
    {
        return $this->firstName;
```

```
    }

    public function lastName()
    {
        return $this->lastName;
    }
}
```

Objects Vs. Primitive Types

Most of the time, the Identity of an Entity is represented as a primitive type — usually a string or an integer. But using a Value Object to represent it has more advantages:

- Value Objects are immutable, so they can't be modified.
- Value Objects are complex types that can have custom behaviors, something which primitive types can't have. Take, as an example, **the equality operation**. With Value Objects, equality operations can be modeled and encapsulated in their own classes, making concepts go from implicit to explicit.

Let's see a possible implementation for `OrderId`, the `Order` Identity that has evolved into a Value Object:

```
namespace Ddd\Billing\Domain\Model;

class OrderId
{
    private $id;

    public function __construct($anId)
    {
        $this->id = $anId;
    }

    public function id()
    {
        return $this->id;
    }

    public function equalsTo(OrderId $anOrderId)
    {
        return $anOrderId->id === $this->id;
    }
}
```

There are different implementations you can consider for implementing the OrderId. The example shown above is quite simple. As explained in the Chapter 3, *Value Objects*, you can make the __constructor method private and use static factory methods to create new instances. Talk with your team, experiment, and agree. Because Entity Identities are not complex Value Objects, our recommendation is that you shouldn't worry too much here.

Going back to the Order, it's time to update references to OrderId:

```
class Order
{
    private $id;
    private $amount;
    private $firstName;
    private $lastName;

    public function __construct(
        OrderId $anOrderId, Amount $amount, $aFirstName, $aLastName
    ) {
        $this->id = $anOrderId;
        $this->amount = $amount;
        $this->firstName = $aFirstName;
        $this->lastName = $aLastName;
    }

    public function id()
    {
        return $this->id;
    }

    public function firstName()
    {
        return $this->firstName;
    }

    public function lastName()
    {
        return $this->lastName;
    }

    public function amount()
    {
        return $this->amount;
    }
}
```

Our Entity has an Identity modeled using a Value Object. Let's consider different ways of creating an OrderId.

Identity Operation

As stated before, the Identity of an Entity is what defines it. So then, handling it is an important aspect of the Entity. There are usually four ways to define the Identity of an Entity: the persistence mechanism provides the Identity, a client provides the Identity, the application itself provides the Identity, or another Bounded Context provides the Identity.

Persistence Mechanism Generates Identity

Usually, the simplest way of generating the Identity is to delegate it to the persistence mechanism, because the vast majority of persistence mechanisms support some kind of Identity generation — like MySQL's AUTO_INCREMENT attribute or Postgres and Oracle sequences. This, although simple, has a major drawback: we won't have the Identity of the Entity until we persist it. So to some degree, if we're going with persistence mechanism-generated Identities, we'll couple the Identity operation with the underlying persistence store:

```
CREATE TABLE `orders` (
    `id` int(11) NOT NULL auto_increment,
    `amount` decimal (10,5) NOT NULL,
    `first_name` varchar(100) NOT NULL,
    `last_name` varchar(100) NOT NULL,
    PRIMARY KEY (`id`)
) ENGINE=InnoDB DEFAULT CHARSET=utf8mb4 COLLATE=utf8mb4_unicode_ci;
```

And then we might consider this code:

```
namespace Ddd\Identity\Domain\Model;

class Person
{
    private $identificationNumber;
    private $firstName;
    private $lastName;

    public function __construct(
        $anIdentificationNumber, $aFirstName, $aLastName
    ) {
        $this->identificationNumber = $anIdentificationNumber;
        $this->firstName = $aFirstName;
        $this->lastName = $aLastName;
    }

    public function identificationNumber()
```

```
    {
        return $this->identificationNumber;
    }

    public function firstName()
    {
        return $this->firstName;
    }

    public function lastName()
    {
        return $this->lastName;
    }
}
```

If you've ever tried to build your own ORM, you've already experienced this situation. What's the approach for creating a new Person? If the database is going to generate the Identity, do we have to pass it in the constructor? When and where is the magic that will update the Person with its Identity? What happens if we end up not persisting the Entity?

Surrogate Identity

Sometimes when using an ORM to map Entities to a persistence store, some constraints are imposed — for example, Doctrine demands an integer field if an IDENTITY generator strategy is used. This can conflict with the Domain Model if it requires another kind of Identity.

The simplest way to handle such a situation is by using a Layer Supertype, where the Identity field created for the persistence store is placed:

```
namespace Ddd\Common\Domain\Model;

abstract class IdentifiableDomainObject
{
    private $id;

    protected function id()
    {
        return $this->id;
    }

    protected function setId($anId)
    {
        $this->id = $anId;
    }
}
```

```
namespace Acme\Billing\Domain;

use Acme\Common\Domain\IdentifiableDomainObject;

class Order extends IdentifiableDomainObject
{
    private $orderId;

    public function orderId()
    {
        if (null === $this->orderId) {
            $this->orderId = new OrderId($this->id());
        }

        return $this->orderId;
    }
}
```

Active Record Vs. Data Mapper for Rich Domain Models

Every project always faces the decision of which ORM should be used. There are a lot of good ORMs for PHP out there: Doctrine, Propel, Eloquent, Paris, and many more.

Most of them are `Active Record` implementations. An Active Record implementation is fine mostly for CRUD applications, but it's not the ideal solution for Rich Domain Models for the following reasons:

- The Active Record pattern assumes a one-to-one relation between an Entity and a database table. So it couples the design of the database to the design of the object system. And in a Rich Domain Model, sometimes Entities are constructed with information that may come from different data sources.
- Advanced things like collections and inheritance are tricky to implement.
- Most of the implementations force the use, through inheritance, of some sort of constructions that impose several conventions. This can lead to persistence leakage into the Domain Model by coupling the Domain Model with the ORM. The only Active Record implementation we've seen that doesn't impose inheriting from a base class is `Castle ActiveRecord` from `Castle Project`, a .NET framework. While this leads to some degree of separation between persistence and Domain concerns in the produced Entities, it doesn't decouple the low-level persistence details from high-level Domain design.

As mentioned in the previous chapter, currently the best ORM for PHP is `Doctrine` , which is an implementation of the `Data Mapper pattern`. Data Mapper decouples persistence concerns from Domain concerns, leading to persistence-free Entities. This makes the tool the best for someone wanting to build a Rich Domain Model.

Client Provides Identity

Sometimes, when dealing with certain Domains, the Identities come naturally, with the client consuming the Domain Model. This is likely the ideal case, because the Identity can be modeled easily. Let's take a look at the book-selling market:

```
namespace Ddd\Catalog\Domain\Model\Book;

class ISBN
{
    private $isbn;

    private function __construct($anIsbn)
    {
        $this->setIsbn($anIsbn);
    }

    private function setIsbn($anIsbn)
    {
        $this->assertIsbnIsValid($anIsbn, 'The ISBN is invalid.');

        $this->isbn = $anIsbn;
    }

    public static function create($anIsbn)
    {
        return new static($anIsbn);
    }

    private function assertIsbnIsValid($anIsbn, $string)
    {
        // ... Validates an ISBN code
    }
}
```

According to `Wikipedia`: The **International Standard Book Number** (**ISBN**) is a unique numeric commercial book identifier. An ISBN is assigned to each edition and variation (except re-printings) of a book. For example, an e-book, a paperback and a hardcover edition of the same book would each have a different ISBN. The ISBN is 13 digits long if assigned on or after 1 January 2007, and 10 digits long if assigned before 2007. The method of assigning an ISBN is nation-based and varies from country to country, often depending on how large the publishing industry is within a country.

The cool thing about the ISBN is that it's already defined in the Domain, it's a valid identifier because it's unique, and it can be easily validated. This is a good example of an Identity provided by the client:

```
class Book
{
    private $isbn;
    private $title;

    public function __construct(ISBN $anIsbn, $aTitle)
    {
        $this->isbn  = $anIsbn;
        $this->title = $aTitle;
    }
}
```

Now, it's just a matter of using it:

```
$book = new Book(
    ISBN::create('...'),
    'Domain-Driven Design in PHP'
);
```

Exercise
Think about other Domains where Identities are built in and model one.

Application Generates Identity

If the client can't provide the Identity generally, the preferred way to handle the Identity operation is to let the application generate the Identities, usually through a UUID. This is our recommended approach in the case that you don't have a scenario as shown in the previous section.

According to `Wikipedia`:

The intent of UUIDs is to enable distributed systems to uniquely identify information without significant central coordination. In this context the word unique should be taken to mean *practically unique* rather than *guaranteed unique*. Since the identifiers have a finite size, it is possible for two differing items to share the same identifier. This is a form of hash collision. The identifier size and generation process need to be selected so as to make this sufficiently improbable in practice. Anyone can create a UUID and use it to identify something with reasonable confidence that the same identifier will never be unintentionally created by anyone to identify something else. Information labeled with UUIDs can therefore be later combined into a single database without needing to resolve identifier (ID) conflicts.

 There are several libraries in PHP that generate UUIDs, and they can be found at Packagist: `https://packagist.org/search/?q=uuid`. The best recommendation is the one developed by Ben Ramsey at the following link: `https://github.com/ramsey/uuid`because it has tons of watchers on GitHub and millions of installations on Packagist.

The preferred place to put the creation of the Identity would be inside a Repository (we'll go deeper into this in the `Chapter 10`, *Repositories*:

```
namespace Ddd\Billing\Domain\Model\Order;

interface OrderRepository
{
    public function nextIdentity();
    public function add(Order $anOrder);
    public function remove(Order $anOrder);
}
```

When using Doctrine, we'll need to create a custom Repository that implements such an interface. It will basically create the new Identity and use the `EntityManager` in order to persist and delete Entities. A small variation is to put the `nextIdentity` implementation into the interface that will become an abstract class:

```
namespace Ddd\Billing\Infrastructure\Domain\Model\Order;

use Ddd\Billing\Domain\Model\Order\Order;
use Ddd\Billing\Domain\Model\Order\OrderId;
use Ddd\Billing\Domain\Model\Order\OrderRepository;

use Doctrine\ORM\EntityRepository;

class DoctrineOrderRepository
```

```
        extends EntityRepository
        implements OrderRepository
{
        public function nextIdentity()
        {
            return OrderId::create();
        }

        public function add(Order $anOrder)
        {
            $this->getEntityManager()->persist($anOrder);
        }

        public function remove(Order $anOrder)
        {
            $this->getEntityManager()->remove($anOrder);
        }
}
```

Let's quickly review the final implementation of the `OrderId` Value Object:

```
namespace Ddd\Billing\Domain\Model\Order;

use Ramsey\Uuid\Uuid;

class OrderId
{
    private $id;

    private function __construct($anId = null)
    {
        $this->id = $id ? :Uuid::uuid4()->toString();
    }

    public static function create($anId = null )
    {
        return new static($anId);
    }
}
```

The main concern about this approach, as you'll see in the following sections, is how easy it is to persist Entities that contain Value Objects. However, mapping embedded Value Objects that are inside an Entity can be tricky, depending on the ORM.

Other Bounded Context Generates Identity

This is likely the most complex Identity generation strategy because it forces a local Entity to be dependent not only on local Bounded Context events, but also on external Bounded Contexts events. So in terms of maintenance, the cost would be high.

The other Bounded Context provides an interface to select the Identity from the local Entity. It can take some of the exposed properties as its own.

When synchronization is needed between the Entities of the Bounded Contexts, it can usually be achieved with an Event-Driven Architecture on each of the Bounded Contexts that need to be notified when the original Entity is changed.

Persisting Entities

Currently, as discussed earlier in the chapter, the best tool for saving Entity state to a persistent store is Doctrine ORM. Doctrine has several ways to specify Entity metadata: by annotations in Entity code, by XML, by YAML, or by plain PHP. In this chapter, we'll discuss in depth why annotations are not the best thing to use when mapping Entities.

Setting Up Doctrine

First of all, we need to require Doctrine through Composer. At the root folder of the project, the command below has to be executed:

```
> php composer.phar require "doctrine/orm=^2.5"
```

Then, these lines will allow you to set up Doctrine:

```
require_once '/path/to/vendor/autoload.php';

use Doctrine\ORM\Tools\Setup;
use Doctrine\ORM\EntityManager;

$paths = ['/path/to/entity-files'];
$isDevMode = false;

// the connection configuration
$dbParams = [
    'driver'   => 'pdo_mysql',
    'user'     => 'the_database_username',
    'password' => 'the_database_password',
    'dbname'   => 'the_database_name',
```

```
];

$config = Setup::createAnnotationMetadataConfiguration($paths, $isDevMode);
$entityManager = EntityManager::create($dbParams, $config);
```

Mapping Entities

By default, Doctrine's documentation presents the code examples using annotations. So we begin the code example using annotations and discussing why they should be avoided whenever possible.

To do so, we'll bring back the `Order` class discussed earlier in this chapter.

Mapping Entities Using Annotated Code

When Doctrine was released, a catchy way of showing how to map objects in the code examples was by using annotations.

What's an annotation?

An annotation is a special form of metadata. In PHP, it's put under source code comments. For example, *PHPDocumentor* makes use of annotations to build API information, and `PHPUnit` uses some annotations to specify data providers or to provide expectations about exceptions thrown by a piece of code:

```
class SumTest extends PHPUnit_Framework_TestCase
{
    /** @dataProvider aMethodName */
    public function testAddition() {
        //...
    }
}
```

In order to map the `Order` Entity to the persistence store, the source code for the `Order` should be modified to add the Doctrine annotations:

```
use Doctrine\ORM\Mapping\Entity;
use Doctrine\ORM\Mapping\Id;
use Doctrine\ORM\Mapping\GeneratedValue;
use Doctrine\ORM\Mapping\Column;

/** @Entity */
class Order
```

```
{
    /** @Id @GeneratedValue(strategy="AUTO") */
    private $id;

    /** @Column(type="decimal", precision="10", scale="5") */
    private $amount;

    /** @Column(type="string") */
    private $firstName;

    /** @Column(type="string") */
    private $lastName;

    public function __construct(
        Amount $anAmount,
        $aFirstName,
        $aLastName
    ) {
        $this->amount = $anAmount;
        $this->firstName = $aFirstName;
        $this->lastName = $aLastName;
    }

    public function id()
    {
        return $this->id;
    }

    public function firstName()
    {
        return $this->firstName;
    }

    public function lastName()
    {
        return $this->lastName;
    }

    public function amount()
    {
        return $this->amount;
    }
}
```

Then, to persist the Entity to the persistent store, it's just as easy to do the following:

```
$order = new Order(
    new Amount(15, Currency::EUR()),
    'AFirstName',
    'ALastName'
);
$entityManager->persist($order);
$entityManager->flush();
```

At first glance, this code looks simple, and this can be an easy way to specify mapping information. But it comes at a cost. What's odd about the final code?

First of all, Domain concerns are mixed with Infrastructure concerns. Order is a Domain concept, whereas Table, Column, and so on are infrastructure concerns.

As a result, this Entity is tightly coupled to the mapping information specified by the annotations in the source code. If the Entity were required to be persisted using another Entity manager and with different mapping metadata, this wouldn't be possible.

Annotations tend to lead to side effects and tight coupling, so it would be better to not use them.

So what's the best way to specify mapping information? The best way is the one that allows you to separate the mapping information from the Entity itself. This can be achieved by using XML mapping, YAML mapping, or PHP mapping. In this book, we're going to cover XML mapping.

Mapping Entities Using XML

To map the `Order` Entity using the XML mapping, the setup code of Doctrine should be altered slightly:

```
require_once '/path/to/vendor/autoload.php';

use Doctrine\ORM\Tools\Setup;
use Doctrine\ORM\EntityManager;

$paths = ['/path/to/mapping-files'];
$isDevMode = false;

// the connection configuration
$dbParams = [
    'driver'   => 'pdo_mysql',
    'user'     => 'the_database_username',
```

```
        'password' => 'the_database_password',
        'dbname'   => 'the_database_name',
    ];

    $config = Setup::createXMLMetadataConfiguration($paths, $isDevMode);
    $entityManager = EntityManager::create($dbParams, $config);
```

The mapping file should be created on the path where Doctrine will search for the mapping files, and the mapping files should be named after the fully qualified class name, replacing the backslashes \ with dots. Consider the following:

```
Acme\Billing\Domain\Model\Order
```

The preceding illustration would have the mapping file named like this:

```
Acme.Billing.Domain.Model.Order.dcm.xml
```

Additionally, it's convenient that all the mapping files use a special XML Schema created specially for specifying mapping information:

```
https://raw.github.com/doctrine/doctrine2/master/doctrine-mapping.xsd
```

Mapping Entity Identity

Our Identity, `OrderId`, is a Value Object. As seen in the previous chapter, there are different approaches for mapping a Value Object using Doctrine, embeddables, and custom types. When Value Objects are used as Identities, the best option is custom types.

An interesting new feature in *Doctrine 2.5* is that it's now possible to use Objects as identifiers for Entities, so long as they implement the magic method `__toString()`. So we can add `__toString` to our Identity Value Objects and use them in our mappings:

```
namespace Ddd\Billing\Domain\Model\Order;

use Ramsey\Uuid\Uuid;

class OrderId
{
    // ...

    public function __toString()
    {
        return $this->id;
    }
}
```

Check the implementation of the Doctrine custom types. They inherit from `GuidType`, so their internal representation will be a UUID. We need to specify the database native translation. Then we need to register our custom types before we use them. If you need help with these steps, `Custom Mapping Types` is a good reference.

```php
use Doctrine\DBAL\Platforms\AbstractPlatform;
use Doctrine\DBAL\Types\GuidType;

class DoctrineOrderId extends GuidType
{
    public function getName()
    {
        return 'OrderId';
    }

    public function convertToDatabaseValue(
        $value, AbstractPlatform $platform
    ) {
        return $value->id();
    }

    public function convertToPHPValue(
        $value, AbstractPlatform $platform
    ) {
        return new OrderId($value);
    }
}
```

Lastly, we'll set up the registration of custom types. Again, we have to update our bootstrapping:

```php
require_once '/path/to/vendor/autoload.php';

// ...

\Doctrine\DBAL\Types\Type::addType(
    'OrderId',
    'Ddd\Billing\Infrastructure\Domain\Model\DoctrineOrderId'
);

$config = Setup::createXMLMetadataConfiguration($paths, $isDevMode);
$entityManager = EntityManager::create($dbParams, $config);
```

Final Mapping File

With all the changes, we're finally ready, so let's take a look at the final mapping file. The most interesting detail is to check how the id gets mapped with our defined custom type for OrderId:

```xml
<?xml version="1.0" encoding="UTF-8"?>
<doctrine-mapping
    xmlns="http://doctrine-project.org/schemas/orm/doctrine-mapping"
    xmlns:xsi="http://www.w3.org/2001/XMLSchema-instance"
    xsi:schemaLocation="
        http://doctrine-project.org/schemas/orm/doctrine-mapping
    https://raw.github.com/doctrine/doctrine2/master/doctrine-mapping.xsd">

    <entity
        name="Ddd\Billing\Domain\Model\Order"
        table="orders">

        <id name="id" column="id" type="OrderId" />

        <field
            name="amount"
            type="decimal"
            nullable="false"
            scale="10"
            precision="5"
        />
        <field
            name="firstName"
            type="string"
            nullable="false"
        />
        <field
            name="lastName"
            type="string"
            nullable="false"
        />
    </entity>
</doctrine-mapping>
```

Testing Entities

It's relatively easy to test Entities, simply because they're plain old PHP classes with actions derived from the Domain concept they represent. The focus of the test should be the invariants that the Entity protects, because the behavior on the Entities will likely be modeled around those invariants.

For example, and for the sake of simplicity, suppose a Domain Model for a blog is needed. A possible one could be this:

```php
class Post
{
    private $title;
    private $content;
    private $status;
    private $createdAt;
    private $publishedAt;

    public function __construct($aContent, $title)
    {
        $this->setContent($aContent);
        $this->setTitle($title);

        $this->unpublish();
        $this->createdAt(new DateTimeImmutable());
    }

    private function setContent($aContent)
    {
        $this->assertNotEmpty($aContent);

        $this->content = $aContent;
    }

    private function setTitle($aPostTitle)
    {
        $this->assertNotEmpty($aPostTitle);

        $this->title = $aPostTitle;
    }

    private function setStatus(Status $aPostStatus)
    {
        $this->assertIsAValidPostStatus($aPostStatus);

        $this->status = $aPostStatus;
    }
```

```php
    private function createdAt(DateTimeImmutable $aDate)
    {
        $this->assertIsAValidDate($aDate);

        $this->createdAt = $aDate;
    }

    private function publishedAt(DateTimeImmutable $aDate)
    {
        $this->assertIsAValidDate($aDate);

        $this->publishedAt = $aDate;
    }

    public function publish()
    {
        $this->setStatus(Status::published());
        $this->publishedAt(new DateTimeImmutable());
    }

    public function unpublish()
    {
        $this->setStatus(Status::draft());
        $this->publishedAt = null ;
    }

    public function isPublished()
    {
        return $this->status->equalsTo(Status::published());
    }

    public function publicationDate()
    {
        return $this->publishedAt;
    }
}

class Status
{
    const PUBLISHED = 10;
    const DRAFT = 20;

    private $status;

    public static function published()
    {
        return new self(self::PUBLISHED);
    }
```

```php
public static function draft()
{
    return new self(self::DRAFT);
}

private function __construct($aStatus)
{
    $this->status = $aStatus;
}

public function equalsTo(self $aStatus)
{
    return $this->status === $aStatus->status;
}
}
```

In order to test this Domain Model, we must ensure the test covers all the Post invariants:

```php
class PostTest extends PHPUnit_Framework_TestCase
{
    /** @test */
    public function aNewPostIsNotPublishedByDefault()
    {
        $aPost = new Post(
            'A Post Content',
            'A Post Title'
        );

        $this->assertFalse(
            $aPost->isPublished()
        );

        $this->assertNull(
            $aPost->publicationDate()
        );
    }

    /** @test */
    public function aPostCanBePublishedWithAPublicationDate()
    {
        $aPost = new Post(
            'A Post Content',
            'A Post Title'
        );

        $aPost->publish();

        $this->assertTrue(
```

```
            $aPost->isPublished()
        );

        $this->assertInstanceOf(
            'DateTimeImmutable',
            $aPost->publicationDate()
        );
    }
}
```

DateTimes

Because `DateTimes` are widely used in Entities, we think it's important to point out specific approaches on unit testing Entities that have fields with date types. Consider that a `Post` is new if it was created within the last 15 days:

```
class Post
{
    const NEW_TIME_INTERVAL_DAYS = 15;

    // ...
    private $createdAt;

    public function __construct($aContent, $title)
    {
        // ...
        $this->createdAt(new DateTimeImmutable());
    }

    // ...

    public function isNew()
    {
        return
            (new DateTimeImmutable())
                ->diff($this->createdAt)
                ->days <= self::NEW_TIME_INTERVAL_DAYS;
    }
}
```

The `isNew()` method needs to compare two `DateTimes`; it's a comparison between the date when the Post was created and today's date. We compute the difference and check if it's less than the specified amount of days. How do we unit test the `isNew()` method? As we demonstrated in the implementation, it's difficult to reproduce specific flows in our test suites. What options do we have?

Passing All Dates as Parameters

One possible option could be passing all the dates as parameters when needed:

```
class Post
{
    // ...

    public function __construct($aContent, $title, $createdAt = null)
    {
        // ...
        $this->createdAt($createdAt ?: new DateTimeImmutable());
    }

    // ...

    public function isNew($today = null)
    {
        return
            ($today ? :new DateTimeImmutable())
                ->diff($this->createdAt)
                ->days <= self::NEW_TIME_INTERVAL_DAYS;
    }
}
```

This is the easiest approach for unit testing purposes. Just pass different pairs of dates to test all possible scenarios with 100 percent coverage. However, if you consider the client code that's creating and asking for the `isNew()` method result, things don't look so nice. The resulting code can be a bit weird because of always passing today's `DateTime`:

```
$aPost = new Post(
    'Hello world!',
    'Hi',
    new DateTimeImmutable()
);

$aPost->isNew(
    new DateTimeImmutable()
);
```

Test Class

Another alternative is to use the Test Class pattern. The idea is to extend the `Post` class with a new one that we can manipulate to force specific scenarios. This new class is going to be used only for unit testing purposes. The bad news is that we have to modify the original `Post` class a bit, extracting some methods and changing some fields and methods from `private` to `protected`. Some developers may worry about increasing the visibility of class properties just because of testing reasons. However, we think that in most cases, it's worth it:

```
class Post
{
    protected $createdAt;

    public function isNew()
    {
        return
            ($this->today())
                ->diff($this->createdAt)
                ->days <= self::NEW_TIME_INTERVAL_DAYS;
    }

    protected function today()
    {
        return new DateTimeImmutable();
    }

    protected function createdAt(DateTimeImmutable $aDate)
    {
        $this->assertIsAValidDate($aDate);

        $this->createdAt = $aDate;
    }
}
```

As you can see, we've extracted the logic for getting today's date into the `today()` method. This way, by applying the Template Method pattern, we can change its behavior from a derived class. Something similar happens with the `createdAt` method and field. Now they're protected, so they can be used and overridden in derived classes:

```
class PostTestClass extends Post
{
    private $today;

    protected function today()
    {
```

```
        return $this->today;
    }

    public function setToday($today)
    {
        $this->today = $today;
    }
}
```

With these changes, we can now test our original `Post` class through testing `PostTestClass`:

```
class PostTest extends PHPUnit_Framework_TestCase
{
    // ...

    /** @test */
    public function aPostIsNewIfIts15DaysOrLess()
    {
        $aPost = new PostTestClass(
            'A Post Content' ,
            'A Post Title'
        );

        $format = 'Y-m-d';
        $dateString = '2016-01-01';
        $createdAt = DateTimeImmutable::createFromFormat(
            $format,
            $dateString
        );

        $aPost->createdAt($createdAt);
        $aPost->setToday(
            $createdAt->add(
                new DateInterval('P15D')
            )
        );

        $this->assertTrue(
            $aPost->isNew()
        );

        $aPost->setToday(
            $createdAt->add(
                new DateInterval('P16D')
            )
        );
```

```
        $this->assertFalse(
            $aPost->isNew()
        );
    }
}
```

Just one last small detail: with this approach, it's impossible to achieve 100 percent coverage on the `Post` class, because the `today()` method is never going to be executed. However, it can be covered by other tests.

External Fake

Another option is to wrap calls to the `DateTimeImmutable` constructor or named constructors using a new class and some static methods. In doing so, we can statically change the result of those methods to behave differently based on specific testing scenarios:

```
class Post
{
    // ...
    private $createdAt;

    public function __construct($aContent, $title)
    {
        // ...
        $this->createdAt(MyCustomDateTimeBuilder::today());
    }

    // ...

    public function isNew()
    {
        return
            (MyCustomDateTimeBuilder::today())
                ->diff($this->createdAt)
                ->days <= self::NEW_TIME_INTERVAL_DAYS;
    }
}
```

For getting today's `DateTime`, we now use a static call to
`MyCustomDateTimeBuilder::today()`. This class also has some setter methods to fake
the result to return in the next calls:

```
class PostTest extends PHPUnit_Framework_TestCase
{
    // ...

    /** @test */
    public function aPostIsNewIfIts15DaysOrLess()
    {
        $createdAt = DateTimeImmutable::createFromFormat(
            'Y-m-d',
            '2016-01-01'
        );

        MyCustomDateTimeBuilder::setReturnDates(
            [
                $createdAt,
                $createdAt->add(
                    new DateInterval('P15D')
                ),
                $createdAt->add(
                    new DateInterval('P16D')
                )
            ]
        );

        $aPost = new Post(
            'A Post Content' ,
            'A Post Title'
        );

        $this->assertTrue(
            $aPost->isNew()
        );

        $this->assertFalse(
            $aPost->isNew()
        );
    }
}
```

The main problem with this approach is it's coupled statically with an object.
Depending on your use case, it'll also be tricky to create a flexible fake object.

Reflection

You can also use reflection techniques for building a new `Post` class with custom dates. Consider `Mimic`, a simple functional library for object prototyping, data hydration, and data exposition:

```php
namespace Domain;

use mimic as m;

class ComputerScientist {
    private $name;
    private $surname;

    public function __construct($name, $surname)
    {
        $this->name = $name;
        $this->surname = $surname;
    }

    public function rocks()
    {
        return $this->name . ' ' . $this->surname . ' rocks!';
    }
}

assert(m\prototype('Domain\ComputerScientist')
    instanceof Domain\ComputerScientist);

m\hydrate('Domain\ComputerScientist', [
    'name'   =>'John' ,
    'surname'=>'McCarthy'
])->rocks(); //John McCarthy rocks!

assert(m\expose(
    new Domain\ComputerScientist('Grace', 'Hopper')) ==
    [
        'name'    => 'Grace' ,
        'surname' => 'Hopper'
    ]
)
```

Share and Discuss
Discuss with your workmates how to properly unit test your Entities with fixed `DateTimes` and come up with additional alternatives.

If you want to know more about testing patterns and approaches, take a look at the book *xUnit Test Patterns: Refactoring Test Code* by Gerard Meszaros.

Validation

Validation is a highly important process in our Domain Model. It checks not only for the correctness of attributes, but also for that of entire objects and the composition of those objects. Different levels of validation are required in order to keep this Model in a valid state. Just because an object consists of valid attributes (on a per basis) doesn't necessarily mean the object (as a whole) is valid. And the opposite is true: valid objects don't necessarily equal valid compositions.

Attribute Validation

Some people understand validation as the process whereby a service validates the state of a given object. In this case, the validation conforms to a `Design-by-contract` approach, which consists of preconditions, postconditions, and invariants. One such way to protect a single attribute is by using `Chapter 3`, *Value Objects*. In order to make our design more flexible for change, we focus only on asserting Domain preconditions that must be met. Here, we'll be using guards as an easy way of validating the preconditions:

```php
class Username
{
    const MIN_LENGTH = 5;
    const MAX_LENGTH = 10;
    const FORMAT = '/^[a-zA-Z0-9_]+$/';

    private $username;

    public function __construct($username)
    {
        $this->setUsername($username);
    }

    private setUsername($username)
    {
        $this->assertNotEmpty($username);
        $this->assertNotTooShort($username);
        $this->assertNotTooLong($username);
        $this->assertValidFormat($username);
        $this->username = $username;
    }
```

```php
    private function assertNotEmpty($username)
    {
        if (empty($username)) {
            throw new InvalidArgumentException('Empty username');
        }
    }

    private function assertNotTooShort($username)
    {
        if (strlen($username) < self::MIN_LENGTH) {
            throw new InvalidArgumentException(sprintf(
                'Username must be %d characters or more',
                self::MIN_LENGTH
            ));
        }
    }

    private function assertNotTooLong($username)
    {
        if (strlen( $username) > self::MAX_LENGTH) {
            throw new InvalidArgumentException(sprintf(
                'Username must be %d characters or less',
                self::MAX_LENGTH
            ));
        }
    }

    private function assertValidFormat($username)
    {
        if (preg_match(self:: FORMAT, $username) !== 1) {
            throw new InvalidArgumentException(
                'Invalid username format'
            );
        }
    }
}
```

As you can see in the example above, there are four preconditions that must be satisfied in order to build a Username Value Object. It:

- Must not be empty
- Must be at least 5 characters
- Must be less than 10 characters
- Must follow a format of alphanumeric characters or underscores

If all the preconditions are met, the attribute will be set and the object will be successfully built. Otherwise, an `InvalidArgumentException` will be raised, execution will be halted, and the client will be shown an error.

Some developers may consider this kind of validation defensive programming. However, we're not checking that the input is a string or that nulls are not permitted. We can't avoid people using our code incorrectly, but we can control the correctness of our Domain state. As seen in the `Chapter 3`, *Value Objects*, validation can help us with security too.

`Defensive programming` isn't a bad thing. In general, it makes sense when developing components or libraries that are going to be used as a third party in other projects. However, when developing your own Bounded Context, those extra paranoid checks (nulls, basic types, type hinting, and so on.) can be avoided to increase development speed by relying on the coverage of your unit test suite.

Entire Object Validation

There are times when an object composed of valid properties, as a whole, can still be deemed invalid. It can be tempting to add this kind of validation to the object itself, but generally this is an anti-pattern. Higher-level validation changes at a rhythm different than that of the object logic itself. Also, it's good practice to separate these responsibilities.

The validation informs the client about any errors that have been found or collects the results to be reviewed later, as sometimes we don't want to stop the execution at the first sign of trouble.

An `abstract` and reusable `Validator` could be something like this:

```
abstract class Validator
{
    private $validationHandler;

    public function __construct(ValidationHandler $validationHandler)
    {
        $this->validationHandler = $validationHandler;
    }

    protected function handleError($error)
    {
        $this->validationHandler->handleError($error);
    }

    abstract public function validate();
}
```

As a concrete example, we want to validate an entire `Location` object, composed of valid Country, City, and Postcode Value Objects. However, these individual values might be in an invalid state at the time of validation. Maybe the city doesn't form part of the country, or maybe the postcode doesn't follow the city format:

```
class Location
{
    private $country;
    private $city;
    private $postcode;

    public function __construct(
        Country $country, City $city, Postcode $postcode
    ) {
        $this->country = $country;
        $this->city = $city;
        $this->postcode = $postcode;
    }

    public function country()
    {
        return $this->country;
    }

    public function city()
    {
        return $this->city;
    }

    public function postcode()
    {
        return $this->postcode;
    }
}
```

The validator checks the state of the `Location` object in its entirety, analyzing the meaning of the relationships between properties:

```
class LocationValidator extends Validator
{
    private $location;

    public function __construct(
        Location $location, ValidationHandler $validationHandler
    ) {
        parent::__construct($validationHandler);
        $this->location = $location;
```

```
    }

    public function validate()
    {
        if (!$this->location->country()->hasCity(
            $this->location->city()
        )) {
            $this->handleError('City not found');
        }

        if (!$this->location->city()->isPostcodeValid(
            $this->location->postcode()
        )) {
            $this->handleError('Invalid postcode');
        }
    }
}
```

Once all the properties have been set, we're able to validate the Entity, most likely after some described process. On the surface, it looks as if the Location validates itself. However, this isn't the case. The `Location` class delegates this validation to a concrete validator instance, splitting these two clear responsibilities:

```
class Location
{
    // ...

    public function validate(ValidationHandler $validationHandler)
    {
     $validator = new LocationValidator($this, $validationHandler);
     $validator->validate();
    }
}
```

Decoupling Validation Messages

With some minor changes to our existing implementation, we're able to decouple the validation messages from the validator:

```
class LocationValidationHandler implements ValidationHandler
{
    public function handleCityNotFoundInCountry();

    public function handleInvalidPostcodeForCity();
}
```

```
class LocationValidator
{
    private $location;
    private $validationHandler;

    public function __construct(
        Location $location,
        LocationValidationHandler $validationHandler
    ) {
        $this->location = $location;
        $this->validationHandler = $validationHandler;
    }

    public function validate()
    {
        if (!$this->location->country()->hasCity(
            $this->location->city()
        )) {
            $this->validationHandler->handleCityNotFoundInCountry();
        }

        if (! $this->location->city()->isPostcodeValid(
            $this->location->postcode()
        )) {
            $this->validationHandler->handleInvalidPostcodeForCity();
        }
    }
}
```

We also need to change the signature of the validation method to the following:

```
class Location
{
    // ...

    public function validate(
        LocationValidationHandler $validationHandler
    ) {
        $validator = new LocationValidator($this, $validationHandler);
        $validator->validate();
    }
}
```

Validating Object Compositions

Validating object compositions can be complicated. As such, the preferred way of achieving this is through a Domain Service. The service then communicates with Repositories in order to retrieve the valid Aggregate. Due to the likely complex object graphs that can be created, an Aggregate could be in an intermediate state, requiring other Aggregates to be validated beforehand. We can use Domain Events to notify other parts of the system that a particular element has been validated.

Entities and Domain Events

We'll explore `Chapter 6`, *Domain-Events* in future chapters; however, it's important to highlight that operations performed on Entities can fire Domain Events. This approach is used to communicate the Domain change to other parts of the Application, or even to other Applications, as you'll see in `Chapter 12`, *Integrating Bounded Contexts*:

```
class Post
{
    // ...

    public function publish()
    {
        $this->setStatus(
            Status::published()
        );

        $this->publishedAt(new DateTimeImmutable());

        DomainEventPublisher::instance()->publish(
            new PostPublished($this->id)
        );
    }

    public function unpublish()
    {
        $this->setStatus(
            Status::draft()
        );

        $this-> publishedAt = null;

        DomainEventPublisher::instance()->publish(
            new PostUnpublished($this->id)
        );
```

```
    }

    // ...
}
```

Domain Events can even be fired when a new instance of our Entity is created:

```
class User
{
    // ...

    public function __construct(UserId $userId, $email, $password)
    {
        $this->setUserId($userId);
        $this->setEmail($email);
        $this->setPassword($password);

        DomainEventPublisher::instance()->publish(
            new UserRegistered($this->userId)
        );
    }
}
```

Wrap-Up

Some concepts in the Domain demand Identity — that is, changes to their internal states don't change their own unique identities. We've seen how modeling Identity as a Value Object brings benefits like immutability, in addition to logic for operating the Identity itself. We've also shown several ways of providing Identity, restated in the following pointers:

- Persistence mechanism: Easy to implement, but you won't have the Identity before persisting the object, which delays and complicates event propagation.
- Surrogate ID: Some ORMs require an extra field on your Entity to map the Identity with the persisting mechanism.
- Provided by the client: Sometimes the Identity fits a Domain concept and you can model it inside your Domain.
- Generated by the application: You can use a library to generate IDs.
- Generated by a Bounded Context: Probably the most complex strategy. Other Bounded Contexts provide an interface for generating Identities.

We've seen and discussed Doctrine as a persistence mechanism, we've looked at the drawbacks of using the Active Record pattern, and finally, we've checked different levels of Entity validation:

- Attribute validation: Check for specifics inside the object state through preconditions, postconditions, and invariants.
- Entire object validation: Look for consistency of an object as a whole. Extracting the validation to an external service is a good practice.
- Object compositions: Complex object compositions could be validated through Domain Services. A good way of communicating this to the rest of the application is through Domain Events.

5
Services

You've already seen what Entities and Value Objects are. As basic building blocks, they should contain most of the business logic of any application. However, there are some scenarios where Entities and Value Objects aren't the best solutions. Let's take a look at what Eric Evans has to say about this in his book, `Domain-Driven Design: Tackling Complexity in the Heart of Software`:

> When a significant process or transformation in the domain is not a natural responsibility of an Entity or Value Object, add an operation to the model as standalone interface declared as a Service. Define the interface in terms of the language of the model and make sure the operation name is part of the Ubiquitous Language. Make the Service stateless.

So when there are operations that need to be represented, but Entities and Value Objects aren't the best place, you should consider modeling these operations as Services. In Domain-Driven Design, there are typically three different types of Services you'll encounter:

- **Application Services**: Operate on scalar types, transforming them into Domain types. A scalar type can be considered any type that's unknown to the Domain Model. This includes primitive types and types that don't belong to the Domain. We'll provide an overview in this chapter, but for a deeper look at this topic, check out the `Chapter 11`, *Application*.
- **Domain Services**: Operate only on types belonging to the Domain. They contain meaningful concepts that can be found within the Ubiquitous Language. They hold operations that don't fit well into Value Objects or Entities.
- **Infrastructure Services**: Are operations that fulfill infrastructure concerns, such as sending emails and logging meaningful data. In terms of Hexagonal Architecture, they live outside the Domain boundary.

Application Services

Application Services are the middleware between the outside world and the Domain logic. The purpose of such a mechanism is to transform commands from the outside world into meaningful Domain instructions.

Let's consider the *User signs up to our platform* use case. Starting with an outside-in approach: from the delivery mechanism, we need to compose the input request for our Domain operation. Using a framework like Symfony as the delivery mechanism, the code would look something like this:

```
class SignUpController extends Controller
{
    public function signUpAction(Request $request)
    {
        $signUpService = new SignUpUserService(
            $this->get('user_repository')
        );

        try {
            $response = $signUpService->execute(new SignUpUserRequest(
                $request->request->get('email'),
                $request->request->get('password')
            ));
        } catch (UserAlreadyExistsException $e) {
            return $this->render('error.html.twig', $response);
        }

        return $this->render('success.html.twig', $response);
    }
}
```

As you can see, we create a new instance of our Application Services, passing all dependencies needed — in this case, a `UserRepository`. `UserRepository` is an interface that can be implemented with any specific technology (Example: MySQL, Redis, Elasticsearch). Then, we build a request object for our Application Service in order to abstract the delivery mechanism — in this example, a web request — from the business logic. Last, we execute the Application Service, get the response, and use that response for rendering the result. On the Domain side, let's check a possible implementation for the Application Service that coordinates the logic that fulfills the *User signs up* use case:

```
class SignUpUserService
{
    private $userRepository;

    public function __construct(UserRepository $userRepository)
```

```
    {
        $this->userRepository = $userRepository;
    }

    public function execute(SignUpUserRequest $request)
    {
        $user = $this->userRepository->userOfEmail($request->email);
        if ($user) {
            throw new UserAlreadyExistsException();
        }

        $user = new User(
            $this->userRepository->nextIdentity(),
            $request->email,
            $request->password
        );

        $this->userRepository->add($user);

        return new SignUpUserResponse($user);
    }
}
```

Everything in the code is about the Domain problem we want to solve, and not about the specific technology we're using to solve it. With this approach, we can decouple the high-level policies from the low-level implementation details. The communication between the delivery mechanism and the Domain is carried by data structures called DTOs, which we introduced in the Chapter 2, *Architectural Styles*:

```
class SignUpUserRequest
{
    public $email;
    public $password;

    public function __construct($email, $password)
    {
        $this->email = $email;
        $this->password = $password;
    }
}
```

There are different strategies for returning content, but for now, consider that we shouldn't return our Entities so that they can't be modified from outside our Application Services. That's why it's common to return another DTO with information, rather than the whole Entity. Let's see a simple example:

```
class SignUpUserResponse
{
    public $id;
    public $email;

    public function __construct(User $user)
    {
        $this->id = $user->id();
        $this->email = $user->email();
    }
}
```

For creating your responses, you can use getters or public instance variables. Application Services should take care with transaction scopes and security. However, you'll delve into more detail about these and other things related to Application Services in the `Chapter 11`, *Application*.

Domain Services

Throughout conversations with Domain Experts, you'll come across concepts in the Ubiquitous Language that can't be neatly represented as either an Entity or a Value Object, such as:

- Users being able to sign into systems by themselves
- A shopping cart being able to become an order by itself

The preceding example are two concrete concepts, neither of which can naturally be bound to either an Entity or a Value Object. Further highlighting this oddity, we can attempt to model the behavior as follows:

```
class User
{
    public function signUp($aUsername, $aPassword)
    {
        // ...
    }
}
```

```
class Cart
{
    public function createOrder()
    {
        // ...
    }
}
```

In the case of the first implementation, we're not able to know that the given username and password relate to the invoked-upon user instance. Clearly, this operation doesn't suit this Entity; instead, it should be extracted out into a separate class, making its intention explicit.

With this in mind, we could create a Domain Service with the sole responsibility of authenticating users:

```
class SignUp
{
    public function execute($aUsername, $aPassword)
    {
        // ...
    }
}
```

Similarly, as in the case of the second example, we could create a Domain Service specialized in creating orders from a supplied cart:

```
class CreateOrderFromCart
{
    public function execute(Cart $aCart)
    {
        // ...
    }
}
```

A Domain Service can be defined as an operation that fulfills a Domain task and naturally doesn't fit into either an Entity or a Value Object. As concepts that represent operations in the Domain, Domain Services should be used by clients regardless of their run history. Domain Services don't hold any kind of state by themselves, so Domain Services are stateless operations.

Domain Services and Infrastructure Services

It's common to encounter infrastructural dependencies when modeling a Domain Service — for example, in the case where an authentication mechanism that handles password hashing is required. In this instance, you could use a `Separated Interface`, which allows for multiple hashing mechanisms to be defined. Using this pattern still provides you with a clear Separation of Concerns between the Domain and the Infrastructure:

```
namespace Ddd\Auth\Domain\Model;

interface SignUp
{
    public function execute($aUsername, $aPassword);
}
```

Using the preceding interface found in the Domain, we could create an implementation in the Infrastructure layer, like the following:

```
namespace Ddd\Auth\Infrastructure\Authentication;

class DefaultHashingSignUp implements Ddd\Auth\Domain\Model\SignUp
{
    private $userRepository;

    public function __construct(UserRepository $userRepository)
    {
        $this->userRepository = $userRepository;
    }

    public function execute($aUsername, $aPassword)
    {
        if (!$this->userRepository->has($aUsername)) {
            throw UserDoesNotExistException::fromUsername($aUsername);
        }

        $aUser = $this->userRepository->byUsername($aUsername);

        if (!$this->isPasswordValidForUser($aUser, $aPassword)) {
            throw new BadCredentialsException($aUser, $aPassword);
        }

        return $aUser;
    }

    private function isPasswordValidForUser(
        User $aUser, $anUnencryptedPassword
    ) {
```

```php
        return password_verify($anUnencryptedPassword,$aUser->hash());
    }
}
```

Here is another implementation based instead on the MD5 algorithm:

```php
namespace Ddd\Auth\Infrastructure\Authentication;

use Ddd\Auth\Domain\Model\SignUp

class Md5HashingSignUp implements SignUp
{
    const SALT = 'S0m3S4lT' ;

    private $userRepository;

    public function __construct(UserRepository $userRepository)
    {
        $this->userRepository = $userRepository;
    }

    public function execute($aUsername, $aPassword)
    {
        if (!$this->userRepository->has($aUsername)) {
            throw new InvalidArgumentException(
                sprintf('The user "%s" does not exist.', $aUsername)
            );
        }

        $aUser = $this->userRepository->byUsername($aUsername);

        if ($this->isPasswordInvalidFor($aUser, $aPassword)) {
            throw new BadCredentialsException($aUser, $aPassword);
        }

        return $aUser;
    }

    private function salt()
    {
        return md5(self::SALT);
    }

    private function isPasswordInvalidFor(
        User $aUser, $anUnencryptedPassword
    ) {
        $encryptedPassword = md5(
            $anUnencryptedPassword . '_' .$this->salt()
```

```
        );

        return $aUser->hash() !== $encryptedPassword;
    }
}
```

Opting for this choice allows us to have multiple implementations of the Domain Service interface at the Infrastructure layer. In other words, we end up with several Infrastructure Domain Services. Each Infrastructure service will be responsible for handling a different hash mechanism. Depending on the implementation, the use can easily be managed through a Dependency Injection container — for example, through Symfony's Dependency Injection component:

```xml
<?xml version="1.0"?>
<container
    xmlns="http://symfony.com/schema/dic/services"
    xmlns:xsi="http://www.w3.org/2001/XMLSchema-instance"
    xsi:schemaLocation="
        http://symfony.com/schema/dic/services
        http://symfony.com/schema/dic/services/services-1.0.xsd">

    <services>

        <service id="sign_in" alias="sign_in.default" />

        <service id="sign_in.default"
            class="Ddd\Auth\Infrastructure\Authentication
            \DefaultHashingSignUp">
            <argument type="service" id="user_repository"/>
        </service>

        <service id="sign_in.md5"
            class="Ddd\Auth\Infrastructure\Authentication
                \Md5HashingSignUp">
            <argument type="service" id="user_repository"/>
        </service>

    </services>
</container>
```

If, in the future, we wish to handle a new type of hashing, we can simply start by implementing the Domain Service interface. Then it's a matter of declaring the service in the Dependency Injection container and replacing the service alias dependency with the newly created one.

An Issue of Code Reuse

Although the implementation described previously clearly defines the Separation of Concerns, we're required to repeat the password verification algorithm every time we wish to implement a new hashing mechanism. An alternative for solving this problem, which improves code reuse, is by separating out these two responsibilities. We could instead extract the password hashing logic out into a specialized class, using the `Strategy Pattern` for all defined hashing algorithms. This leaves the design open for extension and closed for modification:

```
namespace Ddd\Auth\Domain\Model;

class SignUp
{
    private $userRepository;
    private $passwordHashing;

    public function __construct(
        UserRepository $userRepository, PasswordHashing $passwordHashing
    ) {
        $this->userRepository = $userRepository;
        $this->passwordHashing = $passwordHashing;
    }

    public function execute($aUsername, $aPassword)
    {
        if (!$this->userRepository->has($aUsername)) {
            throw new InvalidArgumentException(
                sprintf('The user "%s" does not exist.', $aUsername)
            );
        }

        $aUser = $this->userRepository->byUsername($aUsername);

        if ($this->isPasswordInvalidFor($aUser, $aPassword)) {
            throw new BadCredentialsException($aUser, $aPassword);
        }

        return $aUser;
    }

    private function isPasswordInvalidFor(User $aUser, $plainPassword)
    {
        return !$this->passwordHashing->verify(
            $plainPassword,
            $aUser->hash()
        );
```

```
        }
    }

    interface PasswordHashing
    {
        /**
         * @param string $password
         * @param string $hash
         * @return boolean
         */
        public function verify($plainPassword, hash);
    }
```

Defining different hashing strategies is as easy as implementing the `PasswordHashing` interface:

```
    namespace Ddd\Auth\Infrastructure\Authentication;

    class BasicPasswordHashing
        implements \Ddd\Auth\Domain\Model\PasswordHashing
    {
        public function verify($plainPassword, $hash)
        {
            return password_verify($plainPassword, $hash);
        }
    }

    class Md5PasswordHashing
        implements Ddd\Auth\Domain\Model\PasswordHashing
    {
        const SALT = 'S0m3S4lT' ;

        public function verify($plainPassword, $hash)
        {
            return $hash === $this-> calculateHash($plainPassword);
        }

        private function calculateHash($plainPassword)
        {
            return md5($plainPassword . '_' .$this-> salt());
        }

        private function salt()
        {
            return md5(self::SALT);
        }
    }
```

Testing Domain Services

Given the user authentication example from multiple Domain Service implementations, it's extremely beneficial to be able to easily test the service. Typically, however, testing the Template Method implementations can be tricky. As a result, we'll be using a plain password hashing implementation for testing purposes:

```
class PlainPasswordHashing implements PasswordHashing
{
    public function verify($plainPassword, $hash)
    {
        return $plainPassword === $hash;
    }
}
```

Now we can test all cases in the Domain Service:

```
class SignUpTest extends PHPUnit_Framework_TestCase
{
    private $signUp;
    private $userRepository;

    protected function setUp()
    {
        $this->userRepository = new InMemoryUserRepository();
        $this->signUp = new SignUp(
            $this->userRepository,
            new PlainPasswordHashing()
        );
    }

    /**
     * @test
     * @expectedException InvalidArgumentException
     */
    public function itShouldComplainIfTheUserDoesNotExist()
    {
        $this->signUp->execute('test-username', 'test-password');
    }

    /**
     * @test
     * @expectedException BadCredentialsException
     */
    public function itShouldTellIfThePasswordDoesNotMatch()
    {
        $this->userRepository->add(
```

```
            new User(
                'test-username',
                'test-password'
            )
        );

        $this->signUp->execute('test-username', 'no-matching-password')
    }

    /**
     * @test
     */
    public function itShouldTellIfTheUserMatchesProvidedPassword()
    {
        $this->userRepository->add(
            new User(
                'test-username',
                'test-password'
            )
        );

        $this->assertInstanceOf(
            'Ddd\Domain\Model\User\User',
            $this->signUp->execute('test-username', 'test-password')
        );
    }
}
```

Anemic Domain Models Vs Rich Domain Models

You must be cautious not to overuse Domain Service abstractions within your system. Following this path can lead to Entities and Value Objects being stripped of all behavior and becoming mere data containers. This is contrary to the goal of Object-Oriented Programming, which can be thought of as the gathering of both data and behavior into semantic units called objects, with the intent of expressing real-world concepts and problems. Domain Service overuse can be considered an anti-pattern and is referred to as the Anemic Domain Model.

Typically, when starting a new project or feature, it's easy to fall into the trap of modeling the data first. This commonly includes thinking that each database table has a direct one-to-one object form representation. However, this thinking may or may not be the exact case all the time.

Suppose we're tasked with modeling an order processing system. If we start by modeling the data first, we could end up with an SQL script like this:

```
CREATE TABLE `orders` (
    `ID` INTEGER NOT NULL AUTO_INCREMENT,
    `CUSTOMER_ID` INTEGER NOT NULL,
    `AMOUNT` DECIMAL(17, 2) NOT NULL DEFAULT '0.00',
    `STATUS` TINYINT NOT NULL DEFAULT 0,
    `CREATED_AT` DATETIME NOT NULL,
    `UPDATED_AT` DATETIME NOT NULL,
    PRIMARY KEY (`ID`)
) ENGINE=INNODB DEFAULT CHARSET=utf8mb4 COLLATE=utf8mb4_unicode_ci;
```

From this, it's relatively easy to create an `Order` class representation. This representation includes the required accessor methods, which are used to set or get data to and from the underlying orders database table:

```php
class Order
{
    const STATUS_CREATED   = 10;
    const STATUS_ACCEPTED  = 20;
    const STATUS_PAID      = 30;
    const STATUS_PROCESSED = 40;

    private $id;
    private $customerId;
    private $amount;
    private $status;
    private $createdAt;
    private $updatedAt;

    public function __construct(
        $customerId,
        $amount,
        $status,
        DateTimeInterface $createdAt,
        DateTimeInterface $updatedAt
    ) {
        $this->customerId = $customerId;
        $this->amount = $amount;
        $this->status = $status;
        $this->createdAt = $createdAt;
```

```
        $this->updatedAt = $updatedAt;
    }

    public function setId($id)
    {
        $this->id = $id;
    }

    public function getId()
    {
        return $this->id;
    }

    public function setCustomerId($customerId)
    {
        $this->customerId = $customerId;
    }

    public function getCustomerId()
    {
        return $this->customerId;
    }

    public function setAmount($amount)
    {
        $this->amount = $amount;
    }

    public function getAmount()
    {
        return $this->amount;
    }

    public function setStatus($status)
    {
        $this->status = $status;
    }

    public function getStatus()
    {
        return $this->status;
    }

    public function setCreatedAt(DateTimeInterface $createdAt)
    {
        $this->createdAt = $createdAt;
    }
```

```
    public function getCreatedAt()
    {
        return $this->createdAt;
    }

    public function setUpdatedAt(DateTimeInterface $updatedAt)
    {
        $this->updatedAt = $updatedAt;
    }

    public function getUpdatedAt()
    {
        return $this->updatedAt;
    }
}
```

An example use case for this implementation could be to update the order status as follows:

```
// Fetch an order from the database
$anOrder = $orderRepository->find( 1 );

// Update order status
$anOrder->setStatus(Order::STATUS_ACCEPTED);

// Update updatedAt field
$anOrder->setUpdatedAt(new DateTimeImmutable());

// Save the order to the database
$orderRepository->save($anOrder);
```

With regard to code reuse, this code has a problem similar to the initial user authentication solution. To resolve this issue, defenders of such a practice suggest the use of a `Service` `layer`, thereby making the operations explicit and reusable. This preceding implementation could now instead be encapsulated into a separate class:

```
class ChangeOrderStatusService
{
    private $orderRepository;

    public function __construct(OrderRepository $orderRepository)
    {
        $this->orderRepository = $orderRepository;
    }

    public function execute($anOrderId, $anOrderStatus)
    {
        // Fetch an order from the database
        $anOrder = $this->orderRepository->find($anOrderId);
```

```
        // Update order status
        $anOrder->setStatus($anOrderStatus);

        // Update updatedAt field
        $anOrder->setUpdatedAt(new DateTimeImmutable());

        // Save the order to the database
        $this->orderRepository->save($anOrder);
    }
}
```

Or, in the case of updating an order amount, consider this:

```
class UpdateOrderAmountService
{
    private $orderRepository;

    public function __construct(OrderRepository $orderRepository)
    {
        $this->orderRepository = $orderRepository;
    }

    public function execute( $orderId, $amount)
    {
        $anOrder = $this->orderRepository->find(1);

        $anOrder->setAmount($amount);
        $anOrder->setUpdatedAt(new DateTimeImmutable());
        $this->orderRepository->save($anOrder);
    }
}
```

The client code would be drastically reduced following a clearly intentioned operation:

```
$updateOrderAmountService = new UpdateOrderAmountService(
    $orderRepository
);

$updateOrderAmountService->execute(1, 20.5);
```

Implementing this approach can result in a large degree of code reusability. Someone who wishes to update the order amount simply has to retrieve an instance of UpdateOrderAmountService and invoke the execute method with the appropriate parameters.

However, choosing this path breaks the discussed Object-Oriented Design principles and incurs the costs of building a Domain Model without taking advantage of any of the benefits.

Anemic Domain Model Breaks Encapsulation

If we revisit the code used to define the services within our Service layer, we can see that as a client making use of the Order Entity, we're required to know every detail of its internal representation. This finding goes against the fundamental rule of Object-Oriented Programming, which is combining data with subsequent behavior

Anemic Domain Model Brings a False Sense of Code Reuse

Say there's an instance where a client bypasses `UpdateOrderAmountService` and instead fetches, updates, and persists directly to `OrderRepository`. Then, all the extra business logic that the `UpdateOrderAmountService` service might have won't be executed. This could lead to the order being stored in an inconsistent state. As such, invariants should be correctly guarded, and the best way to do this is to let the true Domain Model handle it. In the case of this example, the Order Entity would be the best place to ensure this:

```
class Order
{
    // ...
    public function changeAmount($amount)
    {
        $this->amount = $amount;
        $this->setUpdatedAt(new DateTimeImmutable());
    }
}
```

Note that by pushing this action down into the Entity and naming it in terms of the Ubiquitous Language, the system achieves great code reuse. Anyone who now wishes to change the amount of the order has to invoke the `Order::changeAmount` method directly.

This leads to far richer classes, where behavior is the goal for code reuse. This is commonly referred to as a Rich Domain Model.

How to Avoid Anemic Domain Models

The way to avoid falling into an Anemic Domain Model is to, when starting a new project or feature, think of the behavior first. Databases, ORMs, and so on are just implementation details, and we should strive to push the decision to use these tools as late in the development process as we can. In doing so, we can focus on the one true attribute that matters: the behavior.

Just as is the case with Entities, Domain Services can also fire `Chapter 6`, *Domain-Events*. However, when events are mostly fired by Domain Services and not Entities, it's again an indicator that you may be creating an Anemic Domain Model.

Wrap-Up

As we've seen, Services represent operations inside our system, and we can differentiate between three versions of them:

- **Application Services**: Help coordinate requests from the outside world into the Domain. These Services should not contain Domain logic. Transactions are handled in the application level; wrapping your services inside transnational decorators will make your code transaction agnostic.
- **Domain Services**: Operate with Domain concepts only, which are expressed by the Ubiquitous Language. Remember to postpone implementation details and think of behavior first, as abuse of Domain Services will lead to Anemic Domain Models and bad Object-Oriented Design.
- **Infrastructure Services**: Operate over Infrastructure, doing things like sending emails or logging information.

Our most important recommendation is that you should consider all your options before deciding on creating a Domain Service. First try to move your business logic inside an Entity or Value. Check with some workmates. Review again. If, after different approaches, the best option is creating a Domain Service, go for it.

6
Domain-Events

Software Events are things that happened in the system that other components might be interested in knowing about. PHP developers are generally not used to working with Events, which are not a feature in the language. However, it's more common to see how new frameworks and libraries embrace them to provide new ways of decoupling, reusing, and speeding up code.

Domain Events are Events related to Domain changes. Domain Events are things that happen in our Domain that Domain Experts care about.

In Domain-Driven Design, Domain Events are fundamental building blocks that help:

- Communicate with other Bounded Contexts.
- Improve performance and scalability, pushing for eventual consistency.
- Serve as historical checkpoints.

Domain Events represent the essence of asynchronous communication. For more on this topic, we recommend the book *Enterprise Integration Patterns:* `Designing, Building, and Deploying Messaging Solutions` by Gregor Hohpe and Bobby Woolf.

Introduction

Think about a JavaScript 2D platform game. There are tons of different components interacting with each other on the screen, all at the same time. There's a component that indicates the number of lives remaining, another one that shows all the points scored, and another one counting down the time remaining to finish the current level. Each time your character jumps on an enemy, the points increase. When your scoring goes higher than a certain number of points, you get an extra life. When your character picks up a key, a door usually opens. But how do all these components interact with one another? What's the optimal architecture for this scenario?

There are probably two main options: the first one is to couple each component with the ones it's connected to. However, in the above example, that means a lot of components are coupled together, with each new addition requiring the developer to modify the code. But do you remember the **Open Closed Principle** (**OCP**)? Adding a new component shouldn't make it so the first component has to be updated; this would be too much work to maintain.

The second — and better — approach is to connect all the components to a single object that handles all the important Events in the game. It receives Events from each component and forwards them to specific components. For example, the scoring component would be interested in an `EnemyKilled` Event, while the `LifeCaptured` Event is quite useful for the player Entity and the remaining lives component. In this way, all components are coupled to a single component that manages all the notifications. With this approach, adding or removing components doesn't affect the existing ones.

When developing a single application, Events come in handy for decoupling components. When developing a whole Domain in a distributed way, Events are very useful for decoupling each service or application that plays a role in the Domain. The key points are the same, but on a different scale.

Definition

Domain Events are one specific type of Event used for notifying local or remote Bounded Contexts of Domain changes.

Vaughn Vernon `defines` a Domain Event as:

> An occurrence of something that happened in the domain.

Eric Evans `defines` a Domain Event as:

> A full-fledged part of the Domain Model, a representation of something that happened in the Domain. Ignore irrelevant Domain activity while making explicit the events that the Domain Experts want to track or be notified of, or which are associated with state change in the other Model objects.

Martin Fowler `defines` a Domain Event as something that:

> Captures the memory of something interesting which affects the Domain.

Examples of Domain Events in a web application are `UserRegistered`, `OrderPlaced`, `UserRelocated`, and `ProductAdded`.

Short Story

In a ticket sales agency, a content manager decides to increase the price of a U2 show. Using her back office, she edits the show. A `ShowPriceChanged` Domain Event is published and persisted into the database with the new show price in the same transaction.

A batch process takes the Domain Event and queues it into RabbitMQ. The Domain Event gets distributed in two queues: one for the same local Bounded Context, and another remote one for Business Intelligence purposes.

In the first queue, a worker fetches the corresponding Show using the ID in the Event and pushes it into an Elasticsearch server so that the user can see the new price when searching. It could also update the new price in a different database table.

In the second queue, a worker inserts the information into a Logs Server or a Data Lake, where reporting or Data Mining processes can be run.

An external application that can't be integrated using Domain Events could access all the `ShowPriceChanged` Events using a REST API that the local Bounded Context provides.

As you can see, Domain Events are useful for dealing with eventual consistency and integrating different Bounded Contexts. Aggregates create Events and publish them. Subscribers may store Events and then forward them to remote subscribers.

Metaphor

We go to Babur's for a meal on Tuesday and pay by credit card. This might be modeled as an Event with an Event type of `PurchasePlaced`, a subject of my credit card, and a date of occurrence of Tuesday. If Babur's uses an old manual system and doesn't transmit the transaction until Friday, the transaction would be effective on Friday.

Things happen. Not all of them are interesting, and some may be worth recording but don't provoke a reaction. However, the most interesting things cause a reaction. Many systems need to react to interesting Events. Often you need to know why a system reacts in the way it did.

By funneling inputs to a system into streams of Domain Events, you can keep a record of all the inputs to a system. This helps you organize your processing logic, and it also allows you to keep an audit log of the inputs to the system.

Exercise
Try to locate examples of potential Domain Events in your current Domain.

Real-World Example

Before going into detail about Domain Events, let's see a real example of Domain Events and how they can help us in our application and our whole Domain.

Let's consider a simple Application Service that will register a new user — for example, in an e-commerce context. Application Services will be explained in another chapter, so don't worry too much about the interface. Instead, just focus on the execute method:

```
class SignUpUserService implements ApplicationService
{
    private $userRepository;
    private $userFactory;
    private $userTransformer;

    public function __construct(
        UserRepository $userRepository,
        UserFactory $userFactory,
        UserTransformer $userTransformer
    ) {
        $this->userRepository = $userRepository;
        $this->userFactory = $userFactory;
        $this->userTransformer = $userTransformer;
```

```
    }

    /**
     * @param SignUpUserRequest $request
     * @return User
     * @throws UserAlreadyExistsException
     */
    public function execute(SignUpUserRequest $request)
    {
        $email = $request->email();
        $password = $request->password();

        $user = $this->userRepository->userOfEmail($email );
        if ($user) {
            throw new UserAlreadyExistsException();
        }

        $user = $this->userFactory->build(
            $this->userRepository->nextIdentity(),
            $email,
            $password
        );

        $this->userRepository->add($user);
        $this->userTransformer->write($user);
    }

}
```

As shown, the *Application Service* section checks if the user already exists. If not, it creates a new User and adds it to the UserRepository.

Now consider an additional requirement: a new user must be notified by email when registered. Without thinking about it too much, the first approach that comes to mind is to update our Application Service to include a piece of code that would do the job — probably some sort of EmailSender that would be run after the add method. However, let's consider another approach.

What about firing a UserRegistered Event so that another component listening can react and send that email? There are some cool benefits to this new approach. First of all, we don't need to update the code of our Application Service every time a new action must be performed when a new user is registered.

Second, it's easier to test. The Application Service remains simpler, and each time a new action is developed, we just write the tests for the action.

Later in the same e-commerce project, we're told to integrate an open source gamification platform not written in PHP. Each time users place purchases or review products in our e-commerce Bounded Context, they can get badges that can be shown on their e-commerce user profile pages or be notified by email. How could we model the problem?

Following the first approach, we would update the Application Service to integrate with the new platform in a fashion similar to the previous email confirmation approach. With the Domain Event approach, we could create another listener for the `UserRegistered` Event, which will connect directly, by REST or SOA, to the gamification platform. Even better, it could communicate the Event to a messaging system like RabbitMQ so that the gamification Bounded Context can subscribe and get notified automatically. Our e-commerce Bounded Context doesn't need to know about the gamification Bounded Context at all.

Characteristics

Domain Events are ordinarily **immutable**, as they're a record of something in the past. In addition to a description of the Event, a Domain Event typically contains a timestamp for the time the Event occurred and the identity of Entities involved in the Event. Additionally, a Domain Event often has a separate timestamp indicating when the Event was entered into the system, along with the identity of the person who entered it. When useful, an identity for the Domain Event can be based on some set of these properties. So, for example, if two instances of the same Event arrive at a node, they can be recognized as the same.

The essence of a Domain Event is that you use it to capture things that can trigger a change to the state of the application you're developing or to another application in your Domain that's interested in those changes. These Event objects are then processed to cause changes to the system and stored to provide an audit log.

Naming Conventions

All Events should be represented as verbs in the past tense, as they're things that have been completed in the past — for example, `CustomerRelocated`, `CargoShipped`, or `InventoryLossageRecorded`. There are interesting examples in the English language where one may be tempted to use nouns as opposed to verbs in the past tense; an example of this would be *Earthquake* or *Capsize* as relevant Events for a congressperson interested in natural disasters. We suggest avoiding the temptation of using names like those for Domain Events and sticking with verbs in the past tense.

Domain Events and Ubiquitous Language

Consider the differences in the Ubiquitous Language when we discuss the side effects of relocating a customer. The Event makes the concept explicit, whereas previously, the changes that occurred within an Aggregate or between multiple Aggregates were left as an implicit concept that needed to be explored and defined. As an example, in most systems, when a side effect occurs on a library like Hibernate or the Entity Framework, it doesn't affect the Domain. These Events are implicit and transparent from the client point of view. The introduction of the Event makes the concept explicit and part of the Ubiquitous Language. Relocating a customer doesn't just change some stuff; rather it produces a `CustomerRelocatedEvent` that is explicitly defined within the language.

Immutability

As we mentioned already, Domain Events talk about the past and describe changes in your Domain that have already occurred. By definition, it's impossible to change the past, unless you're Marty McFly and have a DeLorean, which is probably not the case. So just remember that Domain Events are immutable.

Symfony Event Dispatcher
Some PHP frameworks support Events. However, don't confuse those Events with Domain Events; they're different in characteristics and goals. For example, Symfony has the Event Dispatcher component, and if you need to implement an Event system for a state machine, you can rely on it. In Symfony, the transformation from requests to responses is handled by Events too. However, Symfony Events are mutable, and each of the listeners is capable of modifying, adding to, or updating the information in the Event.

Modeling Events

In order to describe your business Domain accurately, you'll have to work closely with Domain Experts and define the Ubiquitous Language. This requires crafting Domain concepts using Domain Events, Entities, Value Objects, and so on. When modeling Events, name them and their properties according to the Ubiquitous Language, in the Bounded Context where they originated. If an Event is the result of executing a command operation on an Aggregate, the name is usually derived from the command that was executed. It's important that the Event name reflects the past nature of the occurrence.

Let's consider our user registration feature; the Domain Event needs to represent it. The following code shows a minimal interface for a base Domain Event:

```
interface DomainEvent
{
    /**
     * @return DateTimeImmutable
     */
    public function occurredOn();
}
```

As you can see, the minimum information required is a `DateTimeImmutable`, which is necessary in order to know when the Event happened.

Now let's model the new user registration Event using the following code. As we mentioned above, the name should be a verb in the past tense, so `UserRegistered` is probably a good choice:

```
class UserRegistered implements DomainEvent
{
    private $userId;

    public function __construct(UserId $userId)
    {
        $this->userId = $userId;
        $this->occurredOn = new \DateTimeImmutable();
    }

    public function userId()
    {
        return $this->userId;
    }

    public function occurredOn()
    {
        return $this->occurredOn;
    }
}
```

The minimum amount of information required to notify subscribers about the creation of new users is the `UserId`. With this information, any process, command, or Application Service — from either the same Bounded Context or a different one — may react to this Event.

As a Rule of Thumb

- Domain Events are usually designed as immutable
- The Constructor will initialize the full state of the Domain Event.
- Domain Events will have getters to access their attributes
- Include the identity of the Aggregate that performs the action
- Include other Aggregate identities related to the first one
- Include parameters that caused the Event (if useful)

But what happens if your Domain experts from the same Bounded Context or a different one need more information? Let's see the same Domain Event modeled with more information — for example, the email address:

```
class UserRegistered implements DomainEvent
{
    private $userId;
    private $userEmail ;

    public function __construct(UserId $userId, $userEmail)
    {
        $this-> userId = $userId;
        $this->userEmail = $userEmail ;
        $this->occurredOn = new DateTimeImmutable();
    }

    public function userId()
    {
        return $this->userId;
    }

    public function userEmail ()
    {
        return $this->userEmail ;
    }

    public function occurredOn()
    {
        return $this->occurredOn;
    }
}
```

Above, we've added the email address. Adding more information to a Domain Event can help improve performance or simplify the integration between different Bounded Contexts. Thinking from the point of view of another Bounded Context could help modeling Events. When a new user is created in the upstream Bounded Context, the downstream one would have to create its own user. Adding the user email could possibly save a sync request to the upstream Bounded Context in the case the downstream one needed it.

Do you remember the gamification example? In order to create a user of the gamification platform, probably called Player, the UserId from the e-commerce Bounded Context was probably enough. But what happens if the gamification platform has to notify the users by email about being rewarded? In this case, the email address is also mandatory. So if the email address is included in the original Domain Event, we're done. If that's not the case, the gamification Bounded Context needs to request this information from the e-commerce Bounded Context via REST or SOA integration.

Why Not the Whole User Entity?
Wondering if you should include the whole User Entity from your Bounded Context in the Domain Event? Our suggestion is that you don't. Domain Events might be used to communicate messages internally to a given Bounded Context or externally to other Bounded Contexts. In other words, what can be a `Seller` in a C2C e-commerce product catalog Bounded Context can be an `Author` of a product review in a product feedback one. Both can share the same ID or email, but `Seller` and `Author` are different concepts representing different Entities from different Bounded Contexts. So Entities from one Bounded Context have no meaning or a totally different one in another Bounded Context.

Doctrine Events

Domain Events are not just for doing batch jobs such as sending emails or communicating to other Bounded Contexts; they're also interesting for performance and scalability improvements. Let's see an example.

Consider the following scenario. You have an e-commerce application. Your main persistence mechanism is MySQL, but for browsing and filtering your catalog, you're using a better approach, such as Elasticsearch or Solr. On Elasticsearch, you'll end up with a subset of the information stored in your full database. How do you keep the data in sync? What happens when the Content Team updates the catalog from the back office tool?

There have been people re-indexing the entire catalog from time to time. This is very expensive and slow. A smarter approach may be updating one or some of the documents related to the Product that has been updated. How can we do that? Using Domain Events.

However, if you've been working with Doctrine, this is likely not something that's new to you. According to the `Doctrine 2 ORM 2 Documentation`:

> Doctrine 2 features a lightweight event system that is part of the Common package. Doctrine uses it to dispatch system events, mainly life cycle events. You can also use it for your own custom events.

Furthermore, it `states` that:

> Life cycle Callbacks are defined on an entity class. They allow you to trigger callbacks whenever an instance of that entity class experiences a relevant life cycle event. More than one callback can be defined for each life cycle event. Life cycle Callbacks are best used for simple operations specific to a particular entity class's life cycle.

Let's see an example from the `Doctrine Events Documentation`:

```
/** @Entity @HasLifecycleCallbacks */
class User
{
    // ...

    /**
     * @Column(type="string", length=255)
     */
    public $value;

    /** @Column(name="created_at", type="string", length=255) */
    private $createdAt;

    /** @PrePersist */
    public function doStuffOnPrePersist()
    {
        $this->createdAt = date('Y-m-d H:i:s');
    }

    /** @PrePersist */
    public function doOtherStuffOnPrePersist()
    {
        $this-> value = 'changed from prePersist callback!';
    }
```

```
/** @PostPersist */
public function doStuffOnPostPersist()
{
    $this->value = 'changed from postPersist callback!';
}

/** @PostLoad */
public function doStuffOnPostLoad()
{
    $this->value = 'changed from postLoad callback!';
}

/** @PreUpdate */
public function doStuffOnPreUpdate()
{
    $this->value = 'changed from preUpdate callback!';
}
}
```

You can hook specific tasks on each different important moment in the Doctrine Entity life cycle. For example, on `PostPersist`, you can generate the JSON document of your Entity and put it into Elasticsearch. That way, it's easy to keep data consistent between different persistence mechanisms.

Doctrine Events are a good example of the benefits of Events around your Entities. But you may be wondering what the problem with them is. This is because they're coupled to a framework, they're synchronous, and they act on your application level, but not for communication purposes. So that's why Domain Events, despite being a bit more difficult to implement and handle, are so much more interesting.

Persisting Domain Events

Persisting Events is always a good idea. Some of you may be wondering why you shouldn't publish Domain Events directly to a messaging or logging system. This is because persisting them has interesting benefits:

- You can expose your Domain Events to other Bounded Contexts through a REST interface.
- You can persist the Domain Event and the Aggregate changes in the same database transaction before pushing them to RabbitMQ. (You don't want to send notifications about something that didn't happen, just as you don't want to miss a notification about something that did happen.)

- Business Intelligence can use this data to analyze, forecast, or trend.
- You can audit your Entity changes.
- For Event Sourcing, you can reconstitute Aggregates from Domain Events.

Event Store

Where do we persist Domain Events? In an Event Store. An Event Store is a Domain Event Repository that lives in our Domain space as an abstraction (interface or abstract class). Its responsibility is to append Domain Events and query them. A possible basic interface could be the following:

```
interface EventStore
{
    public function append(DomainEvent $aDomainEvent);
    public function allStoredEventsSince($anEventId);
}
```

However, depending on the usage of your Domain Events, the previous interface can have more methods to query your Events.

In terms of implementation, you can decide to use a Doctrine Repository, a DBAL one, or a plain PDO. Because Domain Events are immutable, using a Doctrine Repository adds an unnecessary performance penalty, though for a small to medium application, Doctrine is probably OK. Let's look at a possible implementation with Doctrine:

```
class DoctrineEventStore extends EntityRepository implements EventStore
{
    private $serializer;

    public function append(DomainEvent $aDomainEvent)
    {
        $storedEvent = new StoredEvent(
            get_class($aDomainEvent),
            $aDomainEvent->occurredOn(),
            $this->serializer()->serialize($aDomainEvent, 'json')
        );

        $this->getEntityManager()->persist($storedEvent);
    }

    public function allStoredEventsSince($anEventId)
    {
        $query = $this->createQueryBuilder('e');
        if ($anEventId) {
```

```
            $query->where('e.eventId > :eventId');
            $query->setParameters(['eventId' => $anEventId]);
        }
        $query->orderBy('e.eventId');

        return $query->getQuery()->getResult();
    }

    private function serializer()
    {
        if (null === $this->serializer) {
            /** \JMS\Serializer\Serializer\SerializerBuilder */
            $this->serializer = SerializerBuilder::create()->build();
        }

        return $this->serializer;
    }
}
```

`StoredEvent` is the Doctrine Entity needed to map to the database. As you may have seen, when appending and after persisting the `Store`, there's no `flush` call. If this operation is inside a Doctrine transaction, it's not needed. So, let's leave it without the call and we'll go into more details when talking about Application Services.

Now let's see the `StoredEvent` implementation:

```
class StoredEvent implements DomainEvent
{
    private $eventId;
    private $eventBody;
    private $occurredOn;
    private $typeName;

    /**
     * @param string $aTypeName
     * @param \DateTimeImmutable $anOccurredOn
     * @param string $anEventBody
     */
    public function __construct(
        $aTypeName, \DateTimeImmutable $anOccurredOn, $anEventBody
    ) {
        $this->eventBody = $anEventBody;
        $this->typeName = $aTypeName;
        $this->occurredOn = $anOccurredOn;
    }

    public function eventBody()
    {
```

```
            return $this->eventBody;
        }

    public function eventId()
    {
        return $this->eventId;
    }

    public function typeName()
    {
        return $this->typeName;
    }

    public function occurredOn()
    {
        return $this->occurredOn;
    }
}
```

And here is its mapping:

```
Ddd\Domain\Event\StoredEvent:
    type: entity
    table: event
    repositoryClass:
        Ddd\Infrastructure\Application\Notification\DoctrineEventStore
    id:
        eventId:
            type: integer
            column: event_id
            generator:
            strategy: AUTO
    fields:
        eventBody:
            column: event_body
            type: text
        typeName:
            column: type_name
            type: string
            length: 255
        occurredOn:
            column: occurred_on
            type: datetime
```

In order to persist Domain Events with different fields, we'll have to join those fields as a serialized string. `typeName` identifies the Domain-wide Domain Event. An Entity or Value Object makes sense inside a Bounded Context, but Domain Events define a communication protocol between Bounded Contexts.

In distributed systems, shit happens. You'll have to deal with Domain Events that aren't published, are lost somewhere in the chain, or are published more than once. That's why it's important to persist a Domain Event with an ID, so that it's easy to track which Domain Events have been published and which are missing.

Publishing Events from the Domain Model

Domain Events should be published when the fact they represent occurs. For instance, when a new user has been registered, a new `UserRegistered` Event should be published.

Following the newspaper metaphor:

- **Modeling** a Domain Event is like writing a news article
- **Publishing** a Domain Event is like printing the article in the paper
- **Spreading** a Domain Event is like delivering the newspaper so everyone can read the article

The recommended approach for publishing Domain Events is to use a simple Listener-Observer pattern to implement a `DomainEventPublisher`.

Publishing a Domain Event from an Entity

Continuing with the example of a new user who has been registered in our application, let's see how the corresponding Domain Event can be published:

```
class User
{
    protected $userId;
    protected $email ;
    protected $password;

    public function __construct(UserId $userId, $email, $password)
    {
        $this->setUserId($userId);
        $this->setEmail($email);
        $this->setPassword($password);

        DomainEventPublisher::instance()->publish(
            new UserRegistered($this->userId)
        );
    }
}
```

```
    // ...
}
```

As seen in the example, when the `User` is created, a new `UserRegistered` Event is published. It's done in the Entity constructor and not outside because, with this approach, it's easier to keep our Domain consistent; any client who creates a new `User` will publish its corresponding Event. On the other hand, this makes it a bit more complex to use an infrastructure that needs to create a `User` Entity without using its constructor. For example, Doctrine uses the `serialize` and `unserialize` technique that recreates an object without calling its constructor. However, if you have to create your own, this isn't going to be as easy as in Doctrine.

In general, constructing an object from plain data such as an array is called **hydration**. Let's see an easy approach to building a new `User` fetched from a database. First of all, let's extract the Domain Event publication to its own method by applying the `Factory Method pattern`.

According to `Wikipedia`:

> The template method pattern is a behavioral design pattern that defines the program skeleton of an algorithm in an operation, deferring some steps to subclasses:

```
class User
{
    protected $userId;
    protected $email ;
    protected $password;

    public function __construct(UserId $userId, $email, $password)
    {
        $this->setUserId($userId);
        $this->setEmail($email);
        $this->setPassword($password);
        $this->publishEvent();

    }

    protected function publishEvent()
    {
        DomainEventPublisher::instance()->publish(
            new UserRegistered($this->userId)
        );
    }
```

```
        // ...
    }
```

Now, let's extend our current `User` with a new infrastructure Entity that will do the job for us. The trick here is make `publishEvent` do nothing so that the Domain Event isn't published:

```
class CustomOrmUser extends User
{
    protected function publishEvent()
    {

    }

    public static function fromRawData($data)
    {
        return new self(
            new UserId($data['user_id']),
            $data['email'],
            $data['password']
        );
    }
}
```

Remember to be careful with this approach; you might fetch invalid objects from the persistence mechanism, as Domain rules change all the time. Another approach without using the parent constructor could be the following:

```
class CustomOrmUser extends User
{
    public function __construct()
    {
    }

    public static function fromRawData($data)
    {
        $user = new self();
        $user->userId = new UserId($data['user_id']);
        $user->email = $data['email'];
        $user->password = $data['password'];

        return $user;
    }
}
```

With this approach, the parent constructor isn't called and User attributes must be protected. Other alternatives are Reflection, passing flags in the constructor, using a proxy library like `Proxy-Manager`, or using an ORM like Doctrine.

> **Other Strategy for Publishing Domain Events**
> As you can see in the previous example, we're using a static class for publishing our Domain Events. Other people, as an alternative, and especially when using `Event Sourcing`, will suggest that Entities hold all the fired Events internally within a field. In order to access all the Events, a getter is used in the Aggregate. This is also a valid approach. However, sometimes it's a bit difficult to keep track of which Entities have fired an Event. It can also be difficult to fire Events from places that aren't just Entities, example: Domain Services. On the plus side, testing if an Entity has fired an Event is much easier.

Publishing your Domain Events from Domain or Application Services

You should struggle to publish Domain Events from deeper in the chain. The closer to the inside of the Entity or the Value Object, the better. As we saw in the previous section, sometimes this isn't easy, but the final result is simpler for the clients. We've seen developers publishing Domain Events from the Application Services or Domain Services. This looks easier to do, but it will eventually lead to an Anemic Domain Model. This is not unlike when pushing business logic in Domain Services instead of placing it into your Entities.

How the Domain Event Publisher Works

A Domain Event Publisher is a Singleton class available from our Bounded Context needed to publish Domain Events. It also has support to attach listeners — Domain Event Subscribers — that will be listening for any Domain Event they're interested in. This isn't much different from subscribing to an Event with jQuery using the on method:

```
class DomainEventPublisher
{
    private $subscribers;
    private static $instance = null;

    public static function instance()
    {
```

```
        if (null === static::$instance) {
            static::$instance = new static();
        }

        return static::$instance;
    }

    private function __construct()
    {
        $this->subscribers = [];
    }

    public function __clone()
    {
        throw new BadMethodCallException('Clone is not supported');
    }

    public function subscribe(
        DomainEventSubscriber $aDomainEventSubscriber
    ) {
        $this->subscribers[] = $aDomainEventSubscriber;
    }

    public function publish(DomainEvent $anEvent)
    {
        foreach ($this->subscribers as $aSubscriber) {
            if ($aSubscriber->isSubscribedTo($anEvent)) {
                $aSubscriber->handle($anEvent);
            }
        }
    }
}
```

The `publish` method goes through all the possible subscribers, checking if they're interested in the published Domain Event. If that's the case, the `handle` method of the subscriber is called.

The `subscribe` method adds a new `DomainEventSubscriber` that will be listening to specific Domain Event types:

```
interface DomainEventSubscriber
{
    /**
     * @param DomainEvent $aDomainEvent
     */
    public function handle($aDomainEvent);

    /**
```

```
    * @param DomainEvent $aDomainEvent
    * @return bool
    */
    public function isSubscribedTo($aDomainEvent);
}
```

As we've already discussed, persisting all the Domain Events is a great idea. We can easily persist all the Domain Events published in our app by using a specific subscriber. Let's create a `DomainEventSubscriber` that will listen to all Domain Events, no matter what type, and persist them using our `EventStore`:

```
class PersistDomainEventSubscriber implements DomainEventSubscriber
{
    private $eventStore;

    public function __construct(EventStore $anEventStore)
    {
        $this->eventStore = $anEventStore;
    }

    public function handle($aDomainEvent)
    {
        $this->eventStore->append($aDomainEvent);
    }

    public function isSubscribedTo($aDomainEvent)
    {
        return true;
    }
}
```

`$eventStore` could be a custom Doctrine Repository, as already seen, or any other object capable of persisting `DomainEvents` into a database.

Setting Up DomainEventListeners

Where's the best place to set up the subscribers to the `DomainEventPublisher`? It depends. For global subscribers that will potentially affect the entire request cycle, the best place might be on the `DomainEventPublisher` initialization itself. For subscribers affected by a specific Application Service, the service instantiation might be a better place. Let's see an example using Silex.

In `Silex`, the best way to register a Domain Event Publisher that will persist all Domain Events is by using an Application Middleware. According to the `Silex 2.0 Documentation`:

> A *before* application middleware allows you to tweak the Request before the controller is executed.

This is the correct place to subscribe the listener responsible for persisting to the database those Events that will be sent to RabbitMQ later:

```
// ...
$app['em'] = $app-> share(function () {
    return (new EntityManagerFactory())->build();
});

$app['event_repository'] = $app->share(function ($app) {
    return $app['em']->getRepository(
        'Ddd\Domain\Model\Event\StoredEvent'
    );
});

$app['event_publisher'] = $app->share(function($app) {
    return DomainEventPublisher::instance();
});

$app->before(
    function(Symfony\Component\HttpFoundation\Request $request)
        use ($app) {

        $app['event_publisher']->subscribe(
            new PersistDomainEventSubscriber(
                $app['event_repository']
            )
        );
    }
);
```

With this setup, each time an Aggregate publishes a Domain Event, it will get persisted into the database. Mission accomplished.

Exercise
If you're working with Symfony, Laravel, or another PHP framework, find a way to subscribe globally specific subscribers for performing tasks around your Domain Events.

In case you want to perform any action on all Domain Events when the request is about to finish, you can create a Listener that will store all published Domain Events in memory. If you add a getter to that Listener to return all Domain Events, you can then decide what to do. This can be useful if you don't want to or if you can't persist the Events in the same transaction, as suggested before.

Testing Domain Events

You already know how to publish Domain Events, but how can you unit test this and ensure that `UserRegistered` is really fired? The easiest way we suggest is to use a specific `EventListener` that will work as a `Spy` to record whether or not the Domain Event was published. Let's see an example of the `User` Entity unit test:

```php
use Ddd\Domain\DomainEventPublisher;
use Ddd\Domain\DomainEventSubscriber;

class UserTest extends \PHPUnit_Framework_TestCase
{
    // ...

    /**
     * @test
     */
    public function itShouldPublishUserRegisteredEvent()
    {
        $subscriber = new SpySubscriber();
        $id = DomainEventPublisher::instance()->subscribe($subscriber);

        $userId = new UserId();
        new User($userId, 'valid@email.com', 'password');
        DomainEventPublisher::instance()->unsubscribe($id);

        $this->assertUserRegisteredEventPublished($subscriber, $userId);
    }

    private function assertUserRegisteredEventPublished(
        $subscriber, $userId
    ) {
        $this->assertInstanceOf(
            'UserRegistered', $subscriber->domainEvent
        );
        $this->assertTrue(
            $subscriber->domainEvent->serId()->equals($userId)
        );
    }
```

```
    }

    class SpySubscriber implements DomainEventSubscriber
    {
        public $domainEvent;

        public function handle($aDomainEvent)
        {
            $this->domainEvent = $aDomainEvent;
        }

        public function isSubscribedTo($aDomainEvent)
        {
            return true;
        }
    }
```

There are some alternatives to the above. You could use a static setter for the `DomainEventPublisher` or some reflection framework to detect the call. However, we think the approach we've shared is more natural. Last but not least, remember to clean up the Spy subscription so it won't affect the execution of the rest of the unit tests.

Spreading the news to Remote Bounded Contexts

In order to communicate a set of Domain Events to local or remote Bounded Contexts, there are two main strategies: messaging and a REST API. The first plans to use a messaging system such as RabbitMQ to transmit the Domain Events. The second plans to create a REST API for accessing the Domain Events of a specific Bounded Context.

Messaging

With all Domain Events persisted into the database, the only thing remaining to spread the news is to push them to our favorite messaging system. We prefer `RabbitMQ`, but any other system, such as ActiveMQ or ZeroMQ, will do the job. For integrating with RabbitMQ using PHP, there aren't many options, but `php-amqplib` will do the work.

First of all, we need a service capable of sending persisted Domain Events to RabbitMQ. You may want to query EventStore for all the Events and send each one, which isn't a bad idea. However, we could push the same Domain Event more than once, and generally speaking, *we need to minimize the number of Domain Events republished*. If the number of Domain Events republished is 0, that's even better. In order to not republish Domain Events, we need some sort of component to track which Domain Events have already been pushed and which ones are remaining. Last but not least, once we know which Domain Events we have to push, we send them and keep track of the last one published into our messaging system. Let's see a possible implementation for this service:

```php
class NotificationService
{
    private $serializer;
    private $eventStore;
    private $publishedMessageTracker;
    private $messageProducer;

    public function __construct(
        EventStore $anEventStore,
        PublishedMessageTracker $aPublishedMessageTracker,
        MessageProducer $aMessageProducer,
        Serializer $aSerializer
    ) {
        $this->eventStore = $anEventStore;
        $this->publishedMessageTracker = $aPublishedMessageTracker;
        $this->messageProducer = $aMessageProducer;
        $this->serializer = $aSerializer;
    }

    /**
     * @return int
     */
    public function publishNotifications($exchangeName)
    {
        $publishedMessageTracker = $this->publishedMessageTracker();
        $notifications = $this->listUnpublishedNotifications(
            $publishedMessageTracker
                ->mostRecentPublishedMessageId($exchangeName)
        );

        if (!$notifications) {
            return 0;
        }

        $messageProducer = $this->messageProducer();
        $messageProducer->open($exchangeName);
        try {
```

```
                $publishedMessages = 0;
                $lastPublishedNotification = null;
                foreach ($notifications as $notification) {
                    $lastPublishedNotification = $this->publish(
                        $exchangeName,
                        $notification,
                        $messageProducer
                    );
                    $publishedMessages++;
                }
        } catch (\Exception $e) {
            // Log your error (trigger_error, Monolog, etc.)
        }

        $this->trackMostRecentPublishedMessage(
            $publishedMessageTracker,
            $exchangeName,
            $lastPublishedNotification
        );

        $messageProducer->close($exchangeName);

        return $publishedMessages;
    }

    protected function publishedMessageTracker()
    {
        return $this->publishedMessageTracker;
    }

    /**
     * @return StoredEvent[]
     */
    private function listUnpublishedNotifications(
        $mostRecentPublishedMessageId
    ) {
        return $this
            ->eventStore()
            ->allStoredEventsSince($mostRecentPublishedMessageId);
    }

    protected function eventStore()
    {
        return $this->eventStore;
    }

    private function messageProducer()
    {
```

```
        return $this->messageProducer;
    }

    private function publish(
        $exchangeName,
        StoredEvent $notification,
        MessageProducer $messageProducer
    ) {
        $messageProducer->send(
            $exchangeName,
            $this->serializer()->serialize($notification, 'json'),
            $notification->typeName(),
            $notification->eventId(),
            $notification->occurredOn()
        );

        return $notification;
    }

    private function serializer()
    {
        return $this->serializer;
    }

    private function trackMostRecentPublishedMessage(
        PublishedMessageTracker $publishedMessageTracker,
        $exchangeName,
        $notification
    ) {
        $publishedMessageTracker->trackMostRecentPublishedMessage(
            $exchangeName, $notification
        );
    }
}
```

NotificationService depends on three interfaces. We've already seen EventStore, which is responsible for appending and querying Domain Events. The second one is PublishedMessageTracker, which is responsible for keeping track of pushed messages. The third one is MessageProducer, an interface representing our messaging system:

```
interface PublishedMessageTracker
{
    /**
     * @param string $exchangeName
     * @return int
     */
    public function mostRecentPublishedMessageId($exchangeName);
```

```
    /**
     * @param string $exchangeName
     * @param StoredEvent $notification
     */
    public function trackMostRecentPublishedMessage(
        $exchangeName, $notification
    );
}
```

The `mostRecentPublishedMessageId` method returns the ID of last `PublishedMessage`, so that the process can start from the next one. `trackMostRecentPublishedMessage` is responsible for tracking which message was sent last, in order to be able to republish messages in case you need to. `$exchangeName` represents the communication channel we're going to use to send out our Domain Events. Let's see a Doctrine implementation of `PublishedMessageTracker`:

```
class DoctrinePublishedMessageTracker extends EntityRepository\
implements PublishedMessageTracker
{
    /**
     * @param $exchangeName
     * @return int
     */
    public function mostRecentPublishedMessageId($exchangeName)
    {
        $messageTracked = $this->findOneByExchangeName($exchangeName);
        if (!$messageTracked) {
            return null ;
        }

        return $messageTracked->mostRecentPublishedMessageId();
    }

    /**
     *@param $exchangeName
     * @param StoredEvent $notification
     */
    public function trackMostRecentPublishedMessage(
        $exchangeName, $notification
    ) {
        if(!$notification) {
            return;
        }

        $maxId = $notification->eventId();

        $publishedMessage= $this->findOneByExchangeName($exchangeName);
```

```
        if(null === $publishedMessage){
            $publishedMessage = new PublishedMessage(
                $exchangeName,
                $maxId
            );
        }

        $publishedMessage->updateMostRecentPublishedMessageId($maxId);

        $this->getEntityManager()->persist($publishedMessage);
        $this->getEntityManager()->flush($publishedMessage);
    }
}
```

This code is quite straightforward. The only edge case we have to consider is when no Domain Event has already been published.

Why an Exchange Name?

We'll see this in more detail in the `Chpater 12`, *Integrating Bounded Contexts*. However, when a system is running and a new Bounded Context comes into play, you might be interested in resending all the Domain Events to the new Bounded Context. So keeping track of the last Domain Event published and the channel where it was sent might come in handy later.

In order to keep track of published Domain Events, we need an exchange name and a notification ID. Here's a possible implementation:

```
class PublishedMessage
{
    private $mostRecentPublishedMessageId;
    private $trackerId;
    private $exchangeName;

    /**
     * @param string $exchangeName
     * @param int $aMostRecentPublishedMessageId
     */
    public function __construct(
        $exchangeName, $aMostRecentPublishedMessageId
    ) {
        $this->mostRecentPublishedMessageId =
            $aMostRecentPublishedMessageId;
        $this->exchangeName = $exchangeName;
    }

    public function mostRecentPublishedMessageId()
```

```
    {
        return $this->mostRecentPublishedMessageId;
    }

    public function updateMostRecentPublishedMessageId($maxId)
    {
        $this->mostRecentPublishedMessageId = $maxId;
    }

    public function trackerId()
    {
        return $this->trackerId;
    }
}
```

And here is its corresponding mapping:

```
Ddd\Domain\Event\PublishedMessage:
    type: entity
    table: event_published_message_tracker
    repositoryClass:
        Ddd\Infrastructure\Application\Notification\
            DoctrinePublished\MessageTracker
    id:
        trackerId:
            column: tracker_id
            type: integer
            generator:
            strategy: AUTO
    fields:
        mostRecentPublishedMessageId:
            column: most_recent_published_message_id
            type: bigint
        exchangeName:
            type: string
            column: exchange_name
```

Now let's see what the MessageProducer interface is used for, along with its implementation details:

```
interface MessageProducer
{
    public function open($exchangeName);

    /**
     * @param $exchangeName
     * @param string $notificationMessage
     * @param string $notificationType
```

```
 * @param int $notificationId
 * @param \DateTimeImmutable $notificationOccurredOn
 * @return
 */
public function send(
    $exchangeName,
    $notificationMessage,
    $notificationType,
    $notificationId,
    \DateTimeImmutable $notificationOccurredOn
);

public function close($exchangeName);
}
```

Easy. The open and close methods open and close a connection with the messaging system. send takes a message body — message name and message ID — and sends them to our messaging engine, whatever it is. Because we've chosen RabbitMQ, we need to implement the connection and sending process:

```
abstract class RabbitMqMessaging
{
    protected $connection;
    protected $channel ;

    public function __construct(AMQPConnection $aConnection)
    {
        $this->connection =$aConnection;
        $this->channel = null ;
    }

    private function connect($exchangeName)
    {
        if (null !== $this->channel ) {
            return;
        }

        $channel = $this->connection->channel();
        $channel->exchange_declare(
            $exchangeName, 'fanout', false, true, false
        );
        $channel->queue_declare(
            $exchangeName, false, true, false, false
        );
        $channel->queue_bind($exchangeName, $exchangeName);

        $this->channel = $channel ;
    }
```

```php
    public function open($exchangeName)
    {

    }

    protected function channel ($exchangeName)
    {
        $this->connect($exchangeName);

        return $this->channel;
    }

    public function close($exchangeName)
    {
        $this->channel->close();
        $this->connection->close();
    }
}

class RabbitMqMessageProducer
    extends RabbitMqMessaging
    implements MessageProducer
{
    /**
     * @param $exchangeName
     * @param string $notificationMessage
     * @param string $notificationType
     * @param int $notificationId
     * @param \DateTimeImmutable $notificationOccurredOn
     */
    public function send(
        $exchangeName,
        $notificationMessage,
        $notificationType,
        $notificationId,
        \DateTimeImmutable $notificationOccurredOn
    ) {
        $this->channel ($exchangeName)->basic_publish(
            new AMQPMessage(
                $notificationMessage,
                [
                  'type'=>$notificationType,
                  'timestamp'=>$notificationOccurredOn->getTimestamp(),
                  'message_id'=>$notificationId
                ]
            ),
            $exchangeName
        );
```

```
        }
    }
```

Now that we have a `DomainService` for pushing Domain Events into a messaging system like RabbitMQ, it's time to execute them. We need to choose a delivery mechanism to run the service. We personally suggest creating a `Symfony Console` Command:

```
class PushNotificationsCommand extends Command
{
    protected function configure()
    {
        $this
            ->setName('domain:events:spread')
            ->setDescription('Notify all domain events via messaging')
            ->addArgument(
                'exchange-name',
                InputArgument::OPTIONAL,
                'Exchange name to publish events to',
                'my-bc-app'
            );
    }

    protected function execute(
        InputInterface $input, OutputInterface $output
    ) {
        $app = $this->getApplication()->getContainer();

        $numberOfNotifications =
            $app['notification_service']
                ->publishNotifications(
                    $input->getArgument('exchange-name')
                );

        $output->writeln(
            sprintf(
                '<comment>%d</comment>' .
                '<info>notification(s) sent!</info>',
                $numberOfNotifications
            )
        );
    }
}
```

Following the Silex example, let's see the definition of the `$app['notification_service']` defined in the `Silex Pimple Service Container`:

```
// ...
$app['event_store']=$app->share( function ($app) {
```

```
        return $app['em']->getRepository('Ddd\Domain\Event\StoredEvent');
    });

    $app['message_tracker'] = $app->share(function($app) {
        return $app['em']
            ->getRepository('Ddd\Domain\Event\Published\Message');
    });

    $app['message_producer'] = $app->share(function () {
        return new RabbitMqMessageProducer(
            new AMQPStreamConnection('localhost', 5672, 'guest', 'guest')
        );
    });

    $app['message_serializer'] = $app->share(function () {
        return SerializerBuilder::create()->build();
    });

    $app['notification_service'] = $app->share(function ($app) {
        return new NotificationService(
            $app['event_store'],
            $app['message_tracker'],
            $app['message_producer'],
            $app['message_serializer']
        );
    });
    //...
```

Syncing Domain Services with REST

With the `EventStore` already implemented in the messaging system, it should be easy to add some pagination capabilities, query for Domain Events, and render a JSON or XML representation publishing a REST API. Why is that interesting? Well, distributed systems using messaging have to face many different problems, such as messages that don't arrive, messages that arrive duplicated, or messages that arrive in an unexpected order. That's why it's nice to provide an API to publish your Domain Events so that other Bounded Contexts can ask for some missing information. Just as an example, consider that you make an HTTP request to an /events endpoint. A possible result would be the following:

```
[
    {
        "id": 1,
        "version": 1,
        "typeName": "Lw\\Domain\\Model\\User\\UserRegistered",
        "eventBody": {
```

```
            "user_id": {
                "id": "459a4ffc-cd57-4cf0-b3a2-0f2ccbc48234"
            }
        },
        "occurredOn": {
            "date": "2016-05-26 06:06:07.000000",
            "timezone_type": 3,
            "timezone": "UTC"
        }
    },
    {
        "id": 2,
        "version": 2,
        "typeName": "Lw\\Domain\\Model\\Wish\\WishWasMade",
        "eventBody": {
            "wish_id": {
                "id": "9e90435a-395c-46b0-b4c4-d4b769cbf201"
            },
            "user_id": {
                "id": "459a4ffc-cd57-4cf0-b3a2-0f2ccbc48234"
            },
            "address": "john@example.com",
            "content": "This is my new wish!"
        },
        "occurredOn": {
            "date": "2016-05-26 06:06:27.000000",
            "timezone_type": 3,
            "timezone": "UTC"
        },
        "timeTaken": "650"
    },
    //...
]
```

As you can see in the previous example, we're exposing a set of Domain Events in a JSON
REST API. In the output example, you can see a JSON representation of each of the Domain
Events. There are some interesting points. First, the version field. Sometimes your Domain
Events will evolve: they'll include more fields, they'll change the behavior of some existing
fields, or they'll remove some existing fields. That's why it's important to add a version field
in your Domain Events. If other Bounded Contexts are listening to such Events, they can
use the version field to parse the Domain Event in different ways. You may have faced the
same problem when versioning REST APIs.

Another point is the name. If you want to use the `classname` of the Domain Event, it may work in most cases. The problem is when a team decides to change the name of the class because of a refactoring. In this case, all Bounded Contexts listening to that name would stop working. This problem only occurs if you publish different Domain Events in the same queue. If you publish each Domain Event type in a different queue, it's not a real problem, but if you choose this approach, you'll face a different set of problems, such as receiving unordered events. Like in many other instances, there's a tradeoff involved. We strongly recommend you read *Enterprise Integration Patterns:* `Designing, Building, and Deploying Messaging Solutions`. In this book, you'll learn different patterns for integrating multiple applications using asynchronous methods. Because Domain Events are messages sent in an integration channel, all messaging patterns also apply to them.

Exercise
Think about the pros and cons of having a REST API for Domain Events. Consider Bounded Context coupling. You can also try to implement a REST API for your current application.

Wrap-Up

We've seen the tricks to model a proper `DomainEvent` with a base interface, we've seen where to publish the `DomainEvent` (the nearer to the Entities the better), and we've seen the strategies for spreading those `DomainEvents` to local and remote Bounded Contexts. Now, the only thing remaining is listening for a notification in the messaging system, reading it, and executing the corresponding Application Service or Command. We'll see how to do this in `Chapter 12`, *Integrating Bounded Contexts* and `Chapter 5`, *Services*.

7
Modules

When you place some classes together in a Module, you are telling the next developer who looks at your design to think about them together. If your model is telling a story, the Modules are chapters.

Domain-Driven Design:Tackling Complexity in the Heart of Software
-Eric Evans

A common concern when building an Application following Domain-Driven Design is where to place the code. Specifically if you're using a PHP framework, it's important to know the recommended way to place the code, where to place Infrastructure code, and how the different concepts inside the model should be structured.

In Domain-Driven Design, there's a tactical pattern for this: **modules**. Nowadays, everyone structures code in modules. All languages have some sort of tool to group classes and language definitions together. Java has packages. Ruby has modules. **PHP has namespaces**.

Domain-Driven Design goes one step further toward packaging and grouping your classes together and gives semantic meaning to these building blocks. Indeed, **it treats modules as a part of the model**. As part of the model, it's important to find the best naming, group together Domain objects that are close to each other, and keep the Domain objects that aren't related decoupled. **Modules should not be treated as a way to separate code but as a way to separate meaningful concepts in the model**.

General Overview

As explained in the `chapter 1`, *Getting Started with Domain-Driven Design*, our Domain is organized internally into Subdomains. Each Subdomain is ideally modeled and implemented by one Bounded Context, but sometimes more than one is needed. If well designed, each Bounded Context is an independent system that will be developed and managed by a team. Our suggestion is to implement each Bounded Context with a whole Application. This means that two Bounded Contexts won't live in the same code Repository. As such, they can be deployed independently, have a different development cycle, or even be developed using different languages. Inside your Bounded Contexts, you'll use modules to group Domain objects that hold a strong relation to one another.

Leverage Modules in PHP

Until PHP 5.3, modules weren't fully supported. But since the introduction of PHP 5.3, we can use PHP namespaces to implement the module pattern. For historical reasons, we're going to present how namespaces were used before PHP 5.3, but you should strive to use a PHP version that supports PHP namespaces. The best choice is always going to be the latest stable version of PHP.

First-Level Namespacing

A common approach is to use a first-level namespace that identifies your company. This will help in avoiding conflicts with third-party libraries. If you're using PSR-0, you'll have a real folder for the namespace; if you're using PSR-4, you don't need it. We'll go deeper into this shortly. But first, let's take a look at the PHP namespacing conventions.

PEAR-Style Namespacing

Before PHP 5.3, due to the lack of a namespace construction, PEAR-style namespaces were used. PEAR is an acronym for PHP Extension and Application Repository, and in the good old days, it was a Repository of reusable components. It's still active, but it's not very convenient, and not many people use it anymore — particularly since Composer and Packagist were introduced. PEAR, as a source of reusable components, needed a way to avoid class name collisions, so contributors started prefixing class names with namespaces. There are still projects that use this form of namespaces (*PHPUnit* and *Zend* Framework 1, to name a couple). An example of PEAR-style namespaces:

The following would be an example of PEAR-style namespaces:

```
├── composer.json
├── composer.lock
└── src
    └── BuyIt
        └── Billing
            └── Domain
                └── Model
                    └── Bill
                        └── Bill.php
```

The class name for the Bill entity, using PEAR-style namespaces, would become `BuyIt_Billing_Domain_Model_Bill_Bill`. However, this is a bit ugly, and it doesn't follow one of the main Domain-Driven Design mantras: every class name should be named in terms of the Ubiquitous Language. For this reason, we strongly discourage its use.

PSR-0 and PSR-4 Namespacing

Namespaces entered the scene when *PHP 5.3* was introduced, along with other important features. This was a major shift, and a group of the most important framework collaborators emerged with `PHP-FIG`, an acronym of PHP Framework Interop Group, in an attempt to standardize and unify common aspects of the framework and library creation. The first **PHP Standard Recommendation (PSR)** the group released was an autoloading standard that, in short, proposed a one-to-one relation between a class and a PHP file using namespaces. Today, `PSR-4` — a simplification of `PSR-0` that still maintains the relation between classes and physical PHP files — is the preferred and recommended way to structure code. We believe that this should be the one used to implement modules in a project.

Referring back to the same folder structure shown in the previous section, let's see what changes with PSR-0. The class name for the Bill Entity, using namespaces and PSR-0, would simply become Bill, and the fully qualified class name would be `BuyIt\Billing\Domain\Model\Bill\Bill`.

As you can see, this enables us to name Domain objects in terms of the Ubiquitous Language, and this is the preferred way to structure and organize code. If you're using Composer, as you should be doing, you need to set some autoloading configurations in your `composer.json` file:

```
...
"autoload": {
    "psr-0": {
        "BuyIt\\": "src/BuyIt/"
    }
},
"autoload-dev": {
    "psr-0": {
        "BuyIt": "tests/BuyIt/"
    }
},
...
```

If you're not using PSR-4 or you haven't migrated from PSR-0 yet, we strongly recommend doing so. You can get rid of the first-level namespace folder, and your code structure will better match the Ubiquitous Language:

```
├── composer.json
├── composer.lock
└── src
    └── Billing
        └── Domain
            └── Model
                └── Bill
                    └── Bill.php
```

However, in order to avoid the collision with third-party libraries, it's still recommended to add the first-level namespace in your `composer.json` file:

```
...
"autoload": {
    "psr-4": {
        "BuyIt\\": "src/"
    }
},
"autoload-dev": {
    "psr-4": {
```

```
            "BuyIt\\": "tests/"
        }
    },
    ...
```

If you prefer to have a first-level namespace but use PSR-4, there are some small changes to make:

```
├── composer.json
├── composer.lock
└── src
    └── BuyIt
        └── Billing
            └── Domain
                └── Model
                    └── Bill
                        └── Bill.php
```

```
    ...
    "autoload": {
        "psr-4": {
            "BuyIt\\": "src/BuyIt/"
        }
    },
    "autoload-dev": {
        "psr-4": {
            "BuyIt\\": "tests/BuyIt/"
        }
    },
    ...
```

As you may have noticed in the examples, we split the `src` and `tests` folders. This was done in order to optimize the autoloading file generated by Composer, and it will reduce the memory needed to store the classmap. It will also help you set up whitelisting and blacklisting options when generating your unit testing code coverage reports. If you want to know more about Composer's autoloading configuration, take a look at the `documentation`.

What about PHAR files?
They could also be used, however, we don't recommend this. As an exercise, make a list of pros and cons for using PHAR files to model modules.

Bounded Contexts and Applications

If we take the example of a fictional company called BuyIt, which deals with an e-commerce Domain, it may make sense to create a different application for each of the different Bounded Contexts solving specific Domain areas.

If some of the different Bounded Contexts are Order Management, Payment Management, Catalog Management, and Inventory Management, we recommend having an application for each one:

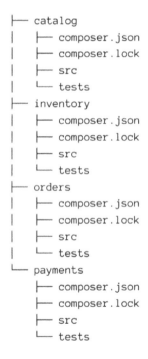

```
├── catalog
│   ├── composer.json
│   ├── composer.lock
│   ├── src
│   └── tests
├── inventory
│   ├── composer.json
│   ├── composer.lock
│   ├── src
│   └── tests
├── orders
│   ├── composer.json
│   ├── composer.lock
│   ├── src
│   └── tests
└── payments
    ├── composer.json
    ├── composer.lock
    ├── src
    └── tests
```

Each application exposes any set of delivery mechanisms needed. With the microservices trend, more and more people build Bounded Contexts that end up exposing REST APIs to the outside world. However, a Bounded Context is more than just an API. Remember that an API is just one of many delivery mechanisms; a Bounded Context can provide a web interface to interact with too.

Can Two Bounded Contexts Be in the Same Application? What about the Other Way Around?

The best option is one Subdomain, one Bounded Context, and one application. If we have a Bounded Context implemented with two applications, the maintenance and the deployment get a bit tricky. And in the case of an application implementing two Bounded Contexts, the deployment process, the time for running the tests, and merging issues can slow down the development.

Beware that each Bounded Context name represents a meaningful concept in our e-commerce Domain and is named in terms of the Ubiquitous Language:

- **Catalog** to hold all the code related to the product descriptions, product combinations, and so on.
- **Inventory** to hold all the code related to the management of product stocks.
- **Orders** to hold all the code related to the order processing systems. It will contain the finite-state machine in charge of processing orders.
- **Payments** to hold all the code related to payments, bills, and waybills.

Structuring Code in Modules

Let's dig a bit further into one of the Bounded Contexts. Take, for example, the Orders context and examine the structure details. As its name suggests, this Bounded Context is responsible for representing all the flows that an order passes — from its creation up to delivering to the customer who has purchased it. Furthermore, it's an independent Application, so it contains a source code folder and a tests folder. The source code folder contains all the code necessary for this Bounded Context to work: the Domain code, the Infrastructure code, and the Application layer.

The following diagram should illustrate the organization:

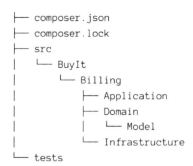

```
├── composer.json
├── composer.lock
├── src
│   └── BuyIt
│       └── Billing
│           ├── Application
│           ├── Domain
│           │   └── Model
│           └── Infrastructure
└── tests
```

All the code is prefixed with a vendor namespace named in terms of the organization name (`BuyIt`, in this case), and contains two subfolders: **Domain** holds all the Domain code, and **Infrastructure** holds the Infrastructure layer, thereby isolating all the Domain logic from the details of the Infrastructure layer. Following this structure, we're making it clear that we're going to use Hexagonal Architecture as a foundational architecture. Below is an example of an alternative structure that could be used:

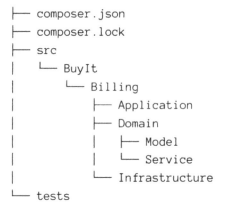

```
├── composer.json
├── composer.lock
├── src
│   └── BuyIt
│       └── Billing
│           ├── Application
│           ├── Domain
│           │   ├── Model
│           │   └── Service
│           └── Infrastructure
└── tests
```

The above style of structure uses an additional subfolder to store the Services defined inside the Domain Model. While this organization may make sense, our preference here is to not use it, since this way of separating code tends to be more focused on the architectural elements rather than the relevant concepts in the model. We believe this style could easily lead to some sort of Service layer on top of the Domain Model, which isn't necessarily a bad thing. Remember that Domain Services are used to describe operations in the Domain that don't belong to Entities or Value Objects. So from now on, we'll stick with the previous code organization.

It's possible to place code directly inside the `Domain/Model` subfolder. For example, it may be customary to place common interfaces and Services, like the `DomainEventPublisher` or the `DomainEventSubscriber`, in it.

If we had to model an Order Management context, we'd probably have an `Order` Entity with its Repository and all the state information. So our first attempt would be to place all those elements directly into the `Domain/Model` subfolder. At first glance, this may seem like the simplest way:

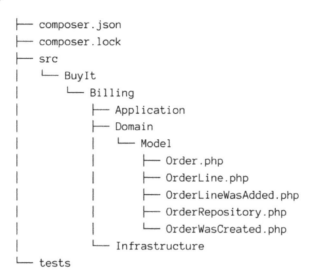

```
├── composer.json
├── composer.lock
├── src
│   └── BuyIt
│       └── Billing
│           ├── Application
│           ├── Domain
│           │   └── Model
│           │       ├── Order.php
│           │       ├── OrderLine.php
│           │       ├── OrderLineWasAdded.php
│           │       ├── OrderRepository.php
│           │       └── OrderWasCreated.php
│           └── Infrastructure
└── tests
```

Design Guidelines

Consider some basic rules and typical issues to pay attention to when implementing modules:

- Namespaces should be named in terms of Ubiquitous Language.
- Don't name your namespaces based on patterns or building blocks (Value Objects, Services, Entities, and so on).
- Create namespaces so that what's inside is as loosely coupled with other namespaces as possible.
- Refactor namespaces the same way as your code. Move them, rename them, group them, extract them, and so on.
- Don't use commercial product names, as they can change. Stick to the Ubiquitous Language.

We've placed the Order and the `OrderLine` Entities, the `OrderLineWasAdded` and the `OrderWasCreated` Event, and the `OrderRepository` into the same subfolder `Domain/Model`. This structure may be fine, but that's because we still have a simple model. What about the `Bill` Entity and its Repository? Or the `Waybill` Entity and its respective Repository? Let's add all those elements and see how they fit into the actual code structure:

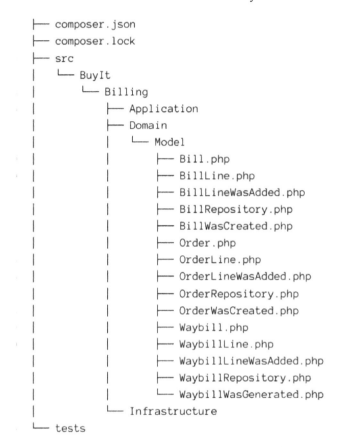

```
├── composer.json
├── composer.lock
├── src
│   └── BuyIt
│       └── Billing
│           ├── Application
│           ├── Domain
│           │   └── Model
│           │       ├── Bill.php
│           │       ├── BillLine.php
│           │       ├── BillLineWasAdded.php
│           │       ├── BillRepository.php
│           │       ├── BillWasCreated.php
│           │       ├── Order.php
│           │       ├── OrderLine.php
│           │       ├── OrderLineWasAdded.php
│           │       ├── OrderRepository.php
│           │       ├── OrderWasCreated.php
│           │       ├── Waybill.php
│           │       ├── WaybillLine.php
│           │       ├── WaybillLineWasAdded.php
│           │       ├── WaybillRepository.php
│           │       └── WaybillWasGenerated.php
│           └── Infrastructure
└── tests
```

While this style of code organization could be fine, it can become non-practical and rather unmaintainable in the long run. Every time we iterate and add new features, the model will become even bigger, and the subfolder will be eating even more code. We need to split the code in a way that give us a perspective of the model at a glance. No technical concerns, just Domain concerns. To reach this, we can split the model using the Ubiquitous Language, by finding meaningful concepts that help us group elements logically in terms of the Domain.

To do this, we could try the following approach:

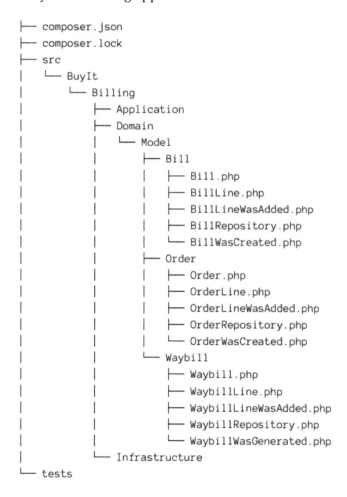

```
├── composer.json
├── composer.lock
├── src
│    └── BuyIt
│         └── Billing
│              ├── Application
│              ├── Domain
│              │    └── Model
│              │         ├── Bill
│              │         │    ├── Bill.php
│              │         │    ├── BillLine.php
│              │         │    ├── BillLineWasAdded.php
│              │         │    ├── BillRepository.php
│              │         │    └── BillWasCreated.php
│              │         ├── Order
│              │         │    ├── Order.php
│              │         │    ├── OrderLine.php
│              │         │    ├── OrderLineWasAdded.php
│              │         │    ├── OrderRepository.php
│              │         │    └── OrderWasCreated.php
│              │         └── Waybill
│              │              ├── Waybill.php
│              │              ├── WaybillLine.php
│              │              ├── WaybillLineWasAdded.php
│              │              ├── WaybillRepository.php
│              │              └── WaybillWasGenerated.php
│              └── Infrastructure
└── tests
```

This way, the code is more organized, conceptually speaking. And as Eric Evans points out in `the Blue Book`, modules are a way to communicate, as they provide us with insights about how the Domain Model works internally, along with helping us increase the cohesion and decrease the coupling between the concepts. If we look at the previous example, we can see that the concepts `Order` and `OrderLine` are strongly related, so they live in the same module. On the other hand, Order and Waybill, although sharing the same context, are different concepts, so they live in different modules. Modules are not just a way to group related concepts in the model, but also a way to express part of the design of the model.

Should We Place Repositories, Factories, Domain Events, and Services in Their Own Subfolders?
Effectively, they could be placed into their own subfolders, but it's strongly discouraged. In doing so, we would be mixing technical concerns and Domain concerns — remember that the module's main interest is to group related concepts from the Domain model and decouple them from non-related concepts. Modules don't separate code but instead separate meaningful concepts.

Modules in the Infrastructure Layer

Thus far, we've been discussing how we structure and organize code in the Domain layer, but we've said almost nothing about the Infrastructure layer. And since we're using Hexagonal Architecture to inverse the dependency between the Domain layer and the Infrastructure layer, we'll need a place where we can put all the implementations of the interfaces defined in the Domain layer. Returning to the example of the billing context, we need a place for the implementations of `BillRepository`, `OrderRepository`, and `WaybillRepository`.

It's clear that they should be placed into the Infrastructure folder, but where? Suppose we decided to use Doctrine ORM to implement the persistence layer. How do we put the Doctrine implementations of our Repositories into the Infrastructure folder? Let's do it directly and see how it looks:

```
├── composer.json
├── composer.lock
├── src
│   └── BuyIt
│       └── Billing
│           ├── Application
│           ├── Domain
│           │   └── Model
│           │       ├── Bill
│           │       └── ...
│           └── Infrastructure
│               ├── DoctrineBillRepository.php
│               ├── DoctrineOrderRepository.php
│               └── DoctrineWaybillRepository.php
└── tests
```

We could leave this as is, but as we saw in the Domain layer, this structure and organization will rot fast and become a mess within a few model iterations. Each time the model grows, it'll probably need even more Infrastructure, and we'll end up mixing different technical concerns such as persistence, messaging, logging, and more. Our first attempt to avoid a tangled mess of Infrastructure implementations is to define a module for each technical concern in the Bounded Context:

```
├── composer.json
├── composer.lock
├── src
│   └── BuyIt
│       └── Billing
│           ├── Application
│           ├── Domain
│           │   └── Model
│           │       ├── Bill
│           │       └── ...
│           └── Infrastructure
│               ├── Logging
│               ├── Messaging
│               └── Persistence
│                   ├── DoctrineBillRepository.php
│                   ├── DoctrineOrderRepository.php
│                   └── DoctrineWaybillRepository.php
└── tests
```

This looks much better and is a lot more maintainable in the long term than our first attempt. However, our namespaces are lacking some sort of relation to the Ubiquitous Language. Let's consider a variation:

```
├── composer.json
├── composer.lock
├── src
│   └── BuyIt
│       └── Billing
│           ├── Application
│           ├── Domain
│           │   └── Model
│           │       ├── Bill
│           │       │   ├── Bill.php
│           │       │   ├── BillLine.php
│           │       │   ├── BillLineWasAdded.php
│           │       │   ├── BillRepository.php
│           │       │   └── BillWasCreated.php
│           │       └── ...
│           └── Infrastructure
│               └── Domain
│                   └── Model
│                       ├── Bill
│                       │   └── DoctrineBillRepository.php
│                       └── ...
└── tests
```

Much better. It matches our Domain Model organization, but inside the Infrastructure layer — plus everything seems easier to find. If you know beforehand that you'll always have a single persistence mechanism, you can stick with this structure and organization. It's rather simple and easy to maintain.

But what about when you have to play with several persistence mechanisms? Nowadays, it's quite common to have a relational persistence mechanism and some kind of shared in-memory persistence like Redis or Riak, or to have some sort of local in-memory implementation to be able to test the code. Let's see how this fits into the actual approach:

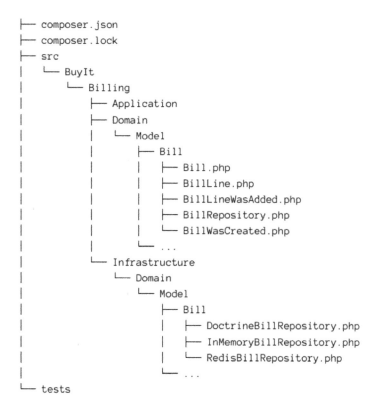

```
├── composer.json
├── composer.lock
├── src
│   └── BuyIt
│       └── Billing
│           ├── Application
│           ├── Domain
│           │   └── Model
│           │       ├── Bill
│           │       │   ├── Bill.php
│           │       │   ├── BillLine.php
│           │       │   ├── BillLineWasAdded.php
│           │       │   ├── BillRepository.php
│           │       │   └── BillWasCreated.php
│           │       └── ...
│           └── Infrastructure
│               └── Domain
│                   └── Model
│                       ├── Bill
│                       │   ├── DoctrineBillRepository.php
│                       │   ├── InMemoryBillRepository.php
│                       │   └── RedisBillRepository.php
│                       └── ...
└── tests
```

We recommend the above. However, all the Repository implementations are living in the same module. This could seem a bit odd when having so many different technologies. In case you find it interesting, you can create an additional module in order to group the related implementations by their underlying technology:

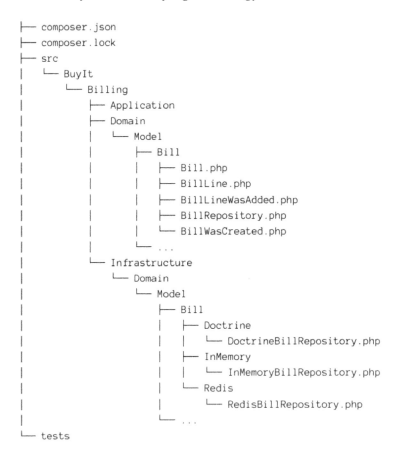

This approach is similar to the unit testing organization. However, there are classes, configurations, templates, and so on. that can't be matched with the Domain Model. That's why you may have additional modules inside the Infrastructure one that are related to specific technologies.

Where should you place Doctrine mapping files or Twig templates?

```
Infrastructure
├── Domain
│     └── ...
├── Logging
├── Messaging
└── Persistence
      └── Doctrine
            ├── BaseDoctrineRepository.php
            ├── EntityManagerFactory.php
            └── Mapping
                  ├── BuyIt.Billing.Domain.Model.Bill.Bill.dcm.yml
                  └── ...
```

As you can see, in order to make Doctrine work, we need an `EntityManagerFactory` and all the mapping files. We may also include any other Infrastructure objects needed as base classes. Because they're not directly related to our Domain Model, it's better to place these resources in a different module. The same things happen with the Delivery Mechanisms (API, Web, Console Commands, and so on.). In fact, you can be using different PHP frameworks or libraries for each delivery mechanism:

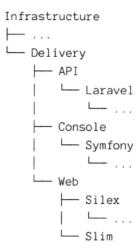

```
Infrastructure
├── ...
└── Delivery
      ├── API
      │     └── Laravel
      │           └── ...
      ├── Console
      │     └── Symfony
      │           └── ...
      └── Web
            ├── Silex
            │     └── ...
            └── Slim
```

In the previous example, we were using the Laravel Framework for serving the API, the Symfony Console Component as the entry point for the command line, and Silex and Slim for the web delivery mechanism. Regarding the `User` Interface, you should place it inside each delivery mechanism. However, if there's any chance to share the UI between different delivery mechanisms, you can create a module called UI at the same level as Persistence or Delivery. In general, our suggestion is struggling with how the frameworks tell you to organize your code. Frameworks should obey you, and not the other way around.

Mixing Different Technologies

In large business-critical applications, it's quite common to have a mix of several technologies. For example, in read-intensive web applications, you usually have some sort of denormalized data source (Solr, Elasticsearch, Sphinx, and so on.) that provides all the reads of the application, while a traditional RDBMS like MySQL or Postgres is mainly responsible for handling all the writes. When this occurs, one of the concerns that normally arises is whether we can have read operations go with the search engine and write operations go with the traditional RDBMS data source. Our general advice here is that these kind of situations are a smell for CQRS, since we need to scale the reads and the writes of the application independently. So if you can go with CQRS, that's likely the best choice.

But if for any reason you can't go with CQRS, an alternative approach is needed. In this situation, the use of the Proxy pattern from the *Gang of Four* comes in handy. We can define an implementation of a Repository in terms of the Proxy pattern:

```php
namespace BuyIt\Billing\Infrastructure\FullTextSearching\Elastica;

use BuyIt\Billing\Domain\Model\Order\OrderRepository;
use BuyIt\Billing\Infrastructure\Domain\Model\Order\Doctrine\
    DoctrineOrderRepository;

class ElasticaOrderRepository implements OrderRepository
{
    private $client;
    private $baseOrderRepository;

    public function __construct(
        Client $client,
        DoctrineOrderRepository $baseOrderRepository
    ) {
        $this->client = $client;
        $this->baseOrderRepository = $baseOrderRepository;
    }

    public function find($id)
```

```
{
    return $this->baseOrderRepository->find($id);
}

public function findBy(array $criteria)
{
    $search = new \Elastica\Search($this->client);
    // ...
    return $this->toOrder($search->search());
}

public function add($anOrder)
{
    // First we attempt to add it to the Elastic index
    $ordersIndex = $this->client->getIndex('orders');
    $orderType = $ordersIndex->getType('order');
    $orderType->addDocument(
        new \ElasticaDocument(
            $anOrder->id(),
            $this->toArray($anOrder)
        )
    );

    $ordersIndex->refresh();

    // When it is done, we attempt to add it to the RDBMS store
    $this->baseOrderRepository->add($anOrder);
}
}
```

This example provides a naive implementation using the `DoctrineOrderRepository` and the Elastica client, a client to interact with an Elasticsearch server. Note that for some operations, we're using the RDBMS datasource, and for others, we're using the Elastica client. Also note that the add operation consists of two parts. The first one attempts to store the Order to the Elasticsearch index, and the second one attempts to store the Order into the relational database, delegating the operation to the Doctrine implementation. Take into account that this is just an example and a way to do it. It can probably be improved — for example, now the whole add operation is synchronous. We could instead enqueue the operation to some sort of messaging middleware that stores the Order in Elasticsearch, for example. There are a lot of possibilities and improvements, depending on your needs.

Modules in the Application Layer

We've seen Domain and Infrastructure modules, so now let's take a look at the Application layer. In Domain-Driven Design, we suggest using Application Services as a way of decoupling the client from both the Domain Model and the necessary knowledge on how to interact with it. As you'll see in Chapter 11, *Application*, an Application Service is built with its dependencies, is executed with a DTO request, and returns a DTO response.

It can also use an output dependency to return the result:

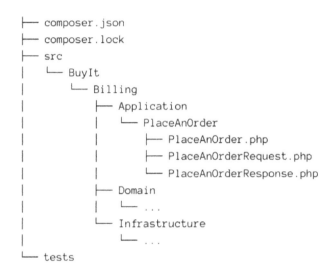

```
├── composer.json
├── composer.lock
├── src
│   └── BuyIt
│       └── Billing
│           ├── Application
│           │   └── PlaceAnOrder
│           │       ├── PlaceAnOrder.php
│           │       ├── PlaceAnOrderRequest.php
│           │       └── PlaceAnOrderResponse.php
│           ├── Domain
│           │   └── ...
│           └── Infrastructure
│               └── ...
└── tests
```

Our suggestion is to create modules around Application Services. Each module will hold its request and response. If you're using the Data Transformer as an output dependency, follow the Infrastructure approach as you would with the UI.

Wrap-Up

Modules are a way of grouping and separating concepts in our application. Modules should be named following the Ubiquitous Language. We shouldn't forget that modules are a way to communicate high-level concepts, which aids us in keeping coupling low and cohesion high. We've seen that we could create meaningful modules even in old versions of PHP by using prefixes. Nowadays, it's easy to build our modules following the PSR-0 and PSR-4 namespacing conventions.

8
Aggregates

Aggregates are probably the most difficult building blocks of Domain-Driven Design. They're hard to understand, and they're even harder to properly design. But don't worry; we're here to help you. However, before jumping into Aggregates, there are some key concepts we need to go through first: transactions and concurrency strategies.

Introduction

If you've worked with e-commerce applications, it's likely you've faced bugs related to data inconsistencies in your database. For example, consider a shopping order with a total amount of $99.99, which doesn't match with the sum of the amounts of each line in the order, $89.99. Where did that extra $10 come from?

Or, consider a website that sells tickets for the cinema. There's a movie theater with 100 available seats, and after a successful movie promotion, everyone is on the website waiting for the tickets to become available for purchase. Once you open the sales, everything happens fast and you somehow end up selling 102 tickets. You may have specified that there are only 100 seats, but for some reason you exceeded that threshold.

You might even have experience with tracking systems such as JIRA or Redmine. Think about a team of Developers, QAs, and a Product Owner. What could happen if everyone sorts and moves around user stories during a planning meeting and then saves? The final backlog or sprint prioritization would be the one from the team member who saved last.

In general, data inconsistencies occur when we deal with our persistence mechanism in a non-atomic way. An example of this is when you send three queries to a database and some of them work and some don't. The final state of the database is inconsistent. Sometimes, you want these three queries to succeed or fail all together, and that can be fixed with transactions. However, be careful, because as you will see in this chapter, not all inconsistencies are fixed with transactions. In fact, sometimes other data inconsistencies need locking or concurrency strategies. These kinds of tools might come up against your application performance, so be aware that there's a tradeoff involved.

You may think that these kinds of data inconsistencies only occur in databases, but that's not true. For example, if we use a document-oriented database such as Elasticsearch, we can have data inconsistency between two documents. Furthermore, most of the NoSQL persistence storage systems don't support ACID transactions. This means you can't persist or update more than one document in a single operation. So, if we make different requests to Elasticsearch, one may fail, leaving the data persisted in Elasticsearch inconsistent.

Keeping data consistent is a challenge. Not leaking infrastructure issues into the Domain is a bigger challenge. Aggregates aim to help you with both of these things.

Key Concepts

Persistence engines — and databases in particular — have some features for fighting data inconsistencies: ACID, constraints, referential integrity, locking, concurrency controls, and transactions. Let's review these concepts before working with Aggregates.

Most of these concepts are on the Internet and available to the public. We want to thank the people at Oracle, PostgreSQL, and Doctrine for doing amazing work with their documentation. They have carefully defined and explained these important terms, and rather than reinvent the wheel, we've compiled some of these official explanations to share with you.

ACID

As discussed in a previous section, **ACID** stands for **atomicity**, **consistency**, **isolation**, and **durability**. According to the `MySQL Glossary`:

> These properties are all desirable in a database system, and are all closely tied to the notion of a transaction. For example, the transactional features of MySQL InnoDB engine adhere to the ACID principles.

Transactions are *atomic* units of work that can be committed or rolled back. When a transaction makes multiple changes to the database, either all the changes succeed when the transaction is committed, or all the changes are undone when the transaction is rolled back.

The database remains in a *consistent* state at all times, after each commit or rollback, and while transactions are in progress. If related data is being updated across multiple tables, queries see either all old values or all new values, not a mix of old and new values.

Transactions are protected *isolated* from each other while they are in progress. They cannot interfere with each other or see each other's uncommitted data. This isolation is achieved through the locking mechanism. Experienced users can adjust the isolation level, trading off less protection in favor of increased performance and concurrency, when they can be sure that the transactions really do not interfere with each other.

The results of transactions are *durable*: once a commit operation succeeds, the changes made by that transaction are safe from power failures, system crashes, race conditions, or other potential dangers that many non-database applications are vulnerable to. Durability typically involves writing to disk storage, with a certain amount of redundancy to protect against power failures or software crashes during write operations.

Transactions

According to the `PostgreSQL 8.2.23 Documentation`:

> Transactions are a fundamental concept of all database systems. The essential point of a transaction is that it bundles multiple steps into a single, all-or-nothing operation. The intermediate states between the steps are not visible to other concurrent transactions, and if some failure occurs that prevents the transaction from completing, then none of the steps affect the database at all.

For example, consider a bank database that contains balances for various customer accounts, as well as total deposit balances for branches. Suppose that we want to record a payment of $100.00 from Alice's account to Bob's account. Simplifying outrageously, the SQL commands for this might look like:

```
UPDATE accounts
    SET balance = balance - 100.00
WHERE name = 'Alice';

UPDATE branches
    SET balance = balance - 100.00
WHERE name = (SELECT branch_name FROM accounts WHERE name ='Alice');

UPDATE accounts
    SET balance = balance + 100.00
WHERE name = 'Bob';

UPDATE branches
    SET balance = balance + 100.00
WHERE name = (SELECT branch_name FROM accounts WHERE name ='Bob');
```

The details of these commands are not important here. The important point is that there are several separate updates involved to accomplish this rather simple operation. Our bank's officers will want to be assured that either all these updates happen, or none of them happen. It would certainly not do for a system failure to result in Bob receiving $100.00 that was not debited from Alice. Nor would Alice long remain a happy customer if she was debited without Bob being credited. We need a guarantee that if something goes wrong partway through the operation, none of the steps executed so far will take effect. Grouping the updates into a transaction gives us this guarantee. A transaction is said to be atomic: from the point of view of other transactions, it either happens completely or not at all.

We also want a guarantee that once a transaction is completed and acknowledged by the database system, it has indeed been permanently recorded and won't be lost even if a crash ensues shortly thereafter. For example, if we are recording a cash withdrawal by Bob, we do not want any chance that the debit to his account will disappear in a crash just after he walks out the bank door. A transactional database guarantees that all the updates made by a transaction are logged in permanent storage (That is: on disk) before the transaction is reported complete.

Another important property of transactional databases is closely related to the notion of atomic updates: when multiple transactions are running concurrently, each one should not be able to see the incomplete changes made by others. For example, if one transaction is busy totalling all the branch balances, it would not do for it to include the debit from Alice's branch but not the credit to Bob's branch, nor vice versa. So transactions must be all-or-nothing not only in terms of their permanent effect on the database, but also in terms of their visibility as they happen. The updates made so far by an open transaction are invisible to other transactions until the transaction completes, whereupon all the updates become visible simultaneously.

In PostgreSQL, for example, a transaction is set up by surrounding the SQL commands of the transaction with BEGIN and COMMIT commands. So our banking transaction would actually look like:

```
BEGIN;
UPDATE accounts
    SET balance = balance - 100.00
WHERE name = 'Alice';
-- etc etc
COMMIT;
```

If, partway through the transaction, we decide we do not want to commit (perhaps we just noticed that Alice's balance went negative), we can issue the command ROLLBACK instead of COMMIT, and all our updates so far will be canceled.

PostgreSQL actually treats every SQL statement as being executed within a transaction. If you do not issue a BEGIN command, then each individual statement has an implicit BEGIN and (if successful) COMMIT wrapped around it. A group of statements surrounded by BEGIN and COMMIT is sometimes called a transaction block.

All this is happening within the transaction block, so none of it is visible to other database sessions. When and if you commit the transaction block, the committed actions become visible as a unit to other sessions, while the rolled-back actions never become visible at all.

Isolation Levels

According to the MySQL Glossary, transaction isolation is:

> One of the foundations of database processing. Isolation is the "I" in the acronym ACID. The isolation level is the setting that fine-tunes the balance between performance and reliability, consistency, and reproducibility of results when multiple transactions are making changes and performing queries at the same time.

> From highest amount of consistency and protection to the least, the isolation levels supported by InnoDB, for example, are: SERIALIZABLE, REPEATABLE READ, READ COMMITTED, and READ UNCOMMITTED.

> With InnoDB tables, many users can keep the default isolation level REPEATABLE READ for all operations. Expert users might choose the read committed level as they push the boundaries of scalability with OLTP processing, or during data warehousing operations where minor inconsistencies do not affect the aggregate results of large amounts of data. The levels on the edges (SERIALIZABLE and READ UNCOMMITTED) change the processing behavior to such an extent that they are rarely used.

Referential Integrity

According to the MySQL Glossary, referential integrity is:

> The technique of maintaining data always in a consistent format, part of the ACID philosophy. In particular, data in different tables is kept consistent through the use of foreign key constraints, which can prevent changes from happening or automatically propagate those changes to all related tables. Related mechanisms include the unique constraint, which prevents duplicate values from being inserted by mistake, and the NOT NULL constraint, which prevents blank values from being inserted by mistake.

Locking

According to the MySQL Glossary, locking is:

> The system of protecting a transaction from seeing or changing data that is being queried or changed by other transactions. The locking strategy must balance reliability and consistency of database operations (the principles of the ACID philosophy) against the performance needed for good concurrency. Fine-tuning the locking strategy often involves choosing an isolation level and ensuring all your database operations are safe and reliable for that isolation level.

Concurrency

According to the MySQL Glossary, concurrency is:

> The ability of multiple operations (in database terminology, transactions) to run simultaneously, without interfering with each other. Concurrency is also involved with performance, because ideally the protection for multiple simultaneous transactions works with a minimum of performance overhead, using efficient mechanisms for locking.

Pessimistic Concurrency Control (PCC)

The book Elasticsearch: The Definitive Guide by Clinton Gormley and Zachary Tong discusses PCC, saying that:

> Widely used by relational databases, this approach assumes that conflicting changes are likely to happen and so blocks access to a resource in order to prevent conflicts. A typical example is locking a row before reading its data, ensuring that only the thread that placed the lock is able to make changes to the data in that row.

With Doctrine

According to the `Doctrine 2 ORM Documentation` on locking support:

> Doctrine 2 offers support for Pessimistic- and Optimistic-locking strategies natively. This allows to take very fine-grained control over what kind of locking is required for your Entities in your application.

According to the `Doctrine 2 ORM Documentation` on pessimistic locking:

> Doctrine 2 supports Pessimistic Locking at the database level. No attempt is being made to implement pessimistic locking inside Doctrine, rather vendor-specific and ANSI-SQL commands are used to acquire row-level locks. Every Doctrine Entity can be part of a pessimistic lock, there is no special metadata required to use this feature.

> However for Pessimistic Locking to work you have to disable the Auto-Commit Mode of your Database and start a transaction around your pessimistic lock use-case using the *Explicit Transaction Demarcation*. Doctrine 2 will throw an Exception if you attempt to acquire an pessimistic lock and no transaction is running.

Doctrine 2 currently supports two pessimistic lock modes:

- Pessimistic Write `Doctrine\DBAL\LockMode::PESSIMISTIC_WRITE`, locks the underlying database rows for concurrent Read and Write Operations.
- Pessimistic Read `Doctrine\DBAL\LockMode::PESSIMISTIC_READ`, locks other concurrent requests that attempt to update or lock rows in write mode.

You can use pessimistic locks in three different scenarios:

- Using `EntityManager#find($className, $id, \Doctrine\DBAL\LockMode::PESSIMISTIC_WRITE)` or `EntityManager#find($className, $id, \Doctrine\DBAL\LockMode::PESSIMISTIC_READ)`
- Using `EntityManager#lock($entity, \Doctrine\DBAL\LockMode::PESSIMISTIC_WRITE)` or `EntityManager#lock($entity, \Doctrine\DBAL\LockMode::PESSIMISTIC_READ)`
- Using `Query#setLockMode(\Doctrine\DBAL\LockMode::PESSIMISTIC_WRITE)` or `Query#setLockMode(\Doctrine\DBAL\LockMode::PESSIMISTIC_READ)`

Optimistic Concurrency Control

According to `Wikipedia`:

> **Optimistic concurrency control** (OCC) is a concurrency control method applied to transactional systems such as relational database management systems and software transactional memory. OCC assumes that multiple transactions can frequently complete without interfering with each other. While running, transactions use data resources without acquiring locks on those resources. Before committing, each transaction verifies that no other transaction has modified the data it has read. If the check reveals conflicting modifications, the committing transaction rolls back and can be restarted. Optimistic concurrency control was first proposed by H.T. Kung.
>
> OCC is generally used in environments with low data contention. When conflicts are rare, transactions can complete without the expense of managing locks and without having transactions wait for other transactions' locks to clear, leading to higher throughput than other concurrency control methods. However, if contention for data resources is frequent, the cost of repeatedly restarting transactions hurts performance significantly; it is commonly thought that other concurrency control methods have better performance under these conditions. However, locking-based "pessimistic" methods also can deliver poor performance because locking can drastically limit effective concurrency even when deadlocks are avoided.

With Elasticsearch

According to `Elasticsearch: The Definitive Guide`, when OCC is used by Elasticsearch:

> This approach assumes that conflicts are unlikely to happen and doesn't block operations from being attempted. However, if the underlying data has been modified between reading and writing, the update will fail. It is then up to the application to decide how it should resolve the conflict. For instance, it could reattempt the update, using the fresh data, or it could report the situation to the user.
>
> Elasticsearch is distributed. When documents are created, updated, or deleted, the new version of the document has to be replicated to other nodes in the cluster. Elasticsearch is also asynchronous and concurrent, meaning that these replication requests are sent in parallel, and may arrive at their destination out of sequence. Elasticsearch needs a way of ensuring that an older version of a document never overwrites a newer version.

Every document has a _version number that is incremented whenever a document is changed. Elasticsearch uses this _version number to ensure that changes are applied in the correct order. If an older version of a document arrives after a new version, it can simply be ignored.

We can take advantage of the _version number to ensure that conflicting changes made by our application do not result in data loss. We do this by specifying the version number of the document that we wish to change. If that version is no longer current, our request fails.

Let's create a new blog post:

```
PUT /website/blog/1/_create
{
    "title": "My first blog entry",
    "text": "Just trying this out..."
}
```

The response body tells us that this newly created document has _version number 1. Now imagine that we want to edit the document: we load its data into a web form, make our changes, and then save the new version.

First we retrieve the document:

```
GET /website/blog/1
```

The response body includes the same _version number of 1:

```
{
    "index": "website",
    "type": "blog",
    "id": "1",
    "version": 1,
    "found": true,
    "_source": {
        "title": "My first blog entry",
        "text": "Just trying this out..."
    }
}
```

Now, when we try to save our changes by reindexing the document, we specify the version to which our changes should be applied. We want this update to succeed only if the current _version of this document in our index is version 1:

```
PUT /website/blog/1?version=1
{
    "title": "My first blog entry",
```

```
            "text": "Starting to get the hang of this..."
    }
```

This request succeeds, and the response body tells us that the _version has been incremented to 2:

```
{
    "index": "website",
    "type": "blog",
    "id": "1",
    "version": 2,
    "created": false
}
```

However, if we were to rerun the same index request, still specifying version=1, Elasticsearch would respond with a 409 Conflict HTTP response code, and a body like the following:

```
{
    "error": {
        "root_cause": [{
            "type": "version_conflict_engine_exception",
            "reason":
                "[blog][1]: version conflict,current[2],provided
[1]",
            "index": "website",
            "shard": "3"
        }],
        "type": "version_conflict_engine_exception" ,
        "reason":
            "[blog][1]:version conflict,current [2],provided[1]",
        "index": "website",
        "shard": "3"
    },
    "status": 409
}
```

This tells us that the current _version number of the document in Elasticsearch is 2, but that we specified that we were updating version 1.

What we do now depends on our application requirements. We could tell the user that somebody else has already made changes to the document, and to review the changes before trying to save them again. Alternatively, as in the case of the widget stock_count previously, we could retrieve the latest document and try to reapply the change.

All APIs that update or delete a document accept a version parameter, which allows you to apply optimistic concurrency control to just the parts of your code where it makes sense.

With Doctrine

According to the `Doctrine 2 ORM Documentation` on optimistic locking:

Database transactions are fine for concurrency control during a single request. However, a database transaction should not span across requests, the so-called "user think time". Therefore a long-running "business transaction" that spans multiple requests needs to involve several database transactions. Thus, database transactions alone can no longer control concurrency during such a long-running business transaction. Concurrency control becomes the partial responsibility of the application itself.

Doctrine has integrated support for automatic optimistic locking via a version field. In this approach any entity that should be protected against concurrent modifications during long-running business transactions gets a version field that is either a simple number (mapping type: `integer`) or a timestamp (mapping type: `datetime`). When changes to such an entity are persisted at the end of a long-running conversation the version of the entity is compared to the version in the database and if they don't match, an `OptimisticLockException` is thrown, indicating that the entity has been modified by someone else already.

You designate a version field in an entity as follows. In this example we'll use an integer:

```
class User
{
    // ...
    /** @Version @Column(type="integer") */
    private $version;
    // ...
}
```

When a version conflict is encountered during `EntityManager#flush()`, an `OptimisticLockException` is thrown and the active transaction rolled back (or marked for rollback). This exception can be caught and handled. Potential responses to an `OptimisticLockException` are to present the conflict to the user or to refresh or reload objects in a new transaction and then retrying the transaction.

With PHP promoting a share-nothing architecture, the time between showing an update form and actually modifying the entity can in the worst scenario be as long as your applications session timeout. If changes happen to the entity in that time frame you want to know directly when retrieving the entity that you will hit an optimistic locking exception:

You can always verify the version of an entity during a request either when calling `EntityManager#find()`:

```
use Doctrine\DBAL\LockMode;
use Doctrine\ORM\OptimisticLockException;

$theEntityId = 1;
$expectedVersion = 184;
try{
    $entity = $em->find(
        'User',
        $theEntityId,
        LockMode::OPTIMISTIC,
        $expectedVersion
    );
    // do the work
    $em->flush();
} catch (OptimisticLockException $e){
    echo
        'Sorry, someone has already changed this entity.' .
        'Please apply the changes again!';
}
```

Or you can use `EntityManager#lock()` to find out:

```
use DoctrineDBALLockMode;
use DoctrineORMOptimisticLockException;

$theEntityId = 1;
$expectedVersion = 184;
$entity = $em->find('User', $theEntityId);
try {
    // assert version em->lock(entity, LockMode::OPTIMISTIC,
    $expectedVersion);
} catch (OptimisticLockException $e){
    echo
        'Sorry, someone has already changed this entity.' .
        'Please apply the changes again!';
}
```

According to `Doctrine 2 ORM Documentation's` important implementation notes:

> You can easily get the optimistic locking workflow wrong if you compare the wrong versions. Say you have Alice and Bob editing a hypothetical blog post:
>
> - Alice reads the headline of the blog post being "Foo", at optimistic lock version 1 (GET Request)
> - Bob reads the headline of the blog post being "Foo", at optimistic lock version 1 (GET Request)
> - Bob updates the headline to "Bar", upgrading the optimistic lock version to 2 (POST Request of a Form)
> - Alice updates the headline to "Baz", ... (POST Request of a Form)
>
> Now at the last stage of this scenario the blog post has to be read again from the database before Alice's headline can be applied. At this point you will want to check if the blog post is still at version 1 (which it is not in this scenario).
>
> Using optimistic locking correctly, you have to add the version as an additional hidden field (or into the SESSION for more safety). Otherwise you cannot verify the version is still the one being originally read from the database when Alice performed her GET request for the blog post. If this happens you might see lost updates you wanted to prevent with Optimistic Locking.
>
> See the example code, The form (GET Request):
>
> ```
> $post = $em->find('BlogPost', 123456);
> echo '<input type="hidden" name="id" value="' .
>         $post->getId() . '"/>';
> echo '<input type="hidden" name="version" value="' .
>         $post->getCurrentVersion() . '" />';
> ```
>
> And the change headline action (POST Request):
>
> ```
> $postId = (int) $_GET['id'];
> $postVersion = (int) $_GET['version'];
> $post = $em->find(
>     'BlogPost',
>     $postId,
>     DoctrineDBALLockMode::OPTIMISTIC,
>     $postVersion
> );
> ```

Wow — that was a lot of information to take in. However, don't worry if you don't completely understand everything. The more you work with Aggregates and Domain-Driven Design, the more you'll encounter moments when transactionality has to be considered in designing your Application.

To summarize, if you want to keep your data consistent, use transactions. However, be careful about overusing transactions or locking strategies because these can slow your Application down or make it unusable. If you want to have a really fast Application, optimistic concurrency can help you. Last but not least, some data can eventually be consistent. This means that we allow our data to not be consistent for a particular window of time. During that time, some inconsistencies are acceptable. Eventually, an asynchronous process will perform the final task to remove such inconsistencies.

What Is an Aggregate?

Aggregates are Entities that hold other Entities and Value Objects that help keep data consistent. From Vaughn Vernon's `Implementing Domain-Driven Design`:

> Aggregates are carefully crafted consistency boundaries that cluster Entities and Value Objects.

Another amazing book that you should definitely buy and read is `NoSQL Distilled: A Brief Guide to the Emerging World of Polyglot Persistence` by Pramod J. Sadalage and Martin Fowler. This book says that:

> In Domain-Driven Design, an aggregate is a collection of related objects that we wish to treat as a unit. In particular, it is a unit for data manipulation and management of consistency. Typically, we like to update aggregates with atomic operations and communicate with our data storage in terms of aggregates.

What Martin Fowler Says...

From `http://martinfowler.com/bliki/DDD_Aggregate.html`:

> Aggregate is a pattern in Domain-Driven Design. A DDD aggregate is a cluster of domain objects that can be treated as a single unit. An example may be an order and its line-items, these will be separate objects, but it is useful to treat the order (together with its line items) as a single aggregate.

An aggregate will have one of its component objects be the aggregate root. Any references from outside the aggregate should only go to the aggregate root. The root can thus ensure the integrity of the aggregate as a whole.

Aggregates are the basic element of transfer of data storage you request to load or save whole aggregates. Transactions should not cross aggregate boundaries.

DDD Aggregates are sometimes confused with collection classes (lists, maps, and so on). DDD aggregates are domain concepts (order, clinic visit, playlist), while collections are generic. An aggregate will often contain multiple collections, together with simple fields. The term *aggregate* is a common one, and is used in various different contexts (example: UML), in which case it does not refer to the same concept as a DDD aggregate.

What Wikipedia Says...

From `https://en.wikipedia.org/wiki/Domain-driven_design#Building_blocks_of_D DD`:

Aggregate: A collection of objects that are bound together by a root entity, otherwise known as an aggregate root. The aggregate root guarantees the consistency of changes being made within the aggregate by forbidding external objects from holding references to its members.

Example: When you drive a car, you do not have to worry about moving the wheels forward, making the engine combust with spark and fuel, etc.; you are simply driving the car. In this context, the car is an aggregate of several other objects and serves as the aggregate root to all of the other systems.

Why Aggregates?

The avid reader will probably be wondering what all of this has to do with Aggregates and Aggregate Design. And actually, that's a pretty good question. There's a direct relation, so let's explore it. The Relational Model uses tables to store data. Those tables are composed of rows, where each row usually represents an instance of a concept of the application's interest. Additionally, each row can point to other rows on other tables of the same database, and the consistency between this relationship can be kept by the use of referential integrity. This model is fine; however, it lacks a very basic word: the *object* word.

Indeed, when we talk about the Relational Model, we're namely talking about tables, rows, and relationships between rows. And when we talk about the Object-Oriented Model, we're talking mainly about compositions of objects. So every time we fetch data — a set of rows — from a relational database, we run a translation process responsible for building an in-memory representation we can operate with. The same applies to the opposite direction. Every time we need to store an object in the database, we should run the other translation process to translate that object to a given set of rows or tables. This translation, from object to rows or tables, means that you may run different queries against your database. As such, without using any specific tool, such as transactions, it's impossible to guarantee the data will be persisted consistently. This problem is the so-called **impedance mismatch**.

Impedance Mismatch

The object-relational impedance mismatch is a set of conceptual and technical difficulties that are often encountered when a **relational database management system** (**RDBMS**) is being used by a program written in an object-oriented programming language or style, particularly when objects or class definitions are mapped in a straightforward way to database tables or relational schemata.

Extracted from `Wikipedia`

The impedance mismatch `is not an easy problem to solve`, so we highly discourage trying to solve it on your own. It would be a huge undertaking, and it's simply not worth the effort. Luckily, there are some libraries out there that take care of this translation process. They're commonly known as Object-Relational Mappers (which we've discussed in earlier chapters) and their primary concern is to ease the process of translating from the Relational Model to the Object-Oriented Model, and vice versa.

This is an issue that also affects NoSQL persistence engines and not just databases. Most NoSQL engines use documents. An Entity is translated into a document representation such as JSON, XML, binary, and so on. and then persisted. The main difference with RDBMS databases is that if a main Entity (such as `Order`) has other related Entities (such as `OrderLines`), you can more easily design a single JSON document that will contain all the information. With this approach, with a single request to your NoSQL engine, you don't need transactions.

Nevertheless, if you're using NoSQL or RDBMS for fetching and persisting your Entities, you'll need one or more queries. In order to ensure data consistency, those queries or requests need to be executed as a single operation. Running as a single operation can guarantee that data will be consistent.

What does consistent mean? It means that all data persisted into our database must be compliant with all business rules, also known as invariants. An example of a business invariant could be how on GitHub, a user is able to have unlimited public repositories but no private repositories. However, if this user pays $12 per month, then they're able to have up to 10 private repositories.

Relational databases provide three main tools for helping us with data consistency: * **Referential** integrity: Foreign keys, nullable checks, and so on. * **Transactions**: Run multiple queries as a single operation. The problem with transactions is the same as that of branches and merges in your code repository. Keeping a branch has a performance cost (memory, CPU, storage, indexing, and so on.). If too many people (concurrency) are touching the same data, conflicts will occur and transaction commits will fail. * **Locking**: Block rows or tables. Other queries around the same tables and rows must wait for the block to be removed. Locking has a negative impact on the performance of your application.

Suppose we have an e-commerce application we want to expand to other countries and regions, and suppose the release goes fairly well and sales increase. A pretty evident side effect of the release is that the database should be able to handle the additional load increase. As seen earlier, there are two scaling methods: up or out.

Scaling up means we improve the hardware infrastructure we have (For example: better CPU, more memory, better hard disks). Scaling out means adding more machines that will organize in a cluster for doing specific work. In this case, we could have a cluster of databases.

But relational databases aren't designed to scale horizontally, since we can't configure them to save one set of rows to a given machine and another set of rows to a different one. Relational databases are easy to scale up, but **the Relational Model doesn't scale horizontally**.

In the NoSQL world, data consistency is a bit more difficult: transactions and referential integrity aren't generally supported, while locking is supported but generally not encouraged.

NoSQL databases aren't affected as drastically by the impedance mismatch. They match perfectly with Aggregate Design because they enable us to easily store and retrieve single units atomically. For example, when using a key-value store such as Redis, an Aggregate could be serialized and stored on a specific key. On a document-oriented store such as Elasticsearch, an Aggregate would be serialized into a JSON and persisted as a document. As mentioned before, the problem comes when multiple documents must be updated at once.

For that reason, when persisting any object with a single representation (one document, so no multiple queries needed), it's easy to distribute those single units across several machines, called nodes, which make up a cluster of NoSQL databases. It's common knowledge that these databases are easy to distribute, which means that the style of databases is easy to scale horizontally.

A Bit of History

Around the beginning of the 21st century, companies such as Amazon and Google grew massively. In order to consolidate their growth, they used clustering techniques: not only did they have better servers, but they also relied on many more of them working together.

In a scenario such as this, deciding how to store your data is key. If you take an Entity and spread its information throughout multiple servers, in multiple nodes of a cluster, the effort needed to control transactions is high. The same thing applies if you want to fetch an Entity. So if you can design your Entity in a way that is persisted in the node of a cluster, it makes things much easier. That's one of the reasons why Aggregate Design is so important.

If you want to know more about the history of Aggregate Design outside of Domain-Driven Design, take a look at `NoSQL Distilled: A Brief Guide to the Emerging World of Polyglot Persistence`.

Anatomy of an Aggregate

An Aggregate is an Entity that may hold other Entities and Value Objects. The parent Entity is known as the root Entity.

A single Entity without any child Entities or Value Objects is also an Aggregate by itself. That's why in some books, the term Aggregates is used instead of the term Entity. When we use them here, Entity and Aggregate mean the same thing.

The main goal of an Aggregate is to keep your Domain Model consistent. Aggregates centralize most of the business rules. Aggregates are persisted atomically in your persistence mechanism. No matter how many child Entities and Value Objects live inside the root Entity, all of them will be persisted atomically, as a single unit. Let's see an example.

Consider an e-commerce application, website, and so on. Users can place orders, which have multiple lines that define what product was bought, the price, the quantity, and the line total amount. An order has a total amount too, which is the sum of all line amounts.

What could happen if you update a line amount but not the order amount? Data inconsistency. To fix this, any modification to any Entity or Value Object within the Aggregate is performed through the root Entity. Most PHP developers we've worked with are more comfortable building objects and then handling their relationships from the client code, rather than pushing the business logic inside the Entities:

```
$order = ...
$orderLine = new OrderLine(
    'Domain-Driven Design in PHP', 24.99
);
$order->addOrderLine($orderLine);
```

As seen in the previous code example, newbie or even average developers generally build child objects first and then relate them to the parent object using a setter. Consider the following approach:

```
$order = ...
$orderLine = $order->addOrderLine(
    'Domain-Driven Design in PHP', 24.99
);
```

Or, consider this approach:

```
$order = ...
$order->addOrderLine(
    'Domain-Driven Design in PHP', 24.99
);
```

These approaches are very interesting because they follow two Software Design principles: Tell-Don't-Ask and Law of Demeter.

According to `Martin Fowler`:

> Tell-Don't-Ask is a principle that helps people remember that object-orientation is about bundling data with the functions that operate on that data. It reminds us that rather than asking an object for data and acting on that data, we should instead tell an object what to do. This encourages to move behavior into an object to go with the data.

According to `Wikipedia`:

> The **Law of Demeter** (**LoD**) or principle of least knowledge is a design guideline for developing software, particularly object-oriented programs. In its general form, the LoD is a specific case of loose coupling...and can be succinctly summarized in each of the following ways:
>
> - Each unit should have only limited knowledge about other units: only units "closely" related to the current unit.
> - Each unit should only talk to its friends; don't talk to strangers.
> - Only talk to your immediate friends.
>
> The fundamental notion is that a given object should assume as little as possible about the structure or properties of anything else (including its subcomponents), in accordance with the principle of "information hiding".

Let's continue with the order example. You've already learned how to run operations through the root Entity. Now let's update a product quantity of a line in an order. This increases the quantity, the line total amount, and the order amount. Great! Now it's time to persist the order with the changes.

If you're using MySQL, you can imagine that we'll need two UPDATE statements: one for the orders table, and another one for the `order_lines` table. What could happen if these two queries aren't performed inside a transaction?

Let's assume that the UPDATE statement that updates the line order works properly. However, the UPDATE on the order total amount fails due to network connectivity issues. In such a scenario, you would end up with a data inconsistency in your Domain Model. Transactions help you keep this consistency.

If you're using Elasticsearch, the situation is a bit different. You can map the order with a JSON document that holds order lines internally, so just a single request is needed. However, if you decide to map the order with one JSON document and each of its order lines with another JSON document, you're in trouble, as Elasticsearch doesn't support transactions. Ouch!

An Aggregate is fetched and persisted using its own Chapter 10, *Repositories*. If two Entities don't belong to the same Aggregate, both will have their own Repository. If a true business invariant exists and two Entities belong to the same Aggregate, you'll only have one Repository. This Repository will be the one for the root Entity.

What are the cons of Aggregates? The problem when dealing with transactions is the possibility of performance issues and operation errors. We'll explore this in depth soon.

Aggregate Design Rules

When designing an Aggregate, there are some rules and considerations to follow in order to get all the benefits and minimize the negative effects. Don't worry too much if you don't understand everything now; as an example, we'll show you a small application where we'll be referencing the rules we introduce you to.

Design Aggregates Based in Business True Invariants

First of all, what's an invariant? An invariant is a rule that must be true and consistent during code execution. For example, a `stack` is a **LIFO** (**Last In, First Out**) data structure that we can *push* items into and *pop* items out of. We can also ask how many items are inside of the stack; this is what's called the size of the stack. Consider a pure PHP implementation without using any specific PHP array functions such as `array_pop`:

```php
class Stack
{
    private $data;

    public function __construct()
    {
        $this->data = [];
    }

    public function push($value)
    {
        $this->data[] = $value;
    }

    public function size()
    {
        $size = 0;
        for ($i = 0; $i < count($this->data); $i++) {
            $size++;
        }

        return $size;
    }

    /**
     * @return mixed
     */
    public function pop()
```

```
    {
        $topIndex = $this->size() - 1;
        $top = $this->data[$topIndex];
        unset($this->data[$topIndex]);
        return $top;
    }
}
```

Consider the previous `size` method implementation. It's far from perfect, but it works. However, as it's implemented in the code above, it's a CPU-intensive and high-cost call. Luckily, there's an option to improve this method, by introducing a private attribute to keep track of the number of elements in the internal array:

```
class Stack
{
    private $data;
    private $size;

    public function __construct()
    {
        $this->data = [];
        $this->size = 0;
    }

    public function push($value)
    {
        $this->data[] = $value;
        $this->size++;
    }

    public function size()
    {
        return $this->size;
    }

    /**
     * @return mixed
     */
    public function pop()
    {
        $topIndex = $this->size--;
        $top = $this->data[$topIndex];
        unset($this->data[$topIndex]);

        return $top;
    }
}
```

With these changes, the `size` method is now a fast operation, as it just returns the value of the `size` field. To accomplish this, we introduced a new integer attribute called `size`. When a new `Stack` is created, the value of `size` is 0, and there's no element in the Stack. When we add a new element into the Stack using the `push` method, we also increase the value of the `size` field. Similarly, we reduce the value of `size` when we remove a value from the Stack using the `pop` method.

By incrementing and decreasing the value of size, we keep it consistent with the real number of elements that are inside the `Stack`. The size value is consistent right before and right after calling any public method in the `Stack` class. As a result, the size value is always equal to the number of elements in the `Stack`. That's an invariant! We could write it down as `$this->size === count($this->data)`.

A true business invariant is a business rule that must always be true and transactionally consistent within an Aggregate. By transactionally consistent, we mean that updating an aggregate must be an atomic operation. All the data contained inside an Aggregate must be persisted atomically. If we don't follow this rule, we could persist data representing a non-valid Aggregate.

According to `Vaughn Vernon`:

> A properly designed Aggregate is one that can be modified in any way required by the business with its invariants completely consistent within a single transaction. And a properly designed Bounded Context modifies only one Aggregate instance per transaction in all cases. What is more, we cannot correctly reason on Aggregate design without applying transactional analysis.

As discussed in the introduction, in an e-commerce application, the amount of an order must match the sum of the amounts of every line in that order. That's an invariant, or business rule. We have to persist the `Order` and its `OrderLines` into the database in the same transaction. This forces us to make `Order` and `OrderLine` be part of the same Aggregate, where `Order` would be the Aggregate Root. Because `Order` is the root, all operations related to `OrderLines` must go through the Order. So no more instantiating `OrderLine` objects outside of an `Order` and then using a setter method to add `OrderLines` to the `Order`. Instead, we must use Factory Methods on the `Order`.

With this approach, we have a single entry point to perform operations on the Aggregate: the `Order`. It means there's no chance of invoking a method to break such a rule. Each time you add or update an `OrderLine` through the `Order`, the `Order` amount gets recalculated internally. Making all operations go through the root help us keep the Aggregate consistent. In this way, it's more difficult to break any invariant.

Small Aggregates Vs. Big Aggregates

For most of the websites and projects where we've worked, almost 95 percent of Aggregates were formed by one single root Entity and some Value Objects. No other Entities were required to be in the same Aggregate. So in most cases, there was no real true business invariant to keep consistent.

Be careful with the has-a/has-many relations that don't necessarily make two Entities become one Aggregate, with one of those being the root. Relations, as we will see, can be handled by referencing Entity Identities.

As explained in the introduction, an Aggregate is a transactional boundary. The smaller the boundary is, the fewer chances there are for conflicts when committing multiple concurrent transactions. When designing Aggregates, you should strive to create them small. If there's no true invariant to protect, that means all single Entities form an Aggregate by themselves. That's great, because it's the best scenario for achieving the best performance. Why? Because locking issues and failed transaction issues are minimized.

If you decide to go for big Aggregates, keeping data consistent can be easier but is probably impractical. When applications with big Aggregates run in production, they start to experience issues when multiple users perform operations. When using optimistic concurrency, the main problem is transactional failures. When using locking, the problem is slowness and timeouts.

Let's consider some radical examples. When using optimistic concurrency, imagine that the whole Domain is versioned, and each operation on any Entity creates a new version for the whole Domain. With this scenario, if two users were performing different operations on different Entities that couldn't be related at all, the second request would experience a transaction failure because of a different version. On the other hand, when using pessimistic concurrency, imagine a scenario where we lock the database on each operation. That would block all the users until the lock is released. This means many requests would be waiting, and at some point, probably timed out. Both of these examples keep data consistent, but the application can't be used by more than one user.

Last but not least, when designing big Aggregates, because they may hold collections of Entities, it's important to consider the performance implications of loading such collections in memory. Even using an ORM such as Doctrine, which can lazy load collections (load collections only when they are needed), if a collection is too big, it can't fit into memory.

Reference Other Entities by Identity

When two Entities don't form an Aggregate but are related, the best option to have Entities reference one another is by using *Identities*. Identities were already explained in the `Chapter 4`, *Entities*.

Consider a `User` and their `Orders`, and assume we haven't found any true invariant. `User` and `Order` wouldn't be part of the same Aggregate. If you need to know which `User` owns a specific `Order`, you can probably ask the `Order` what its `UserId` is. `UserId` is a Value Object that holds the `User` Identity. We get the whole `User` by using its Repository, the `UserRepository`. This code generally lives in the Application Service.

As a general explanation, each Aggregate has its own Repository. If you've fetched a specific Aggregate and you need to fetch another related Aggregate, you'll do it in your Application Services or Domain Services. The Application Service will depend on Repositories to fetch the Aggregates needed.

Jumping from one Aggregate to another is what's generally called traversing or navigating your Domain. With ORMs, it's easy to do it by mapping all the relations between your Entities. However, it's also really dangerous, as you can easily end up running countless queries in a specific feature. As a rule, you shouldn't do this. Don't map all the relations between your Entities because you can. Instead, only map the relations between Entities inside an Aggregate in your ORM if two Entities form an Aggregate. If this isn't the case, you'll use Repositories to get referenced Aggregates.

Modify One Aggregate Per Transaction and Request

Consider the following scenario: you make a request, it gets into your controller, and it intends to update two different Aggregates. Each Aggregate keeps the data consistent within that Aggregate. However, what would happen if the request goes well over the first Aggregate update but suddenly stops (server restarted, reloaded, out of memory, and so on.) and the second Aggregate isn't updated? Is that a data consistency issue? It may be. Let's consider some solutions.

From Vaughn Vernon's `Implementing Domain-Driven Design`:

> In a properly designed Bounded Context modifies only one Aggregate instance per transaction in all cases. What is more, we cannot correctly reason on Aggregate design without applying transactional analysis. Limiting modification to one Aggregate instance per transaction may sound overly strict. However, it is a rule of thumb and should be the goal in most cases. It addresses the very reason to use Aggregates.

If, in a single request, you need to update two Aggregates, it may just be that those two Aggregates are a single one and they need to both be updated in the same transaction. If not, you can wrap the entire request in a transaction, but we wouldn't recommend this as the main option because of the performance issues and the transaction errors involved.

If both updates on different Aggregates don't need to be wrapped into a transaction, this means we can assume some delay between one update and the other. In such a scenario, a more Domain-Driven Design approach is to use Domain Events. When doing so, the first Aggregate update will fire a Domain Event. That event will be persisted in the same transaction as the Aggregate update and then published into our message queue. Later, a worker will take the event from the queue and perform the second Aggregate update. Such an approach pushes for Eventual Consistency, reduces the size of the transaction boundaries, improves performance, and reduces transaction errors.

Sample Application Service: User and Wishes

Now you know the basic rules for Aggregate Design.

The best way to learn about Aggregates is by seeing code. So let's consider the scenario of a web application where users can make wishes to be granted if something happens to them, similar to a will. For example, I would like to send an email to my wife explaining what to do with my GitHub account if I die in a horrible accident, or maybe I want to send an email telling her how much I loved her. The way to check that I'm still alive is to answer emails the platform sends to me. (If you want to know more about `this application`, you can visit our `GitHub` account. So we have users and their wishes. Let's consider only one use case: "As a `User`, I want to make a Wish." How could we model this? Using good practices when designing Aggregates, let's try to push for small Aggregates. In this case, that means using two different Aggregates of one Entity each, `User` and `Wish`. For the relationship between them, we should use an identifier, such as `UserId`.

No Invariant, Two Aggregates

We'll discuss Application Services in the following chapters, but for now, let's check different approaches for making a Wish. The first approach, particularly for a novice, would likely be something similar to this:

```
class MakeWishService
{
    private $wishRepository;

    public function __construct(WishRepository $wishRepository)
    {
        $this->wishRepository = $wishRepository;
    }

    public function execute(MakeWishRequest $request)
    {
        $userId = $request->userId();
        $address = $request->address();
        $content = $request->content();

        $wish = new Wish(
            $this->wishRepository->nextIdentity(),
            new UserId($userId),
            $address,
            $content
        );

        $this->wishRepository->add($wish);
    }
}
```

This code probably allows for the best performance possible. You can almost see the INSERT statement behind the scenes; the minimum number of operations for such a use case is one, which is good. With the current implementation, we can create as many wishes as we want, according to the business requirements, which is also good.

However, there may be a potential issue: we can create wishes for a user who may not exist in the Domain. This is a problem, regardless of what technology we're using for persisting Aggregates. Even if we're using an in-memory implementation, we can create a Wish without its corresponding User.

This is broken business logic. Of course, this can be fixed using a foreign key in the database, from wish (user_id) to user(id), but what happens if we're not using a database with foreign keys? And what happens if it's a NoSQL database, such as Redis or Elasticsearch?

If we want to fix this issue so that the same code can work properly in different infrastructures, we need to check if the user exists. It's likely that the easiest approach is in the same Application Service:

```
class MakeWishService
{
    // ...
    public function execute(MakeWishRequest $request)
    {
        $userId = $request->userId();
        $address = $request->address();
        $content = $request->content();

        $user = $this->userRepository->ofId(new UserId($userId));
        if (null === $user) {
            throw new UserDoesNotExistException();
        }

        $wish = new Wish(
            $this->wishRepository->nextIdentity(),
            $user->id(),
            $address,
            $content
        );

        $this->wishRepository->add($wish);
    }
}
```

That could work, but there's a problem performing the check in the Application Service: this check is high in the delegation chain. If any other code snippet that isn't this Application Service — such as a Domain Service or another Entity — wants to create a `Wish` for a non-existing User, it can do it. Take a look at the following code:

```
// Somewhere in a Domain Service or Entity
$nonExistingUserId = new UserId('non-existing-user-id');
    $wish = new Wish(
        $this->wishRepository->nextIdentity(),
        $nonExistingUserId,
        $address,
        $content
);
```

If you've already read `Chapter 9`, *Factories*, then you have the solution. Factories help us keep the business invariants, and that's exactly what we need here.

There's an implicit invariant saying that we're not allowed to make a wish without a valid user. Let's see how a factory can help us:

```php
abstract class WishService
{
    protected $userRepository;
    protected $wishRepository;

    public function __construct(
        UserRepository $userRepository,
        WishRepository $wishRepository
    ) {
        $this->userRepository = $userRepository;
        $this->wishRepository = $wishRepository;
    }

    protected function findUserOrFail($userId)
    {
        $user = $this->userRepository->ofId(new UserId($userId));
        if (null === $user) {
            throw new UserDoesNotExistException();
        }

        return $user;
    }

    protected function findWishOrFail($wishId)
    {
        $wish = $this->wishRepository->ofId(new WishId($wishId));
        if (!$wish) {
            throw new WishDoesNotExistException();
        }

        return $wish;
    }

    protected function checkIfUserOwnsWish(User $user, Wish $wish)
    {
        if (!$wish->userId()->equals($user->id())) {
            throw new \InvalidArgumentException(
                'User is not authorized to update this wish'
            );
        }
    }
}

class MakeWishService extends WishService
{
```

```
public function execute(MakeWishRequest $request)
{
    $userId = $request->userId();
    $address = $request->address();
    $content = $request->content();

    $user = $this->findUserOrFail($userId);

    $wish = $user->makeWish(
        $this->wishRepository->nextIdentity(),
        $address,
        $content
    );

    $this->wishRepository->add($wish);
}
}
```

As you can see, Users make Wishes, and so does our code. makeWish is a Factory Method for building Wishes. The method returns a new Wish built with the UserId from the owner:

```
class User
{
    // ...

    /**
     * @return Wish
     */
    public function makeWish(WishId $wishId, $address, $content)
    {
        return new Wish(
            $wishId,
            $this->id(),
            $address,
            $content
        );
    }

    // ...
}
```

Why are we returning a `Wish` and not just adding the new `Wish` to an internal collection as we would do with Doctrine? To summarize, in this scenario, `User` and `Wish` don't conform to an Aggregate because there's no true business invariant to protect. A `User` can add and remove as many `Wishes` as they want. `Wishes` and their `User` can be updated independently in the database in different transactions, if needed.

Following the rules about Aggregate Design explained before, we should aim for small Aggregates, and that's the result here. Each Entity has its own Repository. Wish references its owning `User` using Identities — `UserId` in this case. Getting all the wishes of a user can be performed by a finder in the `WishRepository` and paginated easily without any performance issues:

```
interface WishRepository
{
    /**
     * @param WishId $wishId
     *
     * @return Wish
     */
    public function ofId(WishId $wishId);

    /**
     * @param UserId $userId
     *
     * @return Wish[]
     */
    public function ofUserId(UserId $userId);

    /**
     * @param Wish $wish
     */
    public function add(Wish $wish);

    /**
     * @param Wish $wish
     */
    public function remove(Wish $wish);

    /**
     * @return WishId
     */
    public function nextIdentity();
}
```

An interesting aspect of this approach is that we don't have to map the relation between `User` and `Wish` in our favorite ORM. Because we reference the `User` from the `Wish` using the `UserId`, we just need the Repositories. Let's consider how the mapping of such Entities using Doctrine might appear:

```
Lw\Domain\Model\User\User:
    type: entity
    id:
        userId:
            column: id
            type: UserId
    table: user
    repositoryClass:
        Lw\Infrastructure\Domain\Model\User\DoctrineUser\Repository
    fields:
        email:
            type: string
        password:
            type: string

Lw\Domain\Model\Wish\Wish:
    type: entity
    table: wish
    repositoryClass:
        Lw\Infrastructure\Domain\Model\Wish\DoctrineWish\Repository
    id:
        wishId:
            column: id
            type: WishId
    fields:
        address:
            type: string
        content:
            type: text
        userId:
            type: UserId
        column: user_id
```

No relation is defined. After making a new wish, let's write some code for updating an existing one:

```
class UpdateWishService extends WishService
{
    public function execute(UpdateWishRequest $request)
    {
        $userId = $request->userId();
        $wishId = $request->wishId();
        $email = $request->email();
        $content = $request->content();

        $user = $this->findUserOrFail($userId);
        $wish = $this->findWishOrFail($wishId);
        $this->checkIfUserOwnsWish($user, $wish);

        $wish->changeContent($content);
        $wish->changeAddress($email);
    }
}
```

Because `User` and `Wish` don't form an Aggregate, in order to update the `Wish`, we need first to retrieve it using the `WishRepository`. Some extra checks ensure that only the owner can update the wish. As you may have seen, `$wish` is already an existing Entity in our Domain, so there's no need to add it back again using the Repository. However, in order to make changes durable, our ORM must be aware of the information updated and flush any remaining changes to the database after the work is done. Don't worry; we'll take a look closer at this in `Chapter 11`, *Application*. In order to complete the example, let's take a look at how to remove a wish:

```
class RemoveWishService extends WishService
{
    public function execute(RemoveWishRequest $request)
    {
        $userId = $request->userId();
        $wishId = $request->wishId();

        $user = $this->findUserOrFail($userId);
        $wish = $this->findWishOrFail($wishId);
        $this->checkIfUserOwnsWish($user, $wish);

        $this->wishRepository->remove($wish);
    }
}
```

As you may have seen, you could refactor some parts of the code, such as the constructor and the ownership checks, to reuse them in both Application Services. Feel free to consider how you would do that. Last but not least, how could we get all the wishes of a specific user:

```
class ViewWishesService extends WishService
{
    /**
     * @return Wish[]
     */
    public function execute(ViewWishesRequest $request)
    {
        $userId = $request->userId();
        $wishId = $request->wishId();

        $user = $this->findUserOrFail($userId);
        $wish = $this->findWishOrFail($wishId);
        $this->checkIfUserOwnsWish($user, $wish);

        return $this->wishRepository->ofUserId($user->id());
    }
}
```

This is quite straightforward. However, we'll go deeper into how to render and return information from Application Services in the corresponding chapter. For now, returning a collection of Wishes will do the job.

Let's sum up this non-Aggregate approach. We couldn't find any true business invariant to consider `User` and `Wish` as an Aggregate, which is why each of them is an Aggregate. `User` has its own `Repository`, `UserRepository`. `Wish` has its own Repository too, `WishRepository`. Each `Wish` holds a `UserId` reference to owner, `User`. Even so, we didn't require a transaction. That's the best scenario in terms of performance and scalability issues. However, life is not always so wonderful. Consider what could happen with a true business invariant.

No More Than Three Wishes Per User

Our application is a huge success and now it's time to get some money from it. We want new users to have a maximum of three wishes available. As a user, if you want to have more wishes, you'll probably have to pay for a premium account in the future. Let's see how we could change our code to follow the new business rule about the maximum number of wishes (in this instance, don't consider the premium user).

Consider the following code for a moment. Apart from what was explained in the previous section about pushing logic into our Entities, could the following code work:

```
class MakeWishService
{
    // ...

    public function execute(MakeWishRequest $request)
    {
        $userId = $request->userId();
        $address = $request->email();
        $content = $request->content();

        $count = $this->wishRepository->numberOfWishesByUserId(
            new UserId($userId)
        );
        if ($count >= 3) {
            throw new MaxNumberOfWishesExceededException();
        }

        $wish = new Wish(
            $this->wishRepository->nextIdentity(),
            new UserId($userId),
            $address,
            $content
        );

        $this->wishRepository->add($wish);
    }
}
```

It looks like it could. That was easy — probably too easy. And here we come across different problems. The first is that Application Services must coordinate but shouldn't contain business logic. Instead, a better place is to put the check for the maximum three wishes into the User, where we could have more control of the relationship between User and Wish. However, for the approach shown here, the code seems to work.

The second problem is that it **doesn't work under race conditions**. Forget about Domain-Driven Design for a moment. What's the problem with this code under heavy traffic? Think for a minute. Is it possible to break the rule of a User to have more than three wishes? Why will your QA be so happy after running some stress tests?

Your QA tries making a wish feature two times and ends up with a user with two wishes. That's correct. Your QA carries on testing the feature. Imagine for a second that they open two tabs in their browser, fill out each of the forms in each tab, and manage to submit the two buttons at the same time. Suddenly, after two requests, the user ends up with four wishes in the database. That's wrong! What happened?

Think as a debugger and consider two different requests getting the if ($count > 3) { line at the same time. Both of the requests will return false because the user has just two wishes. So both requests will create the Wish and both of the requests will add it into the database. The result is four wishes for one User. That's an inconsistency!

We know what you're thinking. It's because we missed putting everything into a transaction. Well, imagine that a user with id 1 already has two wishes, so there's one remaining. Two HTTP requests to create two different wishes arrive at the same time. We start one database transaction per request (we'll review how to deal with transactions and requests in Chapter 11, *Application*). Consider all the queries that the previous PHP code is going to run against our database. Remember that you need to disable any auto-commit flag if you're using any Visual Database Tool:

Request #1	Request#2
START TRANSACTION; – Query OK, 0 rows affected (0.00 sec)	
	START TRANSACTION; – Query OK, 0 rows affected (0.00 sec)
SELECT COUNT(*) FROM wishes WHERE user_id = 1; – 2	
	SELECT COUNT(*) FROM wishes WHERE user_id = 1;

Request #1	Request #2
	– 2

INSERT INTO wishes VALUES (
   3, 1, 'mom@myfamily.com',
   'Mom, I will always love you!');
– Query OK, 1 row affected (0.00 sec)	

	INSERT INTO wishes VALUES (
	   4, 1, 'dad@myfamily.com',
	   'Dad, I will always love you!');
	– Query OK, 1 row affected (0.00 sec)

SELECT COUNT(*) FROM wishes WHERE user_id = 1; – 3	
	SELECT COUNT(*) FROM wishes WHERE user_id = 1; – 3
COMMIT; – Query OK, 0 rows affected (0.00 sec)	
	COMMIT; – Query OK, 0 rows affected (0.00 sec)

How many wishes does the user with id 1 have? That's right, four. How did this happen? If you take this SQL block and execute it line by line in two different connections, you'll see how the wishes table is going to have four rows at the end of both executions. So it looks like it's not about protecting with a transaction. How could we fix this issue? As explained in the introduction, a concurrency control could help.

For those developers more advanced in database techniques, tweaking the isolation level could work. However, we consider that option too complex, as the problem could be solved with other approaches, and we're not always dealing with databases.

Pessimistic Concurrency Control

There's an important consideration when placing locks: any other connection trying to update or query the same data is going to hang until the lock is released. Locks can easily generate most of the performance problems. In MySQL, for example, there are different options for placing locks: explicit locking tables UN/LOCK tables, and locking reads SELECT ... FOR UPDATE and SELECT ... LOCK IN SHARE MODE.

As we already shared above in the beginning, according to the book *Elasticsearch:* `The Definitive Guide` by Clinton Gormley and Zachary Tong:

> Widely used by relational databases, this approach assumes that conflicting changes are likely to happen and so blocks access to a resource in order to prevent conflicts. A typical example is locking a row before reading its data, ensuring that only the thread that placed the lock is able to make changes to the data in that row.

We could `LOCK` the table, but we consider such an approach complex and risky. When using locks, you have to be careful because you can end up with situations where two threads or requests are waiting for the other one to release the lock. This is what's called a deadlock.

Based on our experience, some developers use `SELECT ... FOR UPDATE` approaches. Let's see the same two request scenarios with this option:

Request #1	Request#2
START TRANSACTION; – Query OK, 0 rows affected (0.00 sec)	
	START TRANSACTION; – Query OK, 0 rows affected (0.00 sec)
SELECT COUNT(*) FROM wishes WHERE user_id = 1 FOR UPDATE; – 2	
	SELECT COUNT(*) FROM wishes WHERE user_id = 1 FOR UPDATE; – Waiting for locks to be released…
INSERT INTO wishes VALUES (3, 1, 'mom@myfamily.com', 'Mom, I will always love you!'); – Query OK, 1 row affected (0.00 sec) SELECT COUNT(*) FROM wishes WHERE user_id = 1; – 3 COMMIT; – Query OK, 0 rows affected (0.00 sec)	
	– Lock is released and it returns 3 (consistent) …

As you can see, after the COMMIT of the first request, the count of the number of wishes of the second request is three. That's consistent, but the second request was waiting while the lock wasn't released. That means that in an environment with a lot of requests, it may generate performance issues. If the first request takes too much time to release the lock, the second request may fail due to a timeout:

```
ERROR 1205 (HY000): Lock wait timeout exceeded; try restarting transaction
```

The above looks like it's a valid option, but we need to be aware of the possible performance issues. Is there any other alternative?

Optimistic Concurrency Control

There's another alternative: not using locks at all. Consider adding a version attribute to our Aggregates. When we persist them, the persistence engine sets 1 as the version of the persisted Aggregate. Later, we retrieve the same Aggregate and perform some changes to it. We persist the Aggregate. The persistence engine checks that the version we have is the same as the one that's currently persisted, version 1. The persistence engine persists the Aggregate with the new state and updates its version to 2. If multiple requests retrieve the same Aggregate, make some changes to it, and then try to persist it, the first request will work, and the second will experiment and error. The last request just changed an outdated version, so the persistence engine throws an error. However, the second request can try to retrieve the Aggregate again, merge the new status, attempt to perform the changes, and then persist the Aggregate.

According to Elasticsearch: The Definitive Guide:

> This approach assumes that conflicts are unlikely to happen and does not block operations from being attempted. However, if the underlying data has been modified between reading and writing, the update will fail. It is then up to the application to decide how it should resolve the conflict. For instance, it could reattempt the update, using the fresh data, or it could report the situation to the user.

This idea was covered before, but it bears repeating. If you try to apply Optimistic Concurrency to this scenario where we're checking maximum wishes in the Application Service, it's not going to work. Why? We're making a new wish, so two requests would create two different wishes. How can we make it work? Well, we need an object to centralize adding the wishes. We could apply the Optimistic Concurrency trick on that object, so it looks like we need a parent object that will hold wishes. Any ideas?

To summarize, after reviewing concurrency controls, there's a pessimistic option working, but there are some concerns about performance impact. There's an optimistic option, but we need to find a parent object. Let's consider the final `MakeWishService`, but with some modifications:

```
class WishAggregateService
{
    protected $userRepository;

    public function __construct(UserRepository $userRepository)
    {
        $this->userRepository = $userRepository;
    }

    protected function findUserOrFail($userId)
    {
        $user = $this->userRepository->ofId(new UserId($userId));
        if (null === $user) {
            throw new UserDoesNotExistException();
        }

        return $user;
    }
}

class MakeWishService extends WishAggregateService
{
    public function execute(MakeWishRequest $request)
    {
        $userId = $request->userId();
        $address = $request->address();
        $content = $request->content();

        $user = $this->findUserOrFail($userId);

        $user->makeWish($address, $content);

        // Uncomment if your ORM can not flush
        // the changes at the end of the request
        // $this->userRepository->add($user);
    }
}
```

We don't pass the `WishId` because it should be something internal to the User. `makeWish` doesn't return a `Wish` either; it stores the new wish internally. After the execution of the Application Service, our ORM will flush the changes performed on the `$user` to the database. Depending on how good our ORM is, we may need to explicitly add our `User` Entity again using the Repository. What changes to the `User` class are needed? First of all, there should be a collection that could hold all the wishes inside a user:

```
class User
{
    // ...

    /**
     * @var ArrayCollection
     */
    protected $wishes;

    public function __construct(UserId $userId, $email, $password)
    {
        // ...
        $this->wishes = new ArrayCollection();
        // ...
    }

    // ...
}
```

The `wishes` property must be initialized in the `User` constructor. We could use a plain PHP array, but we've chosen to use an `ArrayCollection`. `ArrayCollection` is a PHP array with some extra features provided by the Doctrine Common Library, and it can be used separate from the ORM. We know that some of you may think that this could be a boundary leaking and that no references to any infrastructure should be here, but we really believe that's not the case. In fact, the same code works using plain PHP arrays. Let's see how the `makeWish` implementation is affected:

```
class User
{
    // ...

    /**
     * @return void
     */
    public function makeWish($address, $content)
    {
        if (count($this->wishes) >= 3) {
            throw new MaxNumberOfWishesExceededException();
        }
```

```
        $this->wishes[] = new Wish(
            new WishId,
            $this->id(),
            $address,
            $content
        );
    }

    // ...
}
```

So far, so good. Now, it's time to review how the rest of the operations are implemented.

Pushing for Eventual Consistency

It looks like the business doesn't want a user to have more than three wishes. That's going to force us to consider `User` as the root Aggregate with `Wish` inside. This will affect our design, performance, scalability issues, and so on. Consider what would happen if we could just let users add as many wishes as they wanted, beyond the limit. We could check who is exceeding that limit and let them know they need to purchase a premium account. Allowing a user to go over the limit and warning them by telephone afterward would be a really nice commercial strategy. That might even allow the developers on your team to avoid designing `User` and `Wish` as part of the same Aggregate, with User as its root. You've already seen the benefits of not designing a single Aggregate: maximum performance.

```
class UpdateWishService extends WishAggregateService
{
    public function execute(UpdateWishRequest $request)
    {
        $userId = $request->userId();
        $wishId = $request->wishId();
        $email = $request->email();
        $content = $request->content();

        $user = $this->findUserOrFail($userId);

        $user->updateWish(new WishId($wishId), $email, $content);
    }
}
```

Because `User` and `Wish` now form an Aggregate, the `Wish` to be updated is no longer retrieved using the `WishRepository`. We fetch the user using the `UserRepository`. The operation of updating a `Wish` is performed via the root Entity, which is the `User` in this case. The `WishId` is necessary in order to identify which `Wish` we want to update:

```
class User
{
    // ...

    public function updateWish(WishId $wishId, $email, $content)
    {
        foreach ($this->wishes as $wish) {
            if ($wish->id()->equals($wishId)) {
                $wish->changeContent($content);
                $wish->changeAddress($address);
                break;
            }
        }
    }
}
```

Depending on the features of your framework, this task may or may not be cheaper to perform. Iterating through all the wishes could mean making too many queries, or even worse, fetching too many rows, which will create a huge impact on memory. In fact, that's one of the main problems of having big Aggregates. So let's consider how to remove a Wish:

```
class RemoveWishService extends WishAggregateService
{
    public function execute(RemoveWishRequest $request)
    {
        $userId = $request->userId();
        $wishId = $request->wishId();

        $user = $this->findUserOrFail($userId);

        $user->removeWish($wishId):
    }
}
```

As seen before, `WishRepository` is no longer necessary. We fetch the `User` using its Repository and perform the action of removing a `Wish`. In order to remove a `Wish`, we need to remove it from the inner collection. An option would be iterating through all the elements and matching the one with the same `WishId`:

```
class User
{
    // ...

    public function removeWish(WishId $wishId)
    {
        foreach ($this->wishes as $k => $wish) {
            if ($wish->id()->equals($wishId)) {
                unset($this->wishes[$k]);
                break;
            }
        }
    }

    // ...
}
```

That's probably the most ORM-agnostic code possible. However, behind the scenes, Doctrine is fetching all the wishes and iterating through all of them. A more specific approach to fetch only the Entity needed that isn't so ORM agnostic would be the following: Doctrine mapping must also be updated in order to make all the magic work as expected. While the Wish mapping remains the same, the `User` mapping has the new `oneToMany` unidirectional relationship:

```
Lw\Domain\Model\Wish\Wish:
    type: entity
    table: lw_wish
    repositoryClass:
        Lw\Infrastructure\Domain\Model\Wish\DoctrineWish\Repository
    id:
        wishId:
            column: id
            type: WishId
    fields:
        address:
            type: string
        content:
            type: text
        userId:
            type: UserId
            column: user_id
```

```
Lw\Domain\Model\User\User:
    type: entity
    id:
    userId:
        column: id
        type: UserId
    table: user
    repositoryClass:
        Lw\Infrastructure\Domain\Model\User\DoctrineUser\Repository
    fields:
        email:
            type: string
        password:
            type: string
    manyToMany:
        wishes:
            orphanRemoval: true
            cascade: ["all"]
            targetEntity: Lw\Domain\Model\Wish\Wish
            joinTable:
                name: user_wishes
                joinColumns:
                    user_id:
                        referencedColumnName: id
                inverseJoinColumns:
                    wish_id:
                        referencedColumnName: id
                        unique: true
```

In the code above, there are two important configurations: `orphanRemoval` and cascade. According to the Doctrine 2 ORM Documentation on `orphan removal` and `transitive persistence / cascade operations`:

> If an Entity of type A contains references to privately owned Entities B then if the reference from A to B is removed the entity B should also be removed, because it is not used anymore. `OrphanRemoval` works with one-to-one, one-to-many and many-to-many associations. When using the `orphanRemoval=true` option Doctrine makes the assumption that the entities are privately owned and will NOT be reused by other entities. If you neglect this assumption your entities will get deleted by Doctrine even if you assigned the orphaned entity to another one.

Persisting, removing, detaching, refreshing and merging individual entities can become pretty cumbersome, especially when a highly interweaved object graph is involved. Therefore Doctrine 2 provides a mechanism for transitive persistence through cascading of these operations. Each association to another entity or a collection of entities can be configured to automatically cascade certain operations. By default, no operations are cascaded.

For more information, please take a closer look at the Doctrine 2 ORM 2 Documentation on `working with associations`.

Finally, let's see how we can get the wishes from a user:

```
class ViewWishesService extends WishService
{
    /**
     * @return Wish[]
     */
    public function execute(ViewWishesRequest $request)
    {
        return $this
            ->findUserOrFail($request->userId())
            ->wishes();
    }
}
```

As mentioned before, especially in this scenario using Aggregates, returning a collection of Wishes is not the best solution. You should never return Domain Entities, as this will prevent code outside of your Application Services — such as Controllers or your UI — from unexpectedly modifying them. With Aggregates, it makes even more sense. Entities that aren't root — the ones that belong to the Aggregate but aren't root — should appear private to others outside.

We'll go deeper into this in the `Chapter 11`, *Application*. For now, to summarize, you have different options:

- The Application Service returns a DTO build accessing Aggregates information.
- The Application Service returns a DTO returned by the Aggregate.
- The Application Service uses an Output dependency where it writes the Aggregate. Such an Output dependency will handle the transformation to a DTO or other format.

Render the Number of Wishes As an exercise, consider that we want to render the number of wishes a user has made on their account page. How would you implement this, considering User and Wish don't form an Aggregate? How would you implement it if User and Wish did form an Aggregate? Consider how Eventual Consistency could help in your solutions.

Transactions

We haven't shown `beginTransaction`, `commit`, or `rollback` in any of the examples. This is because transactions are handled at Application Service level. Don't worry for now; you'll find more details about this in `Chapter 11`, *Application*.

Wrap Up

Aggregates are all about persistence and transactions. In fact, you can't design Aggregates without thinking about how they're going to be persisted. The basic rules to design proper Aggregates are: make them small, find true business invariants, push for eventual consistency using Domain Events, reference other Aggregates by Identity, and modify one Aggregate per request. Review how the code changes if two Entities form a single Aggregate or not. Use factories to enrich your Entities. Finally, relax. In most of the PHP applications we've seen, only five percent of the Entities were Aggregates formed by two Entities or more. Discuss with your workmates when designing and implementing Aggregates.

9
Factories

Factories are a powerful abstraction. They help decouple the client from the details of how to interact with the Domain. The client doesn't need to know how to build complex objects and Aggregates, so you can use Factories to create whole Aggregates, thereby enforcing their invariants.

Factory Method on Aggregate Root

The `Factory Method` pattern, as defined in the classic, `Gang of Four`, is a creational pattern that:

Defines an interface for creating an object, but leaves the choice of its type to the subclasses, creation being deferred at run-time.

Adding a Factory Method in the Aggregate Root hides the internal implementation details of creating Aggregates from any external client. This also moves the responsibility for the integrity of the Aggregate back to the root.

In a Domain Model where we have a `User` Entity and a `Wish` Entity, the `User` acts as the Aggregate root. There's no `Wish` without `User`. The `User` Entity should manage its Aggregates.

The way to move the control of `Wish` back to the `User` Entity is by placing a Factory method in the Aggregate root:

```
class User
{
    // ...

    public function makeWish(WishId $wishId, $email, $content)
    {
        $wish = new WishEmail(
            $wishId,
            $this->id(),
            $email,
            $content
        );

        DomainEventPublisher::instance()->publish(
            new WishMade($wishId)
        );

        return $wish;
    }
}
```

The client doesn't need to know the internal details of how the Aggregate Root handles the creation logic:

```
$wish = $aUser->makeWish(
    $wishRepository->nextIdentity(),
    'user@example.com',
    'I want to be free!'
);
```

Forcing Invariants

Factory Methods in the Aggregate Root are also a good place for invariants.

In a Domain Model with `Forum` and `Post` Entities, where `Post` is an aggregated part of the Aggregate Root `Forum`, publishing a `Post` could look something like this:

```
class Forum
{
    // ...

    public function publishPost(PostId $postId, $content)
    {
```

```
$post = new Post($this->id, $postId, $content);

DomainEventPublisher::instance()->publish(
    new PostPublished($postId)
);

return $post;
    }
}
```

After talking with a Domain Expert, we came to the conclusion that a `Post` shouldn't be published when the `Forum` is closed. This is an invariant, and we could force it directly on `Post` creation, thereby preventing an inconsistent Domain state:

```
class Forum
{
    // ...

    public function publishPost(PostId $postId, $content)
    {
        if ($this->isClosed()) {
            throw new ForumClosedException();
        }

        $post = new Post($this->id, $postId, $content);

        DomainEventPublisher::instance()->publish(
            new PostPublished($postId)
        );

        return $post;
    }
}
```

Factory on Service

Decoupling creation logic also comes in handy in our Services.

Building Specifications

Using Specifications in our Services might be the best example to illustrate how to use Factories within our Services.

Consider the following Service example. Given a request from the outside world, we want to build a feed based on the latest `Posts` added to the system:

```php
namespace Application\Service;

use Domain\Model\Post;
use Domain\Model\PostRepository;

class LatestPostsFeedService
{
    private $postRepository;

    public function __construct(PostRepository $postRepository)
    {
        $this->postRepository = $postRepository;
    }

    /**
     * @param LatestPostsFeedRequest $request
     */
    public function execute($request)
    {
        $posts = $this->postRepository->latestPosts($request->since);

        return array_map(function(Post $post) {
            return [
                'id' => $post->id()->id(),
                'content' => $post->body()->content(),
                'created_at' => $post-> createdAt()
            ];
        }, $posts);
    }
}
```

Finder methods in Repositories like `latestPosts` have some limitations, as they keep adding complexity to our Repositories indefinitely. As we discuss in the `Chapter 10`, *Repositories* Specifications are a better approach.

Lucky for us, we have a nice `query` method in our `PostRepository` that works with Specifications:

```php
class LatestPostsFeedService
{
    // ...

    public function execute($request)
    {
```

```
        $posts = $this->postRepository->query($specification);
    }
}
```

Using a concrete implementation for the Specification is a bad idea:

```
class LatestPostsFeedService
{

    public function execute($request)
    {
        $posts = $this->postRepository->query(
            new SqlLatestPostSpecification($request->since)
        );
    }
}
```

Coupling our high-level application Service with a low-level Specification implementation mixes layers and breaks the Separation of Concerns. In addition, this is a pretty bad way of coupling our Service to a concrete Infrastructure implementation. There's no way you could use this Service outside of the SQL persistence solution. What if we want to test our Service with an in-memory implementation?

The solution to this problem is to decouple Specification creation from the Service itself by using the `Abstract Factory pattern`. According to `OODesign.com`:

> Abstract Factory offers the interface for creating a family of related objects, without explicitly specifying their classes.

As we might have multiple Specification implementations, we first need to create an interface for the Factory:

```
namespace Domain\Model;

interface PostSpecificationFactory
{
    public function createLatestPosts(DateTimeImmutable $since);
}
```

Then we need to create Factories for each `PostRepository` implementation. As an example, a Factory for the in-memory `PostRepository` implementation could look like this:

```
namespace Infrastructure\Persistence\InMemory;

use Domain\Model\PostSpecificationFactory;

class InMemoryPostSpecificationFactory
    implements PostSpecificationFactory
{
    public function createLatestPosts(DateTimeImmutable $since)
    {
        return new InMemoryLatestPostSpecification($since);
    }
}
```

Once we have a centralized place for the creation logic, it's easy to decouple it from the Service:

```
class LatestPostsFeedService
{
    private $postRepository;
    private $postSpecificationFactory;

    public function __construct(
        PostRepository $postRepository,
        PostSpecificationFactory $postSpecificationFactory
    ) {
        $this->postRepository = $postRepository;
        $this->postSpecificationFactory = $postSpecificationFactory;
    }

    public function execute($request)
    {
        $posts = $this->postRepository->query(
            $this->postSpecificationFactory->createLatestPosts(
                $request->since
            )
        );
    }
}
```

Now, unit testing our Service through an in-memory `PostRepository` implementation is pretty easy:

```php
namespace Application\Service;

use Domain\Model\Body;
use Domain\Model\Post;
use Domain\Model\PostId;
use Infrastructure\Persistence\InMemory\InMemoryPostRepositor;

class LatestPostsFeedServiceTest extends PHPUnit_Framework_TestCase
{
    /**
     * @var \Infrastructure\Persistence\InMemory\InMemoryPostRepository
     */
    private $postRepository;

    /**
     * @var LatestPostsFeedService
     */
    private $latestPostsFeedService;

    public function setUp()
    {
        $this->latestPostsFeedService = new LatestPostsFeedService(
            $this->postRepository = new InMemoryPostRepository()
        );
    }

    /**
     * @test
     */
    public function shouldBuildAFeedFromLatestPosts()
    {
        $this->addPost(1, 'first', '-2 hours');
        $this->addPost(2, 'second', '-3 hours');
        $this->addPost(3, 'third', '-5 hours');

        $feed = $this->latestPostsFeedService->execute(
            new LatestPostsFeedRequest(
                new \DateTimeImmutable('-4 hours')
            )
        );

        $this->assertFeedContains([
            ['id' => 1, 'content' => 'first'],
            ['id' => 2, 'content' => 'second']
        ], $feed);
```

```
    }

    private function addPost($id, $content, $createdAt)
    {
        $this->postRepository->add(new Post(
            new PostId($id),
            new Body($content),
            new \DateTimeImmutable($createdAt)
        ));
    }

    private function assertFeedContains($expected, $feed)
    {
        foreach ($expected as $index => $contents) {
            $this->assertArraySubset($contents, $feed[$index]);
            $this->assertNotNull($feed[$index]['created_at']);
        }
    }
}
```

Building Aggregates

Entities are agnostic to the persistence mechanism. You don't want to couple and pollute
your Entities with persistence details. Take a look at the next Application Service:

```
class SignUpUserService
{
    private $userRepository;

    public function __construct(UserRepository $userRepository)
    {
        $this->userRepository = $userRepository;
    }

    /**
     * @param SignUpUserRequest $request
     */
    public function execute( $request)
    {
        $email = $request->email();
        $password = $request->password();

        $user = $this->userRepository->userOfEmail($email);
        if (null !== $user) {
            throw new UserAlreadyExistsException();
        }
```

```
    $this->userRepository->persist(new User(
        $this->userRepository->nextIdentity(),
        $email,
        $password
    ));

    return $user;
    }
}
```

Imagine a `User` Entity like the following one:

```
class User
{
    private $userId;
    private $email;
    private $password;

    public function __construct(UserId $userId, $email, $password)
    {
        // ...
    }

    // ...
}
```

Imagine we want to use Doctrine as our Infrastructure persistence mechanism. Doctrine requires having an `id` as a plain string instance variable in order to work properly. In our Entity, `$userId` is a `UserId` Value Object. Adding an additional `id` to our `User` Entity just because of Doctrine would couple our persistence mechanism with our Domain Model. We saw in the `Chapter 4`, *Entities* that we could solve this problem with a Surrogate ID by creating a wrapper around our `User` Entity in the Infrastructure layer:

```
class DoctrineUser extends User
{
    private $surrogateUserId;

    public function __construct(UserId $userId, $email, $password)
    {
        parent::__construct($userId, $email, $password);
        $this->surrogateUserId = $userId->id();
    }
}
```

As creating the `DoctrineUser` in our Application Service would again couple the persistence layer with our Domain, we need to decouple the creation logic out of the Service with an Abstract Factory.

We could do this by creating an interface in our Domain:

```
interface UserFactory
{
    public function build(UserId $userId, $email, $password);
}
```

Then, we place the implementation of it inside our Infrastructure layer:

```
class DoctrineUserFactory implements UserFactory
{
    public function build(UserId $userId, $email, $password)
    {
        return new DoctrineUser($userId, $email, $password);
    }
}
```

Once decoupled, we only need to inject the Factory into our Application Service:

```
class SignUpUserService
{
    private $userRepository;
    private $userFactory;

    public function __construct(
        UserRepository $userRepository,
        UserFactory $userFactory
    ) {
        $this->userRepository = $userRepository;
        $this->userFactory = $userFactory;
    }

    /**
     * @param SignUpUserRequest $request
     */
    public function execute($request)
    {
        // ...
        $user = $this->userFactory->build(
            $this->userRepository->nextIdentity(),
            $email,
            $password
        );
        $this->userRepository->persist($user);
        return $user;
    }
}
```

Testing Factories

You'll see a common pattern while writing your tests. This is because building Entities and complex Aggregates can be a very tedious and repetitive process. Inevitably, complexity and duplication will start creeping into your test suite. Consider the following Entity:

```
class Author
{
    private $username;
    private $email ;
    private $fullName;

    public function __construct(
        Username $aUsername,
        FullName $aFullName,
        Email $anEmail
    ) {
        $this->username = $aUsername;
        $this->email = $anEmail ;
        $this->fullName = $aFullName;
    }

    // ...
}
```

Somewhere in your system, you'll end up with a test looking like this:

```
class MyTest extends PHPUnit_Framework_TestCase
{
    /**
     * @test
     */
    public function itDoesSomething()
    {
        $author = new Author(
            new Username('johndoe'),
            new FullName('John', 'Doe' ),
            new Email('john@doe.com' )
        );

        //do something with author
    }
}
```

Services inside boundaries share concepts like Entities, Aggregates, and Value Objects. Imagine the clutter of repeating the same building logic over and over across your tests. As we'll see, extracting the building logic out of tests comes in handy and prevents duplication.

Object Mother

An `Object Mother` is a catchy name for a Factory that creates fixed fixtures for your tests. Similar to the previous example, we could extract the duplicated logic to an Object Mother so it could be reused across tests:

```
class AuthorObjectMother
{
    public static function createOne()
    {
        return new Author(
            new Username('johndoe'),
            new FullName('John', 'Doe'),
            new Email('john@doe.com )
        );
    }
}

class MyTest extends PHPUnit_Framework_TestCase
{
    /**
     * @test
     */
    public function itDoesSomething()
    {
        $author = AuthorObjectMother::createOne();
    }
}
```

You'll notice that the more tests and situations you have, the more methods the Factory will have.

As Object Mothers aren't very flexible, they tend to grow in complexity quickly. Luckily, there's a more flexible alternative for your tests.

Test Data Builder

Test Data Builders are just normal Builders with default values used exclusively in your test suites so that you don't have to specify irrelevant parameters on specific test cases:

```php
class AuthorBuilder
{
    private $username;
    private $email ;
    private $fullName;

    private function __construct()
    {
        $this->username = new Username('johndoe');
        $this->email = new Email('john@doe.com');
        $this->fullName = new FullName('John', 'Doe');
    }

    public static function anAuthor()
    {
        return new self();
    }

    public function withFullName(FullName $aFullName)
    {
        $this->fullName = $aFullName;

        return $this;
    }

    public function withUsername(Username $aUsername)
    {
        $this->username = $aUsername;

        return $this;
    }

    public function withEmail(Email $anEmail)
    {
        $this->email = $anEmail ;

        return $this;
    }

    public function build()
    {
        return new Author($this->username, $this->fullName, $this->email);
    }
```

```
    }

    class MyTest extends PHPUnit_Framework_TestCase
    {
        /**
         * @test
         */
        public function itDoesSomething()
        {
            $author = AuthorBuilder::anAuthor()
                ->withEmail(new Email('other@email.com'))
                ->build();
        }
    }
```

We could even combine Test Data Builders to build more complicated Aggregates, like a `Post`:

```
    class Post
    {
        private $id;
        private $author;
        private $body;
        private $createdAt;

        public function __construct(
            PostId $anId, Author $anAuthor, Body $aBody
        ) {
            $this->id = $anId;
            $this->author = $anAuthor;
            $this->body = $aBody;
            $this->createdAt = new DateTimeImmutable();
        }
    }
```

Let's see the corresponding Test Data Builder for our `Post`. We could reuse the `AuthorBuilder` for building a default `Author`:

```
    class PostBuilder
    {
        private $postId;
        private $author;
        private $body;

        private function __construct()
        {
            $this->postId = new PostId();
            $this->author = AuthorBuilder::anAuthor()->build();
```

```php
        $this->body = new Body('Post body');
    }

    public static function aPost()
    {
        return new self();
    }

    public function withAuthor(Author $anAuthor)
    {
        $this->author = $anAuthor;

        return $this;
    }

    public function withPostId(PostId $aPostId)
    {
        $this->postId = $aPostId;

        return $this;
    }

    public function withBody(Body $body)
    {
        $this->body = $body;

        return $this;
    }

    public function build()
    {
        return new Post($this->postId, $this->author, $this->body);
    }
}
```

This solution is now flexible enough to cover any test case, including the possibility of building inner Entities:

```
class MyTest extends PHPUnit_Framework_TestCase
{
    /**
     * @test
     */
    public function itDoesSomething()
    {
        $post = PostBuilder::aPost()
            ->withAuthor(AuthorBuilder::anAuthor()
                ->withUsername(new Username('other'))
                    ->build())
            ->withBody(new Body('Another body'))
                ->build();

        //do something with the post
    }
}
```

Wrap-Up

Factories are a powerful tool for decoupling construction logic from our business logic. The Factory Method pattern not only helps by moving creation responsibility to the Aggregate Root, but it could also force Domain invariants. Using the Abstract Factory pattern in our Services allows us to separate our Domain logic from Infrastructure creation details. A common use case is that of Specifications and their respective persistence implementations. We've seen that Factories come in handy on our test suites too. While we could extract building logic into Object Mother Factories, Test Data Builders provide more flexibility for our tests.

10
Repositories

In order to interact with a Domain object, you need to hold a reference to it. One way of achieving this is by creation. Alternatively, you can traverse an association. In Object-Oriented programs, objects have links (references) to other objects, which makes them easily traversable, thereby contributing to the expressive power of our models. But here's the catch: you need a mechanism to retrieve the first object, the Aggregate Root.

Repositories act as storage locations, where a retrieved object is returned in the exact same state it was persisted in. In Domain-Driven Design, every Aggregate type typically has a unique associated Repository, which is used for its persistence and fetching needs. However, in the case where it's required to share an Aggregate object hierarchy, the types might share a Repository.

Once you've successfully retrieved the Aggregate from the Repository, every change you make is persisted, which removes the need to go back to the Repository.

Definition

Martin Fowler defines a Repository as:

> The mechanism between the domain and data mapping layers, acting like an in-memory domain object collection. Client objects construct query specifications declaratively and submit them to Repository for satisfaction. Objects can be added to and removed from the Repository, as they can from a simple collection of objects, and the mapping code encapsulated by the Repository will carry out the appropriate operations behind the scenes. Conceptually, a Repository encapsulates the set of objects persisted in a data store and the operations performed over them, providing a more object-oriented view of the persistence layer. Repository also supports the objective of achieving a clean separation and one-way dependency between the domain and data mapping layers.

Repositories Are Not DAOs

Data Access Objects (**DAOs**) are a common pattern for persisting Domain objects into the database. It's easy to confuse the DAO pattern with a Repository. The significant difference is that Repositories represent collections, while DAOs are closer to the database and are often far more table-centric. Typically, a DAO would contain CRUD methods for a particular Domain object. Let's see how a common interface for a DAO might look:

```
interface UserDAO
{
    /**
     * @param string $username
     * @return User
     */
    public function get($username);

    public function create(User $user);

    public function update(User $user);

    /**
     * @param string $username
     */
    public function delete($username);
}
```

A DAO interface could have multiple implementations, which could range from using ORM constructions to using plain SQL queries. The main problem with DAOs is that their responsibilities are not clearly defined. DAOs are usually perceived as gateways to the database, so it's relatively easy to greatly decrease cohesion with many specific methods in order to query the database:

```
interface BloatUserDAO
{
    public function get($username);

    public function create(User $user);

    public function update(User $user);

    public function delete($username);

    public function getUserByLastName($lastName);

    public function getUserByEmail($email);

    public function updateEmailAddress($username, $email);

    public function updateLastName($username, $lastName);
}
```

As you can see, the more we add new methods to implement, the harder it becomes to unit test the DAO, and it becomes increasingly coupled to the User object. This problem will grow over time, with many other contributors collaborating in making the Big Ball of Mud even bigger.

Collection-Oriented Repositories

Repositories mimic a collection by implementing their common interface characteristics. As a collection, a Repository shouldn't leak any intentions of persistence behavior, such as the notion of saving to a store.

The underlying persistence mechanism has to support this need. You shouldn't be required to handle changes to the objects over their lifetime. The collection references the most recent changes to the object, meaning that upon each access, you get the latest object state.

Repositories implement a concrete collection type, the Set. A Set is a data structure with an invariant that doesn't contain duplicate entries. If you try to add an element that's already present to a Set, it won't be added. This is useful in our use case, as each Aggregate has a unique identity that's associated with the Root Entity.

Consider, for example, that we have the following Domain Model:

```
namespace Domain\Model;

class Post
{
    const EXPIRE_EDIT_TIME = 120; // seconds

    private $id;
    private $body;
    private $createdAt;

    public function __construct(PostId $anId, Body $aBody)
    {
        $this->id = $anId;
        $this->body = $aBody;
        $this->createdAt = new \DateTimeImmutable();
    }

    public function editBody(Body $aNewBody)
    {
        if($this->editExpired()) {
            throw new RuntimeException('Edit time expired');
        }

        $this->body = $aNewBody;
    }

    private function editExpired()
    {
        $expiringTime= $this->createdAt->getTimestamp() +
            self::EXPIRE_EDIT_TIME;

        return $expiringTime < time();
    }

    public function id()
    {
        return $this->id;
    }

    public function body()
    {
```

```php
        return $this->body;
    }

    public function createdAt()
    {
        return $this->createdAt;
    }
}

class Body
{
    const MIN_LENGTH = 3;
    const MAX_LENGTH = 250;

    private $content;

    public function __construct($content)
    {
        $this->setContent(trim($content));
    }

    private function setContent($content)
    {
        $this->assertNotEmpty($content);
        $this->assertFitsLength($content);

        $this->content = $content;
    }

    private function assertNotEmpty($content)
    {
        if(empty($content)) {
            throw new DomainException('Empty body');
        }
    }

    private function assertFitsLength($content)
    {
        if(strlen($content) < self::MIN_LENGTH) {
            throw new DomainException('Body is too short');
        }

        if(strlen($content) > self::MAX_LENGTH) {
            throw new DomainException('Body is too long');
        }
    }

    public function content()
```

```
    {
        return $this->content;
    }
}

class PostId
{
    private $id;

    public function __construct($id = null)
    {
        $this->id = $id ?: uniqid();
    }

    public function id()
    {
        return $this->id;
    }

    public function equals(PostId $anId)
    {
        return $this->id === $anId->id();
    }
}
```

If we wanted to persist this `Post` Entity, a simple in-memory `Post` Repository could be created like this:

```
class SimplePostRepository
{
    private $post = [];

    public add(Post $aPost)
    {
        $this->posts[(string) $aPost->id()] = $aPost;
    }

    public function postOfId(PostId $anId)
    {
        if (isset($this->posts[(string) $anId])) {
            return $this->posts[(string) $anId];
        }

        return null;
    }
}
```

And, as you would expect, it's handled as a collection:

```
$id = new PostId();
$repository = new SimplePostRepository();
$repository->add(new Post($id, 'Random content'));

// later ...
$post = $repository->postOfId($id);
$post->editBody('Updated content');

// even later ...
$post = $repository->postOfId($id);
assert('Updated content' === $post->body());
```

As you can see, from the collection's point of view, there's no need for a save method in the Repository. Changes affecting the object are correctly handled by the underlying persistence layer. Collection-oriented Repositories are the ones that don't need to add an Aggregate that was persisted before. This mainly happens with the Repositories that are memory based, but we also have ways to do this with the Persisted-Oriented Repositories. We'll look at this in a moment; additionally, we'll cover this more in depth in the Chapter 11, *Application*.

The first step to design a Repository is to define a collection-like interface for it. The interface needs to define the usual collection methods, like so:

```
interface PostRepository
{
    public function add(Post $aPost);
    public function addAll(array $posts);
    public function remove(Post $aPost);
    public function removeAll(array $posts);
    // ...
}
```

For implementing such an interface, you could also use an abstract class. In general, when we talk about an interface, we refer to the general concept and not just the specific PHP interface. To keep your design simple, don't add methods you don't need; the Repository interface definition and its corresponding Aggregate should be placed in the same Module.

Sometimes remove doesn't physically delete the Aggregate from the database. This strategy - where the Aggregate has a status field that's updated to a *deleted* value - is known as a *soft delete*. Why is this approach interesting? It can be interesting for auditing changes and performance. In those cases, you can instead mark the Aggregate as disabled or *logically removed*. The interface could be updated accordingly by removing the removal methods or providing disable behavior in the Repository.

Another important aspect of Repositories are the finder methods, like the following:

```
interface PostRepository
{
    // ...

    /**
     * @return Post
     */
    public function postOfId(PostId $anId);

    /**
     * @return Post[]
     */
    public function latestPosts(DateTimeImmutable $sinceADate);
}
```

As we suggested in `Chapter 4`, *Entities*, we prefer Application-Generated Identities. The best place to generate a new Identity for an Aggregate is its Repository. So to retrieve the globally unique ID for a `Post`, a logical place to include it is in `PostRepository`:

```
interface PostRepository
{
    // ...

    /**
     * @return PostId
     */
    public function nextIdentity();
}
```

The code responsible for building up each `Post` instance calls `nextIdentity` to get a unique identifier, `PostId`:

```
$post = newPost($postRepository->nextIdentity(), $body);
```

Some developers favor placing the implementation close to the interface definition as a subpackage of the Module. However, because we want a clear Separation of Concerns, we recommend instead placing it inside the Infrastructure layer.

In-Memory Implementation

As Uncle Bob wrote in `Screaming Architecture`:

> A good software architecture allows decisions about frameworks, databases, web-servers, and other environmental issues and tools, to be deferred and delayed. A good architecture makes it unnecessary to decide on Rails, or Spring, or Hibernate, or Tomcat or MySql, until much later in the project. A good architecture makes it easy to change your mind about those decisions too. A good architecture emphasizes the use-cases and decouples them from peripheral concerns.

In the early stages of your application, a fast in-memory implementation could come in handy. It's something you could use to mature other parts of your system, allowing you to delay database decisions to the correct moment. An in-memory Repository is simple, fast, and easy to implement.

For our `Post` Repository, an in-memory hash map is enough to provide all the functionality we need:

```
namespace Infrastructure\Persistence\InMemory;

use Domain\Model\Post;
use Domain\Model\PostId;
use Domain\Model\PostRepository;

class InMemoryPostRepository implements PostRepository
{
    private $posts = [];

    public function add(Post $aPost)
    {
        $this->posts[$aPost->id()->id()] = $aPost;
    }

    public function remove(Post $aPost)
    {
        unset($this->posts[$aPost->id()->id()]);
    }

    public function postOfId(PostId $anId)
    {
        if (isset($this->posts[$anId->id()])) {
            return $this->posts[$anId->id()];
        }
```

```
        return null;
    }

    public function latestPosts(\DateTimeImmutable $sinceADate)
    {
        return $this->filterPosts(
            function (Post $post) use($sinceADate) {
                return $post->createdAt() > $sinceADate;
            }
        );
    }

    private function filterPosts(callable $fn)
    {
        return array_values(array_filter($this->posts, $fn));
    }

    public function nextIdentity()
    {
        return new PostId();
    }
}
```

Doctrine ORM

We've talked about Doctrine in past chapters quite a bit. Doctrine is a set of libraries for database storage and object mapping. It comes bundled with the popular Symfony2 web framework by default and, among other features, it allows you to easily decouple your application from the persistence layer, thanks to the Data Mapper pattern.

Meanwhile, the ORM stands over a powerful database abstraction layer that enables database interaction through an SQL dialect called **Doctrine Query Language (DQL)**, which is inspired by the famous Java Hibernate framework.

If we're going to use Doctrine ORM, the first task to complete is adding the dependencies to our project through Composer:

```
composer require doctrine/orm
```

Object Mapping

The mapping between your Domain objects and the database can be considered an implementation detail. The Domain lifecycle shouldn't be aware of these persistence details. As such, the mapping information should be defined as part of the Infrastructure layer, outside the Domain, and as the implementation for the Repositories.

Doctrine Custom Mapping Types

As our Post Entity is composed of Value Objects like Body or PostId, it's a good idea to make Custom Mapping Types or use Doctrine Embeddables for them, as seen in the Value Objects chapter. This will make the object mapping considerably easier:

```php
namespace Infrastructure\Persistence\Doctrine\Types;

use Doctrine\DBAL\Types\Type;
use Doctrine\DBAL\Platforms\AbstractPlatform;
use Domain\Model\Body;

class BodyType extends Type
{
    public function getSQLDeclaration(
        array $fieldDeclaration, AbstractPlatform $platform
    ) {
        return $platform->getVarcharTypeDeclarationSQL(
            $fieldDeclaration
        );
    }

    /**
     * @param string $value
     * @return Body
     */
    public function convertToPHPValue(
        $value, AbstractPlatform $platform
    ) {
        return new Body($value);
    }

    /**
     * @param Body $value
     */
    public function convertToDatabaseValue(
        $value, AbstractPlatform $platform
    ) {
        return $value->content();
```

```
    }

    public function getName()
    {
        return 'body';
    }
}

namespace Infrastructure\Persistence\Doctrine\Types;

use Doctrine\DBAL\Types\Type;
use Doctrine\DBAL\Platforms\AbstractPlatform;
use Domain\Model\PostId;

class PostIdType extends Type
{
    public function getSQLDeclaration(
        array $fieldDeclaration, AbstractPlatform $platform
    ) {
        return $platform->getGuidTypeDeclarationSQL(
            $fieldDeclaration
        );
    }

    /**
     * @param string $value
     * @return PostId
     */
    public function convertToPHPValue(
        $value, AbstractPlatform $platform
    ) {
        return new PostId($value);
    }

    /**
     * @param PostId $value
     */
    public function convertToDatabaseValue(
        $value, AbstractPlatform $platform
    ) {
        return $value->id();
    }

    public function getName()
    {
        return 'post_id';
    }
}
```

Don't forget to implement the __toString magic method on the PostId Value Object, as Doctrine requires this:

```
class PostId
{
    // ...
    public function __toString()
    {
        return $this->id;
    }
}
```

Doctrine offers multiple formats for the mapping, such as YAML, XML, or annotations. XML is our preferred choice, as it provides robust IDE autocompletion:

```xml
<?xml version="1.0" encoding="UTF-8"?>
<doctrine-mapping
    xmlns="http://doctrine-project.org/schemas/orm/doctrine-mapping"
    xmlns:xsi="http://www.w3.org/2001/XMLSchema-instance"
    xsi:schemaLocation="
        http://doctrine-project.org/schemas/orm/doctrine-mapping
        http://raw.github.com/doctrine/doctrine2/master/doctrine-mapping.xsd">

    <entity name="Domain\Model\Post" table="posts">
        <id name="id" type="post_id" column="id">
            <generator strategy="NONE" />
        </id>
        <field name="body" type="body" length="250" column="body"/>
        <field name="createdAt" type="datetime" column="created_at"/>
    </entity>

</doctrine-mapping>
```

Exercise
Write down what the mapping would look like in the case of using the Doctrine Embeddables approach. Take a look at Chapter Value Objects or Chapter Entities if you need some help.

Entity Manager

The `EntityManager` is the central access point for the ORM functionality. Bootstrapping it is easy:

```
use Doctrine\DBAL\Types\Type;
use Doctrine\ORM\EntityManager;
use Doctrine\ORM\Tools;

Type::addType(
    'post_id',
    'Infrastructure\Persistence\Doctrine\Types\PostIdType'
);

Type::addType(
    'body',
    'Infrastructure\Persistence\Doctrine\Types\BodyType'
);

$entityManager = EntityManager::create(
    [
        'driver' => 'pdo_sqlite',
        'path'=> __DIR__ . '/db.sqlite',
    ],
    Tools\Setup::createXMLMetadataConfiguration(
        ['/Path/To/Infrastructure/Persistence/Doctrine/Mapping'],
        $devMode = true
    )
);
```

Remember to configure it according to your needs and setup.

DQL Implementation

In the case of this Repository, we'll only need the `EntityManager` to retrieve Domain objects directly from the database:

```
namespace Infrastructure\Persistence\Doctrine;

use Doctrine\ORM\EntityManager;
use Domain\Model\Post;
use Domain\Model\PostId;
use Domain\Model\PostRepository;

class DoctrinePostRepository implements PostRepository
{
```

```
    protected $em;

    public function __construct(EntityManager $em)
    {
        $this->em = $em;
    }
    public function add(Post $aPost)
    {
        $this->em->persist($aPost);
    }

    public function remove(Post $aPost)
    {
        $this->em->remove($aPost);
    }

    public function postOfId(PostId $anId)
    {
        return $this->em->find('Domain\Model\Post', $anId);
    }

    public function latestPosts(\DateTimeImmutable $sinceADate)
    {
        return $this->em->createQueryBuilder()
            ->select('p')
            ->from('Domain\Model\Post', 'p')
            ->where('p.createdAt > :since')
            ->setParameter(':since', $sinceADate)
            ->getQuery()
            ->getResult();
    }

    public function nextIdentity()
    {
        return new PostId();
    }
}
```

If you check some Doctrine examples out there, you may find that after running persist or remove, flush should be called. But as seen in our proposal, there's no call to `flush`. Flushing and dealing with transactions is delegated to the Application Service. That's why you can work with Doctrine, considering that flushing all the changes on Entities will happen at the end of the request. In terms of performance, one flush call is best.

Persistence-Oriented Repository

There are times when collection-oriented Repositories don't fit well with our persistence mechanism. If you don't have a unit of work, keeping track of Aggregate changes is a difficult task. The only way to persist such changes is by explicitly calling `save`.

The interface definition for a persistence-oriented Repository is similar to how you would define a collection-oriented equivalent:

```
interface PostRepository
{
    public function nextIdentity();
    public function postOfId(PostId $anId);
    public function save(Post $aPost);
    public function saveAll(array $posts);
    public function remove(Post $aPost);
    public function removeAll(array $posts);
}
```

In this case, we now have save and `saveAll` methods, which provide functionality similar to the previous add and `addAll` methods. However, the important difference is how the client uses them. Within a collection-oriented style, you use the add methods just once: when the Aggregate is created. In a persistence-oriented style, you'll not only use the `save` action after creating a new Aggregate, but also when an existing one is modified:

```
$post = new Post(/* ... */);
$postRepository->save($post);

// later ...
$post = $postRepository->postOfId($postId);
$post->editBody(new Body('New body!'));
$postRepository->save($post);
```

Other than this difference, the details are only in the implementation.

Redis Implementation

The `Redis` is an in-memory key value that can be used as a cache or store.

Depending on the circumstances, we could consider using Redis as a store for our Aggregates.

To get started, make sure you have a PHP client to connect to Redis. A good one that we recommend is `Predis`:

```
composer require predis/predis:~1.0
namespace Infrastructure\Persistence\Redis;

use Domain\Model\Post;
use Domain\Model\PostId;
use Domain\Model\PostRepository;
use Predis\Client;

class RedisPostRepository implements PostRepository
{
    private $client;

    public function __construct(Client $client)
    {
        $this->client = $client;
    }

    public function save(Post $aPost)
    {
        $this->client->hset(
            'posts',
            (string) $aPost->id(), serialize($aPost)
        );
    }

    public function remove(Post $aPost)
    {
        $this->client->hdel('posts', (string) $aPost->id());
    }

    public function postOfId(PostId $anId)
    {
        if($data = $this->client->hget('posts', (string) $anId)) {
            return unserialize($data);
        }

        return null;
    }

    public function latestPosts(\DateTimeImmutable $sinceADate)
    {
        $latest = $this->filterPosts(
            function(Post $post) use ($sinceADate) {
                return $post->createdAt() > $sinceADate;
            }
```

```
            );

        $this->sortByCreatedAt($latest);

        return array_values($latest);
    }

    private function filterPosts(callable $fn)
    {
        return array_filter(array_map(function ($data) {
            return unserialize($data);
        },

        $this->client->hgetall('posts')), $fn);
    }

    private function sortByCreatedAt(&$posts)
    {
        usort($posts, function (Post $a, Post $b) {
            if ($a->createdAt() == $b->createdAt()) {
                return 0;
            }
            return ($a->createdAt() < $b->createdAt()) ? -1 : 1;
        });
    }

    public function nextIdentity()
    {
        return new PostId();
    }
}
```

SQL Implementation

In a classic example, we could create a simple PDO implementation for our PostRepository just by using plain SQL queries:

```
namespace Infrastructure\Persistence\Sql;

use Domain\Model\Body;
use Domain\Model\Post;
use Domain\Model\PostId;
use Domain\Model\PostRepository;

class SqlPostRepository implements PostRepository
{
```

```
const DATE_FORMAT = 'Y-m-d H:i:s';

private $pdo;

public function __construct(\PDO $pdo)
{
    $this->pdo = $pdo;
}

public function save(Post $aPost)
{
    $sql ='INSERT INTO posts ' .
        '(id, body, created_at) VALUES ' .
        '(:id, :body, :created_at)';

    $this->execute($sql, [
        'id' => $aPost->id()->id(),
        'body' => $aPost->body()->content(),
        'created_at' => $aPost->createdAt()->format(
            self::DATE_FORMAT
        )
    ]);
}

private function execute($sql, array $parameters)
{
    $st = $this->pdo->prepare($sql);

    $st->execute($parameters);

    return $st;
}

public function remove(Post $aPost)
{
    $this->execute('DELETE FROM posts WHERE id = :id', [
        'id' => $aPost->id()->id()
    ]);
}

public function postOfId(PostId $anId)
{
    $st =$this->execute('SELECT * FROM posts WHERE id = :id',[
        'id' => $anId->id()
    ]);

    if($row = $st->fetch(\PDO::FETCH_ASSOC)) {
        return $this->buildPost($row);
```

```
        }

        return null;
    }

    private function buildPost($row)
    {
        return new Post(
            new PostId($row['id']),
            new Body($row['body']),
            new \DateTimeImmutable($row['created_at'])
        );
    }

    public function latestPosts(\DateTimeImmutable $sinceADate)
    {
        return $this->retrieveAll(
            'SELECT * FROM posts WHERE created_at > :since_date', [
                'since_date' => $sinceADate->format(self::DATE_FORMAT)
            ]
        );
    }

    private function retrieveAll($sql, array $parameters = [])
    {
        $st = $this->pdo->prepare($sql);

        $st->execute($parameters);

        return array_map(function ($row) {
            return $this->buildPost($row);
        }, $st->fetchAll(\PDO::FETCH_ASSOC));
    }

    public function nextIdentity()
    {
        return new PostId();
    }

    public function size()
    {
        return $this->pdo->query('SELECT COUNT(*) FROM posts')
            ->fetchColumn();
    }
}
```

As we don't have any mapping configuration, it would be very useful to have an initialization method for the schema within the same class. **Things that change together should remain together**:

```
class SqlPostRepository implements PostRepository
{
    // ...
    public function initSchema()
    {
        $this->pdo->exec(<<<SQL
DROP TABLE IF EXISTS posts;

CREATE TABLE posts (
    id CHAR(36) PRIMARY KEY,
    body VARCHAR (250) NOT NULL,
    created_at DATETIME NOT NULL
) ENGINE=InnoDB DEFAULT CHARSET=utf8mb4 COLLATE=utf8mb4_unicode_ci;
        SQL);
    }
}
```

Extra Behavior

```
interface PostRepository
{
    // ...
    public function size();
}
```

The implementation could look like this:

```
class DoctrinePostRepository implements PostRepository
{
    // ...

    public function size()
    {
        return $this->em->createQueryBuilder()
            ->select('count(p.id)')
            ->from('Domain\Model\Post', 'p')
            ->getQuery()
            ->getSingleScalarResult();
    }
}
```

Adding additional behavior to a Repository can be very beneficial. An example of this is the ability to count all the items in a given collection. You might think to add a method with the name count; however, as we're trying to mimic a collection, a better name would instead be size:

You're also able to place specific calculations, counters, read-optimized queries, or complex commands (INSERT, UPDATE, or DELETE) into the Repository. However, all behavior should still follow the Repositories' collection characteristics. You're encouraged to move as much logic into Domain-specific stateless Domain Services as possible, instead of simply adding these responsibilities to the Repository.

In some instances, you won't require the entire Aggregate for simply accessing small amounts of information. To solve this, you can add Repository methods to access these as shortcuts. You should make sure to only access data that could be retrieved by navigating through the Aggregate Root. As such, you shouldn't allow access to the private and internal areas of the Aggregate Root, as this would violate the laid out contractual agreement.

For some use cases, you'll require very specific queries that are compositions of multiple Aggregate types, each returning specific information. These queries can be run and then returned as a single Value Object. It's very common for Repositories to return Value Objects.

If you find yourself creating many use case optimal finder methods, you may be introducing a common code smell. This could be an indication of a misjudged Aggregate boundary. If, however, you're confident that the boundaries are correct, it could be time to explore CQRS.

Querying Repositories

Upon comparison, Repositories are different than a collection if we consider their querying ability. A Repository deals with a large set of objects that typically aren't in memory when the query is performed. It's not feasible to load all the instances of a Domain object in memory and perform a query over them.

A good solution is to pass a criterion and let the Repository handle the implementation details to successfully perform the operation. It might translate the criterion to SQL or ORM queries or iterate over an in-memory collection. However, it doesn't matter, because the implementation deals with it.

Specification Pattern

A common implementation for the criterion object is the Specification pattern. A specification is a simple predicate that takes a Domain object and returns a boolean. Given a Domain object, it will return true if it specifies the specification, and false otherwise:

```
interface PostSpecification
{
    /**
     * @return boolean
     */
    public function specifies(Post $aPost);
}
```

We just need to add a query method to our Repository:

```
interface PostRepository
{
    // ...
    public function query($specification);
}
```

In-Memory Implementation

As an example, if we wanted to replicate the latestPosts query method in our PostRepository by using a Specification for an in-memory implementation, it would look like this:

```
namespace Infrastructure\Persistence\InMemory;

use Domain\Model\Post;

interface InMemoryPostSpecification
{
    /**
     * @return boolean
     */
    public function specifies(Post $aPost);
}
```

The in-memory implementation for the `latestPosts` behavior could look like this:

```
namespace Infrastructure\Persistence\InMemory;
use Domain\Model\Post;

class InMemoryLatestPostSpecification
    implements InMemoryPostSpecification
{
    private $since;

    public function __construct(\DateTimeImmutable $since)
    {
        $this->since = $since;
    }

    public function specifies(Post $aPost)
    {
        return $aPost->createdAt() > $this->since;
    }
}
```

The `query` method for our Repository implementation could look like this:

```
class InMemoryPostRepository implements PostRepository
{
    // ...

    /**
     * @param InMemoryPostSpecification $specification
     *
     * @return Post[]
     */
    public function query($specification)
    {
        return $this->filterPosts(
            function (Post $post) use ($specification) {
                return $specification->specifies($post);
            }
        );
    }
}
```

Retrieving all the latest posts from the Repository is as simple as creating a tailored instance of the above implementation:

```
$latestPosts = $postRepository->query(
    new InMemoryLatestPostSpecification(new \DateTimeImmutable('-24'))
);
```

SQL Implementation

A standard specification works well for in-memory implementations. However, as we don't pre-load all the Domain objects in memory for an SQL implementation, we need a more specific specification for these cases:

```
namespace Infrastructure\Persistence\Sql;

interface SqlPostSpecification
{
    /**
     * @return string
     */
    public function toSqlClauses();
}
```

The SQL implementation for this specification could look like this:

```
namespace Infrastructure\Persistence\Sql;

class SqlLatestPostSpecification implements SqlPostSpecification
{
    private $since;

    public function __construct(\DateTimeImmutable $since)
    {
        $this->since = $since;
    }

    public function toSqlClauses()
    {
        return "created_at >'" .
            $this->since->format('Y-m-d H:i:s') .
            "'";
    }
}
```

And here's an example of how to query an `SQLPostRepository` implementation:

```
class SqlPostRepository implements PostRepository
{
    // ...

    /**
     * @param SqlPostSpecification $specification
     *
     * @return Post[]
     */
```

```
public function query($specification)
{
    return $this->retrieveAll(
        'SELECT * FROM posts WHERE ' .
            $specification->toSqlClauses()
    );
}

private function retrieveAll($sql, array $parameters = [])
{
    $st = $this->pdo->prepare($sql);

    $st->execute($parameters);

    return array_map(function ($row) {
        return $this->buildPost($row);
    }, $st->fetchAll(\PDO::FETCH_ASSOC));
}
}
```

Managing Transactions

The Domain Model isn't the place to manage transactions. The operations applied over the Domain Model should be agnostic to the persistence mechanism. A common approach to solving this problem is placing a Facade in the Application layer, thereby grouping related use cases together. When a method of the Facade is invoked from the UI layer, the business method begins a transaction. Once complete, the Facade ends the interaction by committing the transaction. If anything goes wrong, the transaction is rolled back:

```
use Doctrine\ORM\EntityManager;

class SomeApplicationServiceFacade
{
    private $em;

    public function __construct(EntityManager $em)
    {
        $this->em = $em;
    }

    public function doSomeUseCaseTask()
    {
        try {
            $this->em->getConnection()->beginTransaction();
            // Use domain model
```

```
            $this->em->getConnection()->commit();
        } catch (Exception $e) {
            $this->em->getConnection()->rollback();
            throw $e;
        }
    }
}
```

The problem introduced with Facades is that we have to repeat the same boilerplate code over and over. If we unify the way we execute use cases, we could wrap them in a transaction using the Decorator pattern:

```
interface ApplicationService
{
    /**
     * @param $request
     * @return mixed
     */
    public function execute(BaseRequest $request);
}

class SomeApplicationService implements ApplicationService
{
    public function execute(BaseRequest $request)
    {
        // do something
    }
}
```

We don't want to couple our Application layer with the concrete transactional procedure, so instead we can create a simple interface for it:

```
interface TransactionalSession
{
    /**
     * @param callable $operation
     * @return mixed
     */
    public function executeAtomically(callable $operation);
}
```

A Decorator's pattern implementation that can make any Application Service transactional is as easy as this:

```
class TransactionalApplicationService implements ApplicationService
{
    private $session;
    private $service;

    public function __construct(
        ApplicationService $service,
        TransactionalSession $session
    ) {
        $this->session = $session;
        $this->service = $service;
    }

    public function execute(BaseRequest $request)
    {
        $operation = function() use($request) {
            return $this->service->execute($request);
        };

        return $this->session->executeAtomically(
            $operation->bindTo($this)
        );
    }
}
```

Following this, we could alternatively create a Doctrine transactional session implementation:

```
class DoctrineSession implements TransactionalSession
{
    private $entityManager;

    public function __construct(EntityManager $entityManager)
    {
        $this->entityManager = $entityManager;
    }

    public function executeAtomically(callable $operation)
    {
        return $this->entityManager->transactional($operation);
    }
}
```

Now we have everything to execute our use cases within a transaction:

```
$useCase = new TransactionalApplicationService(
    new SomeApplicationService(
        // ...
    ),
    new DoctrineSession(
        // ...
    )
);

$response = $useCase->execute();
```

Testing Repositories

In order to be sure that the Repository will work in production, we'll need to test its implementation. To do this, we have to test the boundaries of the system, making sure that our expectations are correct.

In the case of a Doctrine test, the setup will be a little bit more sophisticated:

```
use Doctrine\DBAL\Types\Type;
use Doctrine\ORM\EntityManager;
use Doctrine\ORM\Tools;
use Domain\Model\Post;

class DoctrinePostRepositoryTest extends \PHPUnit_Framework_TestCase
{
    private $postRepository;

    public function setUp()
    {
        $this->postRepository = $this->createPostRepository();
    }

    private function createPostRepository()
    {
        $this->addCustomTypes();
        $em = $this->initEntityManager();
        $this->initSchema($em);

        return new PrecociousDoctrinePostRepository($em);
    }

    private function addCustomTypes()
    {
```

```php
        if (!Type::hasType('post_id')) {
            Type::addType(
                'post_id',
                'Infrastructure\Persistence\Doctrine\Types\PostIdType'
            );
        }

        if (!Type::hasType('body')) {
            Type::addType(
                'body',
                'Infrastructure\Persistence\Doctrine\Types\BodyType'
            );
        }
    }

    protected function initEntityManager()
    {
        return EntityManager::create(
            ['url' => 'sqlite:///:memory:'],
            Tools\Setup::createXMLMetadataConfiguration(
                ['/Path/To/Infrastructure/Persistence/Doctrine/Mapping'],
                $devMode = true
            )
        );
    }

    private function initSchema(EntityManager $em)
    {
        $tool = new Tools\SchemaTool($em);
        $tool->createSchema([
            $em->getClassMetadata('Domain\Model\Post')
        ]);
    }

    // ...
}

class PrecociousDoctrinePostRepository extends DoctrinePostRepository
{
    public function persist(Post $aPost)
    {
        parent::persist($aPost);

        $this->em->flush();
    }

    public function remove(Post $aPost)
    {
```

```
        parent::remove($aPost);

        $this->em->flush();
    }
}
```

Once we have this environment set up, we can continue to test the Repository's behavior:

```
class DoctrinePostRepositoryTest extends \PHPUnit_Framework_TestCase
{
    // ...

    /**
     * @test
     */
    public function itShouldRemovePost()
    {
        $post = $this->persistPost('irrelevant body');

        $this->postRepository->remove($post);

        $this->assertPostExist($post->id());
    }

    private function assertPostExist($id)
    {
        $result = $this->postRepository->postOfId($id);
        $this->assertNull($result);
    }

    private function persistPost(
        $body,
        \DateTimeImmutable $createdAt = null
    ) {
        $this->postRepository->add(
            $post = new Post(
                $this->postRepository->nextIdentity(),
                new Body($body),
                $createdAt
            )
        );

        return $post;
    }
}
```

Following our earlier assertion, if we save a `Post`, we expect to find it in the exact same state.

Now we can move on to test finding the latest posts by specifying a given date:

```
class DoctrinePostRepositoryTest extends \PHPUnit_Framework_TestCase
{
    // ...

    /**
     * @test
     */
    public function itShouldFetchLatestPosts()
    {
        $this->persistPost(
            'a year ago', new \DateTimeImmutable('-1 year')
        );
        $this->persistPost(
            'a month ago', new \DateTimeImmutable('-1 month')
        );
        $this->persistPost(
            'few hours ago', new \DateTimeImmutable('-3 hours')
        );
        $this->persistPost(
            'few minutes ago', new \DateTimeImmutable('-2 minutes')
        );

        $posts = $this->postRepository->latestPosts(
            new \DateTimeImmutable('-24 hours')
        );

        $this->assertCount(2, $posts);
        $this->assertEquals(
            'few hours ago', $posts[0]->body()->content()
        );
        $this->assertEquals(
            'few minutes ago', $posts[1]->body()->content()
        );
    }
}
```

Testing Your Services with In-Memory Implementations

Setting up a fully persistent Repository implementation can be complex and result in slow execution. You should care about keeping your tests fast. Going through the whole database setup and then querying will slow you down enormously. Having an in-memory implementation could help delay persistence decisions until the end. We can test in the same manner as we did before, but this time, we'll use a full-featured fast and simple in-memory implementation:

```
class MyServiceTest extends \PHPUnit_Framework_TestCase
{
    private $service;

    public function setUp()
    {
        $this->service = new MyService(
            new InMemoryPostRepository()
        );
    }
}
```

Wrap-Up

A Repository is a mechanism that acts as a storage location. The difference between a DAO and a Repository is that a DAO follows a database-first approach, decreasing cohesion with many low-level methods to query the database. Depending on the underlying persistence mechanics, we've seen different Repository approaches:

- **Collection-oriented Repositories** tend to be purer to the Domain model, even if they persist Entities. From the client's point of view, a collection-oriented Repository looks like a collection (Set). There's no need for explicit persistence calls on Entity updates, as the Repository tracks changes on the objects. We explored how to use Doctrine as the underlying persistence mechanism for this type of Repository.
- **Persistence-oriented Repositories** require explicit persistence calls, as they don't track object changes. We explored Redis and plain SQL implementations.

Along the way, we discovered Specifications as a pattern that helps us query the database without sacrificing flexibility and cohesion. We also studied how to manage transactions and how to test our services with simple and fast in-memory Repository implementations.

11
Application

The Application layer is the area that separates the Domain Model from the clients that query or change its state. Application Services are the building blocks for such a layer. As Vaughn Vernon says: "Application Services are the direct clients of the domain model." You could think about an Application Service as a point of contact between the outside world (HTML forms, API clients, the command line, frameworks, UI, and so on.) and the Domain Model itself. It might help by thinking about the top-level use cases that your system exposes to the world, example: "as guest, I want to register," "as a logged user, I want to purchase a product," and so on.

In this chapter, we'll explore how to implement Application Services, understand the role of the Command pattern, and establish the responsibilities of an Application Service. To do this, let's consider the use case of *signing up a new user*.

Conceptually, in order to register a new user, we need to:

- Get an email and password from the client
- Check if the email is already in use
- Create a new user
- Add this new user to the existing user set
- Return the user we've just created

Let's go for it.

Requests

We need to send the `email` and `password` to the Application Service. There are many ways of doing such a thing from the client (HTML form, API client, or even the command line). We could just send standard parameters (email and password) through the method signature or build and send a data structure with this information. The latter approach, sending a `DTO`, brings some interesting features to the table. By sending an object, it'll be possible to serialize and queue it over a Command Bus. It'll also be possible to add type safety and some IDE help, too.

Data Transfer Object
A DTO is a data structure that carries information between processes. Don't mistake it for a full-featured object. A DTO doesn't have any behavior except for storage and retrieval of its own data (accessors and mutators). DTOs are simple objects that shouldn't contain any business logic that would require testing.

As Vaughn Vernon says:

Application Service method signatures use only primitive types (`int`, `strings`, and so on.), and possibly DTOs. As an alternative to these approaches, however, a better approach may be to design Command objects instead. There is not necessarily a right or wrong way. It mostly depends on your tastes and goals.

The implementation for a DTO that holds the data required for the Application Service could be something like this:

```php
namespace Lw\Application\Service\User;

class SignUpUserRequest
{
    private $email;
    private $password;

    public function __construct($email, $password)
    {
        $this->email = $email;
        $this->password = $password;
    }

    public function email()
    {
        return $this->email;
    }
}
```

```
    public function password()
    {
        return $this->password;
    }
}
```

As you see, `SignUpUserRequest` has no behavior, only data. This could have come from an HTML form or an API endpoint, though we don't care which.

Building Application Service Requests

Creating a request from the delivery mechanism, your favorite framework, should be pretty straightforward. On the web, you could pick up parameters from the controller request and pass them down to the Service inside a DTO. The same principle applies for a CLI command: read input parameters and send them down again.

With Symfony, we can extract the data we need from Request object from the `HttpFoundation` component:

```
// ...
class UsersController extends Controller
{
    /**
     * @Route('/signup', name = 'signup')
     * @param Request $request
     * @return Response
     */
    public function signUpAction(Request $request)
    {
        // ...
        $signUpUserRequest = new SignUpUserRequest(
            $request->get('email'),
            $request->get('password')
        );
        // ...
    }
// ...
```

On a more elaborate Silex application that uses the `Form` component to capture and validate parameters, it would look like this:

```
// ...
$app->match('/signup', function (Request $request) use ($app) {
    $form = $app['sign_up_form'];
    $form->handleRequest($request);

    if ($form->isValid()) {
        $data = $form->getData();

        try {
            $app['sign_in_user_application_service']->execute(
                new SignUpUserRequest(
                    $data['email'],
                    $data['password']
                )
            );

            return $app->redirect(
                $app['url_generator']->generate('login')
            );
        } catch (UserAlreadyExistsException $e) {
            $form
                ->get('email')
                ->addError(
                    new FormError(
                        'Email is already registered by another user'
                    )
                );
        } catch (Exception $e) {
            $form
                ->addError(
                    new FormError(
                        'There was an error, please get in touch with us'
                    )
                );
        }
    }

    return $app['twig']->render('signup.html.twig', [
        'form' => $form->createView(),
    ]);
});
```

Request Design

When designing your request objects, you should always follow these principles: use primitives, design for serialization, and don't include business logic inside. This way, you'll be able to save unit testing dollars.

Use Primitives

We recommend using basic types to build up your request objects — that means strings, integers, booleans, and so on. We're just abstracting away input parameters. You should be able to consume Application Services independently from the delivery mechanism. Even pretty complicated HTML forms get translated into basic types all the time at the controller level. You don't want to mix up your framework and your business logic.

With certain scenarios, it's tempting to use Value Objects directly. Don't do it. Updates on the Value Object definition will affect all clients, and you'll be coupling clients with your Domain logic.

Serializable

A cool side effect of using basic types is that any request object can easily be serialized into a string, sent through the wire, and stored in a messaging system or database.

No Business Logic

Avoid putting any business logic — even validation — inside your request objects. Validation should take place inside your Domain — this is inside your Entities, Value Objects, Domain Services, etc. Validation is a way of enforcing business invariants and Domain constraints.

No Tests

Application requests are data structures, not objects. Unit testing data structures is like testing getters and setters. There's no behavior to test, so there isn't much value in trying to unit test request objects and DTOs. These structures will be covered as a side effect of more elaborate tests, such as Integration or Acceptance tests.

Commands are an alternative to request objects. We could design a Service with multiple Application methods, and each one of them with the parameters you'd put inside the Request. This is OK for simple applications, but we'll worry about this topic later.

Anatomy of an Application Service

Once we have the data encapsulated in a request, it's time for the business logic. As Vaughn Vernon says: "Keep Application Services thin, using them only to coordinate tasks on the model."

The first thing to do is to extract the necessary information from the request, That is, the email and password. At a high level, we need to check if there's an existing user with a particular email. If this isn't the case, then we create and add the user to the UserRepository. In the special case of finding a user with the same email, we raise an exception so the client can treat it their own way — by displaying an error, retrying, or just ignoring it:

```
namespace Lw\Application\Service\User;

use Ddd\Application\Service\ApplicationService;
use Lw\Domain\Model\User\User;
use Lw\Domain\Model\User\UserAlreadyExistsException;
use Lw\Domain\Model\User\UserRepository;

class SignUpUserService
{
    private $userRepository;

    public function __construct(UserRepository $userRepository)
    {
        $this->userRepository = $userRepository;
    }

    public function execute(SignUpUserRequest $request)
    {
        $email = $request->email();
        $password = $request->password();

        $user = $this->userRepository->ofEmail($email);
        if ($user) {
            throw new UserAlreadyExistsException();
        }

        $this->userRepository->add(
```

```
            new User(
                $this->userRepository->nextIdentity(),
                $email ,
                $password
            )
        );
    }
}
```

Nice! If you're wondering what this `UserRepository` thing is doing in the constructor, we'll show you that next.

Handling Exceptions
Exceptions raised by Application Services are a way of communicating unusual cases and flows to the client. Exceptions on this layer are related to business logic (like not finding a user), and not implementation details (like `PDOException`, `PredisException`, or `DoctrineException`).

Dependency Inversion

Handling users is not the responsibility of the Service. As we saw in `Chapter 10`, *Repositories*, there's a specialized class that deals with `User` collections: the `User Repository`. This is a dependency from the Application Service to the Repository. We don't want to couple the Application Service with a concrete implementation of the Repository, as then we'd be coupling our Service with Infrastructure details. So we depend on the contract (interface) that concrete implementations depend on, the `UserRepository`.

A specific implementation of the `UserRepository` will be built and passed in at runtime — for example, with `DoctrineUserRepository`, a specific implementation that uses Doctrine. Passing a specific implementation will also work when testing. For example, `NotAvailableUserRepository` can be a specific implementation that will throw exceptions each time an operation is performed. This way, we can test all Application Service behaviors, including *sad* paths, which is when the application must behave properly, even if something goes wrong.

Application Services could depend on Domain Services like `GetBadgesByUser` too. At runtime, the implementation for such a Service could be quite elaborate. Imagine an `HttpGetBadgesByUser` for integrating a Bounded Context through HTTP protocol.

Depending on abstractions, we'll make our Application Service immune to low-level Infrastructure changes.

Instantiating Application Services

Instantiating just your Application Service is easy, but building the dependency tree might be tricky, depending on how complicated the dependencies are to build. For such a purpose, most frameworks come with a Dependency Injection Container. Without one, you'll end up with something like the following code somewhere in your controller:

```
$redisClient = new Predis\Client([
    'scheme' => 'tcp',
    'host' => '10.0.0.1',
    'port' => 6379
]);

$userRepository = new RedisUserRepository($redisClient);
$signUp = new SignUpUserService($userRepository);
$signUp->execute(new SignUpUserRequest(
    'user@example.com',
    'password'
));
```

We decided to use the `Redis` implementation for the `UserRepository`. In the previous code example, we built all dependencies needed for building a Repository that uses Redis internally. Those dependencies are: a `Predis` client, and all parameters to connect to our Redis server. This is not only inefficient, but it also spreads duplication across controllers.

You could refactor the construction logic into a Factory, or you could use a Dependency Injection Container — most modern frameworks come with it.

Is It Bad to Use a Dependency Injection Container?
Not at all. Dependency Injection Containers are just a tool. They help by abstracting away the complexities of building your dependencies. They come in handy for building Infrastructure artifacts. Symfony offers a complete solution.

Take into account the fact that passing the entire container as a whole to one of the Services is a bad practice. That would be like coupling the entire context of your application with the Domain. If a Service needs specific objects, build them from your framework and pass them as dependencies into the Service, but don't make that Service aware of the entire context.

Let's see how would we build dependencies in Silex:

```
$app = new \Silex\Application();
$app['redis_parameters'] = [
    'scheme' => 'tcp',
    'host' => '127.0.0.1',
    'port' => 6379
];

$app['redis'] = $app->share(function ($app) {
    return new Predis\Client($app['redis_parameters']);
});

$app['user_repository'] = $app->share(function($app) {
    return new RedisUserRepository(
        $app['redis']
    );
});

$app['sign_up_user_application_service'] = $app->share(function($app) {
    return new SignUpUserService(
        $app['user_repository']
    );
});

// ...

$app->match('/signup' ,function (Request $request) use ($app) {
    // ...
    $app['sign_up_user_application_service']->execute(
        new SignUpUserRequest(
            $request->get('email'),
            $request->get('password')
        )
    );
    // ...
});
```

As you can see, $app is used as the Service Container. We register all the components needed, along with their dependencies. sign_up_user_application_service depends on the definitions made above. Changing the implementation for the user_repository is as easy as returning something else (MySQL, MongoDB, and so on.), so we don't need to change the Service code at all.

The equivalent for a Symfony application looks like this:

```xml
<?xml version=" 1.0" ?>
<container xmlns="http://symfony.com/schema/dic/services"
    xmlns:xsi="http://www.w3.org/2001/XMLSchema-instance"
    xsi:schemaLocation="
        http://symfony.com/schema/dic/services
        http://symfony.com/schema/dic/services/services-1.0.xsd">
    <services>
        <service
            id="sign_up_user_application_service"
            class="SignUpUserService">
            <argument type="service" id="user_repository" />
        </service>

        <service
            id="user_repository"
            class="RedisUserRepository">
            <argument type="service">
                <service class="Predis\Client" />
            </argument>
        </service>
    </services>
</container>
```

Now that you have the definition of your Application Service in the Symfony Service Container, getting it later is pretty straightforward. All delivery mechanisms — Web Controllers, REST Controllers, and even Console Commands — share the same definition. The Service is available on any class implementing the `ContainerAware` interface. Getting the Service is as easy as calling `$this->get('sign_up_user_application_service'`.

To summarize, how you build your Services (adhoc, using Service Containers, using Factories, and so on.) doesn't matter. However, it's important to keep your Application Services setup out of the Infrastructure boundary.

Customize an Application Service

The main way to customize your Application Service is by choosing which dependencies you're passing in. Depending on your Service Container capabilities, that could be a bit tricky, so you can also add a setter to change the dependency on the fly. For example, you may need to change an output dependency so that you can set up a default one and then change it afterward. If logic gets too complicated, you can create an Application Service Factory that will handle this situation for you.

Execution

There are two different approaches for invoking Application Services: a dedicated class per use case with a single execution method, and multiple Application Services and use cases inside the same class.

One Class Per Application Service

This is our preferred approach, and probably the one that fits all scenarios:

```
class SignUpUserService
{
    // ...
    public function execute(SignUpUserRequest $request)
    {
        // ...
    }
}
```

Using a dedicated class per Application Service makes the code more robust against external changes (Single Responsibility Principle). There are fewer reasons to change the class, as the Service does one and only one thing. The Application Service will be easier to test, seeing as it does less things. It's easier to implement a common Application Service contract, making class decoration easier (check out Sub section *Transactions* of `Chapter 10`, *Repositories*). This will also result in higher cohesion, as all dependencies are exclusively dedicated to a single use case.

The `execution` method could have a more expressive name, like `signUp`. However, the `execute Command pattern` format standardizes a common contract across Application Services, thereby enabling easy decoration, which comes in handy for transactions.

Multiple Application Service Methods per Class

Sometimes it might be a good idea to group cohesive Application Services under the same class:

```
class UserService
{
    // ...
    public function signUp(SignUpUserRequest $request)
    {
        // ...
    }
```

```
public function signIn(SignUpUserRequest $request)
{
    // ...
}

public function logOut(LogOutUserRequest $request)
{
    // ...
}
}
```

We don't recommend such an approach, as not all Application Services are 100 percent cohesive. Some Services will require different dependencies, and you'll end up with Application Services depending on things they don't need. Another issue is that this kind of class grows fast. As it violates the Single Responsibility Principle, there will be multiple reasons to change and maybe even break it.

Returning Values

After signing up, we might be thinking about redirecting the user to a profile page. The natural way of passing the required information back to the controller is to return the User Entity directly from the Service:

```
class SignUpUserService
{
    // ...

    public function execute(SignUpUserRequest $request)
    {
        $user = new User(
            $this->userRepository->nextIdentity(),
            $email,
            $password
        );

        $this->userRepository->add($user);

        return $user;
    }
}
```

Then, from the controller, we would pick up the id field and redirect to some other place. However, think twice about what we've just done. We returned a full-featured Entity to the controller, which will allow the delivery mechanism to bypass the Application Layer and interact directly with the Domain.

Imagine the `User` Entity offers an `updateEmailAddress` method. You could try to prevent it, but at some point in the future, somebody might think about using it:

```
$app-> match( '/signup' , function (Request $request) use ($app) {
    // ...
    $user = $app['sign_up_user_application_service']->execute(
        new SignUpUserRequest(
            $request->get('email'),
            $request->get('password'))
    );
    $user->updateEmailAddress('shouldnotupdate@email.com');
    // ...
});
```

Not only that, but the data that the presentation layer needs is not the same that the Domain manages. We don't want to evolve and couple the Domain layer around the presentation layer. Instead, we want them to evolve freely.

To do this, we need a flexible way of decoupling both layers.

DTO from Aggregate Instances

We could return sterile data structures with the information the presentation layer needs. As we've seen before, DTOs fit with this scenario. We just need to compose them in the Application Service and return them to the client:

```
class UserDTO
{
    private $email ;
    // ...

    public function __construct(User $user)
    {
        $this->email = $user->email ();
        // ...
    }

    public function email ()
    {
        return $this->email ;
    }
}
```

The `UserDTO` will expose whatever read-only data we need from the `User` Entity on the presentation layer, thereby avoiding exposing behavior:

```
class SignUpUserService
{
    public function execute(SignUpUserRequest $request)
    {
        // ...

        $user = // ...

        return new UserDTO($user);
    }
}
```

Mission accomplished. Now we could pass parameters to the template engine and transform them into widgets, tags, or subtemplates, or do whatever we want with the data on the presentation side:

```
$app->match('/signup' , function (Request $request) use ($app) {
    /**
     * @var UserDTO $user
     */
    $userDto=$app['sign_up_user_application_service']->execute(
        new SignUpUserRequest(
            $request->get('email'),
            $request->get('password')
        )
    );

    // ...
});
```

However, letting the Application Service decide how to build the DTO reveals another limitation. As building the DTO depends exclusively on the Application Service, adapting the DTO to different clients will be very difficult. Consider the data needed for a redirect on a Web Controller and the data needed for a REST response for the same use case. Not the same data at all.

Let's allow the client to define how to build the DTO by passing a specific DTO Assembler:

```
class SignUpUserService
{
    private $userDtoAssembler;

    public function __construct(
        UserRepository $userRepository,
        UserDTOAssembler $userDtoAssembler
    ) {
        $this->userRepository = $userRepository;
        $this->userDtoAssembler = $userDtoAssembler;
    }

    public function execute(SignUpUserRequest $request)
    {
        $user = // ...

        return $this->userDtoAssembler->assemble($user);
    }
}
```

Now the client can customize the response by passing a specific `UserDTOAssembler`.

Data Transformers

There are some cases where generating intermediate DTOs for more complex responses like JSON, XML, CSV, and iCAL Contact could be seen as an unnecessary overhead. We could output the representation in a buffer and ask for it later on the delivery side.

Transformers help reduce this overhead by transforming high-level Domain concepts into low-level client details. Let's see an example:

```
interface UserDataTransformer
{
    public function write(User $user);

    /**
     * @return mixed
     */
    public function read();
}
```

Consider the case of generating different data representations for a given product. Usually, the product information is served through a web interface (HTML), but we might be interested in offering other formats, like XML, JSON, or CSV. This might enable integrations with other Services.

Consider a similar case for a blog. We might expose our potential as writers in HTML to the world, but some people will be interested in consuming our articles through RSS. The use cases — Application Services — remain the same. The representation doesn't.

DTOs are a clean and simple solution that could be passed to template engines for different representations, but this might complicate the logic of this last step of data transformation, as the logic for such templates could become a problem to maintain, test, and understand.

Data Transformers might be a better approach on specific cases. These are just black boxes with Domain concepts (Aggregates, Entities, and so on.) as inputs and read-only representations (XML, JSON, CSV, and so on.) as outputs. These transformers could be really easy to test:

```php
class JsonUserDataTransformer implements UserDataTransformer
{
    private $data;

    public function write(User $user)
    {
        // More complex logic could be placed here
        // As using JMSSerializer, native json, etc.
        $this->data = json_encode($user);
    }

    /**
     * @return string
     */
    public function read()
    {
        return $this->data;
    }
}
```

That was easy. Wondering how the XML or CSV one would look? Let's see how to integrate the Data Transformer with our Application Service:

```
class SignUpUserService
{
    private $userRepository;
    private $userDataTransformer;

    public function __construct(
        UserRepository $userRepository,
        UserDataTransformer $userDataTransformer
    ) {
        $this->userRepository = $userRepository;
        $this->userDataTransformer = $userDataTransformer;
    }

    public function execute(SignUpUserRequest $request)
    {
        $user = // ...
        $this->userDataTransformer()->write($user);
    }

    /**
     * @return UserDataTransformer
     */
    public function userDataTransformer()
    {
        return $this->userDataTransformer;
    }
}
```

That's similar to the DTO Assembler approach, but this time without returning a concrete value. The Data Transformer is being used to hold and interact with the data.

The main issue with DTOs is the overhead of writing them. Most of the time, your Domain concepts and DTO representations will present the same structure. Most of the time, you'll feel it's not worth your time to make such a mapping. That said, the relationship between representations and Aggregates is not 1:1. You can represent two Aggregates together in a single representation. You can also represent the same Aggregate in multiple ways. How you do it always depends on your use cases.

However, according to `Martin Fowler`:

> One case where it is useful to use something like a DTO is **when you have a significant mismatch between the model in your presentation layer and the underlying domain model**. In this case it makes sense to make presentation specific facade/gateway that maps from the domain model and presents an interface that's convenient for the presentation. It fits in nicely with Presentation Model. This is worth doing, but it is only worth doing for screens that have this mismatch (in this case it isn't extra work, since you'd have to do it in the screen anyway.)

We think the long-term vision will be worth the investment. On medium to big projects, interface representations and Domain concepts change at very different rhythms. You might want to decouple them from each other to lower the friction for updates. Using DTOs or Data Transformers allows you to evolve your model freely without having to think about breaking the layout all the time.

Multiple Application Services on Compound Layouts

Most of the time, no layout is as simple as a single Application Service. Our projects have pretty complicated interfaces.

Consider the homepage of a specific project. How can we render so many pieces and use cases? There are a few options, so let's check them out.

AJAX Content Integration

You could let the browser ask for different endpoints directly and combine the data in the layout right after through AJAX or `Hijax`. This will avoid mixing a lot of Application Services in your controllers, but it might have a performance penalty, depending on the number of requests triggered.

ESI Content Integration

Edge Side Includes (**ESI**) is a tiny markup language similar to the previous approach, but on the server side. It requires additional effort configuring extra middleware, like NGINX or Varnish, to make it work. Includes (ESI) is a tiny markup language similar to the previous approach, but on the server side. It requires additional effort configuring extra middleware, like NGINX or `Varnish`, to make it work.

Symfony Sub Requests

If you use Symfony, Sub Requests could be an interesting option. According to the `Symfony Documentation`:

In addition to the main request that's sent into `HttpKernel::handle`, you can also send so-called sub request. A sub request looks and acts like any other request, but typically serves to render just one small portion of a page instead of a full page. You'll most commonly make sub-requests from your controller (or perhaps from inside a template, that's being rendered by your controller). This creates another full request-response cycle where this new Request is transformed into a Response. The only difference internally is that some listeners (Example: security) may only act upon the master request. Each listener is passed some sub-class of `KernelEvent`, whose `isMasterRequest()` can be used to check if the current request is a master or sub request.

This is great, as you'll get the benefits of invoking separate Application Services without AJAX penalties or complicated ESI configurations.

One Controller, Multiple Application Services

One last option could be managing multiple Application Services within the same controller, though the controller logic could get a little bit dirty, as it'll handle and merge the responses to pass to the view.

Testing Application Services

As you're interested in testing the behavior of the Application Service itself, there's no need to turn it into an integration test with complicated setups going against a real database. You're not interested in testing the low-level details, so most of the time, a unit test will be enough:

```
class SignUpUserServiceTest extends \PHPUnit_Framework_TestCase
{
    /**
     * @var \Lw\Domain\Model\User\UserRepository
     */
    private $userRepository;

    /**
     * @var SignUpUserService
     */
    private $signUpUserService;

    public function setUp()
    {
        $this->userRepository = new InMemoryUserRepository();
        $this->signUpUserService = new SignUpUserService(
            $this->userRepository
        );
    }

    /**
     * @test
     * @expectedException
     *     \Lw\Domain\Model\User\UserAlreadyExistsException
     */
    public function alreadyExistingEmailShouldThrowAnException()
    {
        $this->executeSignUp();
        $this->executeSignUp();
    }

    private function executeSignUp()
    {
        return $this->signUpUserService->execute(
            new SignUpUserRequest(
                'user@example.com',
                'password'
            )
        );
    }
```

```
/**
 * @test
 */
public function afterUserSignUpItShouldBeInTheRepository()
{
    $user = $this->executeSignUp();

    $this->assertSame(
        $user,
        $this->userRepository->ofId($user->id())
    );
}
}
```

We've used an in-memory implementation for the User Repository. This is what is called a Fake: a fully functional implementation for the Repository that will make our test work as a unit. We don't need to go to the database to test the behavior of this class. That would make our test slow and fragile.

Checking for a Domain Events submission might be interesting too. If creating a user fires a user registered event, ensuring it's been triggered might be a good idea:

```
class SignUpUserServiceTest extends \PHPUnit_Framework_TestCase
{
    // ...

    /**
     * @test
     */
    public function itShouldPublishUserRegisteredEvent()
    {
        $subscriber = new SpySubscriber();
        $id = DomainEventPublisher::instance()->subscribe($subscriber);

        $user = $this->executeSignUp();
        $userId = $user->id();

        DomainEventPublisher::instance()->unsubscribe($id);
        $this->assertUserRegisteredEventPublished(
            $subscriber, $userId
        );
    }

    private function assertUserRegisteredEventPublished(
        $subscriber, $userId
    ) {
        $this->assertInstanceOf(
```

```
                   'UserRegistered', $subscriber->domainEvent
            );
            $this->assertTrue(
                $subscriber->domainEvent->userId()->equals($userId)
            );
        }
    }

    class SpySubscriber implements DomainEventSubscriber
    {
        public $domainEvent;

        public function handle($aDomainEvent)
        {
            $this->domainEvent = $aDomainEvent;
        }

        public function isSubscribedTo($aDomainEvent)
        {
            return true;
        }
    }
```

Transactions

Transactions are an implementation detail related to the persistence mechanism. The Domain layer shouldn't be aware of this low-level implementation detail. Thinking about beginning, committing, or rolling back a transaction at this level is a big smell. This level of detail belongs to the Infrastructure layer.

The best way of handling transactions is to not handle them at all. We could wrap our Application Services with a Decorator implementation for handling the transaction session automatically.

We've implemented a solution to this problem in one of our repositories, and you can check it out here:

```
    interface TransactionalSession
    {
        /**
         * @return mixed
         */
        public function executeAtomically(callable $operation);
    }
```

This contract takes a piece of code and executes it atomically. Depending on your persistence mechanism, you'll end up with different implementations.

Let's see how we could do it with Doctrine ORM:

```
class DoctrineSession implements TransactionalSession
{
    private $entityManager;

    public function __construct(EntityManager $entityManager)
    {
        $this->entityManager = $entityManager;
    }

    public function executeAtomically(callable $operation)
    {
        return $this->entityManager->transactional($operation);
    }
}
```

This is how a client would use the previous code:

```
/** @var EntityManager $em */
$nonTxApplicationService = new SignUpUserService(
    $em->getRepository('BoundedContext\Domain\Model\User\User')
);

$txApplicationService = new TransactionalApplicationService(
    $nonTxApplicationService,
    new DoctrineSession($em)
);

$response = $txApplicationService->execute(
    new SignUpUserRequest(
        'user@example.com',
        'password'
    )
);
```

Now that we have the Doctrine implementation for transactional sessions, it would be great to create a Decorator for our Application Services. With this approach, we make transactional requests transparent to the Domain:

```
class TransactionalApplicationService implements ApplicationService
{
    private $session;
    private $service;
```

```
public function __construct(
    ApplicationService $service, TransactionalSession $session
) {
    $this->session = $session;
    $this->service = $service;
}

public function execute(BaseRequest $request)
{
    $operation = function () use ($request) {
        return $this->service->execute($request);
    };

    return $this->session->executeAtomically($operation);
}
}
```

A nice side effect of using Doctrine Session is that it automatically manages the flush method, so you don't need to add the flush inside your Domain or Infrastructure.

Security

In case you're wondering how to manage and handle user credentials and security in general, unless it's the responsibility of your Domain, we recommend letting the framework handle it. The user session is a concern of the delivery mechanism. Polluting the Domain with such concepts will make it harder to develop.

Domain Events

Domain Event listeners have to be configured before the Application Service gets executed, or nobody will be noticed. There are situations where you'll have to be explicit and configure the listener before executing the Application Service:

```
// ...
$subscriber = new SpySubscriber();
DomainEventPublisher::instance()->subscribe($subscriber);

$applicationService = // ...
$applicationService->execute(...);
```

Most of the time, this will be done by configuring the Dependency Injection Container.

Command Handlers

An interesting way of executing Application Services is through a Command Bus library. A good one is `Tactician`. From the Tactician website:

> What is a Command Bus? The term is mostly used when we combine the `Command` `pattern` with a `service layer`. Its job is to take a Command object (which describes what the user wants to do) and match it to a Handler (which executes it). This can help structure your code neatly.

— our Application Services are the Service Layer, and our Request objects look pretty much like Commands.

Fair enough — our Application Services are the Service Layer, and our Request objects look pretty much like Commands. Wouldn't it be great if we had a mechanism to link all the Application Services, and then based on the Request, execute the correct one? Well, that's actually what a Command Bus is.

Tactician Library and Other Options

Tactician is a Command Bus library, which allows you to use the Command pattern for your Application Services. It's especially convenient for Application Services, but you could use any kind of input.

Let's see an example from the `Tactician` website:

```
// You build a simple message object like this:
class PurchaseProductCommand
{
    protected $productId;
    protected $userId;

    // ...and constructor to assign those properties...
}

// And a Handler class that expects it:
class PurchaseProductHandler
{
    public function handle(PurchaseProductCommand $command)
    {
        // use command to update your models, etc
    }
}
// And then in your Controllers, you can fill in the command using your
```

```
favorite
// form or serializer library, then drop it in the CommandBus and you're
done!
$command = new PurchaseProductCommand(42, 29);
$commandBus->handle($command);
```

That's it. Tactician is the `$commandBus` Service. It does all the plumbing for finding the right handler and method, which can avoid a lot of boilerplate code. Here, Commands and Handlers are just normal classes, but you can configure whichever one fits your app better.

In summary, we can conclude that Commands are just Request objects, and Command Handlers are just Application Services.

A cool thing about Tactician (and Command Buses in general) is that they're really easy to extend. Tactician provides plug-ins for common tasks, like logging and database transactions. That way, you can forget about setting up the wiring on every handler.

Another interesting plug-in for `Tactician is Bernard` integration. Bernard is an asynchronous job queue that allows you to leave some tasks for later processing. Heavy processes block the response. Most of the time, we can branch and delay their execution for later. For the best experience, answer the customer as fast as possible and let them know once the branched processes are done.

Matthias Noback has developed another similar project, called `SimpleBus`, that can be used as an alternative to Tactician. The main difference is that `SimpleBus` Command Handlers don't have a return value.

Wrap-Up

Application Services represent the Application layer of your Bounded Context. These high-level use cases should be relatively simple and skinny, as their purpose evolves around Domain coordination. Application Services are the entry point for Domain logic interaction. We've seen that Requests and Commands keep things organized; that DTOs and Data Transformers allow us to decouple data representation from Domain conceptualization; that building Application Services is pretty straightforward with Dependency Injection Containers; and that we have plenty of options for combining Application Services in complex layouts.

12

Integrating Bounded Contexts

Every enterprise application is typically composed of several areas in which the company operates. Areas such as *billing, inventory, shipping management, catalog,* and so on are common examples. The easiest manner in which to manage all these concerns may seem to lean toward a **monolithic system**. But, you might wonder, does it have to be this way? What if any friction garnered between teams working on these separate areas could be reduced by splitting this big monolithic application into smaller, independent chunks? In this chapter, we'll explore how to do this, so be prepared for insights and heuristics around **strategical design**.

Dealing with Distributed Systems

Dealing with distributed systems is **hard**. Breaking a system into independent autonomous parts has its benefits, but it also increases complexity. For example, the coordination and synchronization of distributed systems is not trivial, and as a result, should be considered carefully. As Martin Fowler said in the PoEAA book, the first law of distributed systems is always: **Don't distribute**.

Integration Through the Data Store

One of the most commonly used techniques to integrate different parts of an application has always been to share the same data store, along with the same code base. This is usually known as a monolithic application, and it often ends up with a single data store that hosts the data related to all the concerns within the application.

Consider an e-commerce application. A shared data store would contain all concerns (Example: tables within a relational database) surrounding the catalog, billing, inventory, and so on. There's nothing wrong with this approach per se—for example, in small linear applications where the complexity is not too high. However, within complex Domains, some issues can arise. If you share data across many tables touching multiple application concerns, transactions will have a big impact on performance.

Another less technical problem that could develop is in regard to the Ubiquitous Language. The main advantage of the separation of Bounded Contexts is having **a single Ubiquitous Language for each one**. In doing so, models will be separated into their own Contexts. Mixing all models together within the same Context can lead to ambiguity and confusion.

Going back to the e-commerce system, imagine we want to introduce the concept of a t-shirt. Within the catalogue Context, a t-shirt would be a *product* with properties like *color*, *size*, *material*, and maybe some fancy *pictures*. In the *inventory* system, however, we don't really want to concern ourselves with these things. Here, a *product* has a different meaning, where we care about different properties like *weight*, *location in the warehouse*, or *dimensions*. Mixing both Contexts together will tangle concepts and complicate the design. In Domain-Driven Design terms, mixing concepts in this manner is what is called a Shared Kernel.

Shared Kernel

Designate some subset of the domain model that the teams agree to share. Of course this includes, along with this subset of the model, the subset of code or of the database design associated with that part of the model. This explicitly shared stuff has special status, and shouldn't be changed without consultation with the other team. Integrate a functional system frequently, but somewhat less often than the pace of CONTINUOUS INTEGRATION within the teams. At these integrations, run the tests of both teams. Eric Evans - `Domain-Driven Design: Tackling Complexity in the Heart of Software`

We don't recommend using a Shared Kernel, as multiple teams can collide within the development of it, which not only results in maintenance issues but also becomes a point of friction. However, if you opt to use a Shared Kernel, changes should be agreed upon beforehand and between all parties involved. Conceptually, this approach has other problems, such as people seeing it as a bag to place *stuff* that doesn't belong anywhere else, and this grows indefinitely. A better way of dealing with the ever-growing complexity of the monolith is to break it up in different autonomous pieces, such as communicating through REST, RPC, or messaging systems. This requires drawing clear boundaries, with each Context likely ending up with its own Infrastructure—data stores, servers, messaging middleware, and so on — and even its own team.

As you might imagine, this could lead to some degree of duplication, but that's a tradeoff that we're willing to make in order to reduce complexity. In Domain-Driven Design, we call these independent pieces **Bounded Contexts**.

Integration Relationships

Customer - Supplier

When there's a unidirectional integration between two Bounded Contexts, where one acts as a provider (**upstream**) and the other as a client (**downstream**), we'll end up with **Customer - Supplier Development Teams**.

Establish a clear customer/supplier relationship between the two teams. In planning sessions, make the downstream team play the customer role to the upstream team. Negotiate and budget tasks for downstream requirements so that everyone understands the commitment and schedule. Jointly develop automated acceptance tests that will validate the interface expected. Add these tests to the upstream team's test suite, to be run as part of its' continuous integration. This testing will free the upstream team to make changes without fear of side effects downstream. Eric Evans - Domain-Driven Design: Tackling Complexity in the Heart of Software.

Customer - Supplier Development Teams are the most common way of integrating Bounded Contexts and usually represent a win-win situation when teams work closely.

Separate Ways

Continuing with the e-commerce example, think about reporting revenue to an old legacy retailer financial system. The integration could be incredibly expensive, resulting in it not being worth the effort to implement. In Domain-Driven Design strategic terms, this is known as **Separate Ways**.

Integration is always expensive. Sometimes the benefit is small. So Declare a BOUNDED CONTEXT to have no connection to the others at all, allowing developers to find simple, specialized solutions within this small scope. Eric Evans - *Domain-Driven Design:* `Tackling Complexity in the Heart of Software.`

Conformist

Consider again the e-commerce example and integration with a third-party shipping service. Both Domains differ in models, teams, and Infrastructure. The team responsible for maintaining the third-party shipping service will not participate in your product planning or provide any solutions to the e-commerce system. These teams don't have a close relationship. We could choose to accept and *conform* to their Domain Model. In strategic design, this is what we call a **Conformist Integration**.

Eliminate the complexity of translation between BOUNDED CONTEXTS by slavishly adhering to the model of the upstream team. Although this cramps the style of the downstream designers and probably does not yield the ideal model for the application, choosing CONFORMITY enormously simplifies integration. Also, you will share a UBIQUITOUS LANGUAGE with your supplier team. The supplier is in the driver's seat, so it is good to make communication easy for them. Altruism may be sufficient to get them to share information with you. Eric Evans - *Domain-Driven Design:* `Tackling Complexity in the Heart of Software.`

Implementing Bounded Context Integrations

To make things easier, we'll assume Bounded Contexts have a Customer - Supplier relationship.

Modern RPC

With modern RPC, we refer to RPC through RESTful resources. A Bounded Context reveals a clear interface to interact with to the outside world. It exposes resources that could be manipulated through HTTP verbs. We could say that the Bounded Context offers a set of services and operations. In strategical terms, this is what is called an **Open Host Service**.

Open Host Service
Define a protocol that gives access to your subsystem as a set of SERVICES. Open the protocol so that all who need to integrate with you can use it. Enhance and expand the protocol to handle new integration requirements, except when a single team has idiosyncratic needs. Then, use a one-off translator to augment the protocol for that special case so that the shared protocol can stay simple and coherent. Eric Evans - *Domain-Driven Design:* `Tackling Complexity in the Heart of Software.`

Let's explore an example provided within the `Last Wishes application` that comes with this book's GitHub organization.

The application is a web platform with the purpose of letting people save their last wills before they die. There are two Contexts: one responsible for handling wills—the Will Bounded Context—and one in charge of giving points to the users of the system—the `Gamification Context`. In the Will Context, the user could have badges related to the number of points the user made on the Gamification Context. This means that we need to integrate both Contexts together in order to show the badges a user has on the Will Context.

The Gamification Context is a full-fledged event-driven application powered by a custom event sourcing engine. It's a full-stack Symfony application that uses `FOSRestBundle`, `BazingaHateoasBundle`, `JMSSerializerBundle`, `NelmioApiDocBundle`, and `OngrElasticsearchBundle` to provide a level 3 and up REST API (commonly known as the Glory of REST), according to the `Richardson Maturity Model`. All the Events triggered within this Context are projected against an Elasticsearch server, in order to produce the data needed for the views. We'll expose the number of points made for a given user through an endpoint like `http://gamification.context.host/api/users/{id}`.

We'll also fetch the user projection from Elasticsearch and serialize it to a format previously negotiated with the client:

```
namespace AppBundle\Controller;

use FOS\RestBundle\Controller\Annotations as Rest;
use FOS\RestBundle\Controller\FOSRestController;
use Nelmio\ApiDocBundle\Annotation\ApiDoc;

class UsersController extends FOSRestController
{
    /**
     * @ApiDoc(
     *     resource = true,
     *     description = "Finds a user given a user ID",
     *     statusCodes = {
```

```
 *          200 = "Returned when the user have been found",
 *          404 = "Returned when the user could not be found"
 *     }
 * )
 *
 * @Rest\View(
 *     statusCode = 200
 * )
 */
public function getUserAction($id)
{
    $repo = $this->get('es.manager.default.user');
    $user = $repo->find($id);

    if (!$user) {
        throw $this->createNotFoundException(
            sprintf(
                'A user with an ID of %s does not exist',
                $id
            )
        );
    }
    return $user;
}
}
```

As we explained in the `Chapter 2`, *Architectural Styles* reads are treated as an Infrastructure concern, so there's no need to wrap them inside a Command / Command Handler flow.

The resulting JSON+HAL representation of a user will be like this:

```
{
    "id": "c3c587c6-610a-42df",
    "points": 0,
    "_links": {
        "self": {
            "href":
            "http://gamification.ctx/api/users/c3c587c6-610a-42df"
        }
    }
}
```

Now we're in a good position to integrate both Contexts. We just need to write the client in the Will Context for consuming the endpoint we've just created. Should we mix both Domain Models? Digesting the Gamification Context directly will mean adapting the Will Context to the Gamification one, resulting in a **Conformist** integration. However, separating these concerns seems worth the effort. We need a layer for guaranteeing the integrity and the consistency of the Domain Model within the Will Context, and we need to translate *points* (Gamification) to *badges* (Will). In Domain-Driven Design, this translation mechanism is what's called an **Anti-Corruption layer**.

Anti-Corruption Layer

Create an isolating layer to provide clients with functionality in terms of their own domain model. The layer talks to the other system through its existing interface, requiring little or no modification to the other system. Internally, the layer translates in both directions as necessary between the two models. Eric Evans - *Domain-Driven Design:* `Tackling Complexity in the Heart of Software`.

So, what does the Anti-Corruption layer look like? Most of the time, Services will be interacting with a combination of Adapters and Facades. The Services encapsulate and hide the low-level complexities behind these transformations. Facades aid in hiding and encapsulating access details required for fetching data from the Gamification model. Adapters translate between models, often using specialized Translators.

Let's see how to define a User Service within the Will's model that will be responsible for retrieving the badges earned by a given user:

```
namespace Lw\Domain\Model\User;

interface UserService
{
    public function badgesFrom(UserId $id);
}
```

Now let's look at the implementation on the Infrastructure side. We'll use an adapter for the transformation process:

```
namespace Lw\Infrastructure\Service;

use Lw\Domain\Model\User\UserId;
use Lw\Domain\Model\User\UserService;

class TranslatingUserService implements UserService
{
    private $userAdapter;
```

```php
    public function __construct(UserAdapter $userAdapter)
    {
        $this->userAdapter = $userAdapter;
    }

    public function badgesFrom(UserId $id)
    {
        return $this->userAdapter->toBadges($id);
    }
}
```

And here's the HTTP implementation for the `UserAdapter`:

```php
namespace Lw\Infrastructure\Service;

use GuzzleHttp\Client;

class HttpUserAdapter implements UserAdapter
{
    private $client;

    public function __construct(Client $client)
    {
        $this->client = $client;
    }

    public function toBadges( $id)
    {
        $response = $this->client->get(
            sprintf('/users/%s', $id),
            [
                'allow_redirects' => true,
                'headers' => [
                    'Accept' => 'application/hal+json'
                ]
            ]
        );

        $badges = [];
        if (200 === $response->getStatusCode()) {
            $badges =
                (new UserTranslator())
                    ->toBadgesFromRepresentation(
                        json_decode(
                            $response->getBody(),
                            true
                        )
                    );
```

```
        }
        return $badges;
    }
}
```

As you can see, the Adapter acts as a **Facade to the Gamification Context** too. We did it this way, as fetching the User resource on the Gamification side is pretty straightforward. The Adapter uses the `UserTranslator` to perform the translation:

```
namespace Lw\Infrastructure\Service;

use Lw\Infrastructure\Domain\Model\User\FirstWillMadeBadge;
use Symfony\Component\PropertyAccess\PropertyAccess;

class UserTranslator
{
    public function toBadgesFromRepresentation($representation)
    {
        $accessor = PropertyAccess::createPropertyAccessor();
        $points = $accessor->getValue($representation, 'points');
        $badges = [];
        if ($points > 3) {
            $badges[] = new FirstWillMadeBadge();
        }
        return $badges;
    }
}
```

The Translator specializes in transforming the points coming from the Gamification Context into badges.

We've shown how to integrate two Bounded Contexts where respective teams share a **Customer-Supplier** relationship. The Gamification Context exposes the integration through an **Open Host Service** implemented by a RESTful protocol. On the other side, the Will Context consumes the service through an **Anti-Corruption layer** responsible for translating the model from one Domain to the other, ensuring the Will Context's integrity.

Message Queues

RESTful resources aren't the only way of enabling integrations between Bounded Contexts. As we'll see, messaging middleware enables decoupled integrations between different Contexts.

Continuing with the Last Wishes application, we've just implemented a unidirectional relationship between two teams to manage points and badges within their respective Contexts. However, we left an important functionality out of scope on purpose: **rewarding the user every time they make a wish**.

We could go for another Open Host Service with a pull strategy. The Will Context will be pulling the Gamification Context periodically to get badges on sync (Example: through an scheduler like Cron). This solution will impact the user's experience, and it'll waste a lot of unnecessary resources.

A better approach is to use a **messaging middleware**. With this solution, Contexts could push messages to a middleware (often a message queue). Interested parties will be able to subscribe, inspect, and consume information on demand in a decoupled fashion. In order to do this, we need a **specialized, shared, and common communication language**, so all the parties can understand the information transmitted. This is what's called the **Published Language**.

Published Language
Use a well-documented shared language that can express the necessary domain information as a common medium of communication, translating as necessary into and out of that language. Eric Evans - *Domain-Driven Design:* Tackling Complexity in the Heart of Software.

In thinking about the format of these messages and looking closer at our Domain Model, we realize we already have what we need: Chapter 6, *Domain-Events*. It's not necessary to define a new way of communicating between Bounded Contexts. Instead, we can just use Domain Events to define a common language across Contexts. The definition of *something that Domain Experts care about that just happened* fits perfectly with what we're looking for: a formal Published Language.

In our example, we could use RabbitMQ as a messaging middleware. This is probably one of the most reliable and robust messaging AMQP protocols out there. We'll also incorporate the widely used PHP libraries php-amqplib and RabbitMQBundle.

Let's start with the Will Context, as it's the one that triggers Events when the user signs up or when making a wish. As we've already seen in the Chapter 6, *Domain-Events*, **it's a good idea to store Domain Events into a persistent mechanism**, so we'll assume that's what was done. We need a message publisher to fetch and publish stored Domain Events from the Event store to the messaging middleware. We already did the integration with RabbitMQ in the Chapter 6, *Domain-Events*, so we just need to implement the code in the Gamification Context. We'll listen for Events triggered by the Will Context. As we're using the Symfony Framework, we take advantage of a Symfony package called RabbitMQBundle.

We define two message consumers for the *User Registered* and *Wish Was Made* events:

```
namespace AppBundle\Infrastructure\Messaging\PhpAmqpLib;

use Lw\Gamification\Command\SignupCommand;
use OldSound\RabbitMqBundle\RabbitMq\ConsumerInterface;
use PhpAmqpLib\Message\AMQPMessage;

class PhpAmqpLibLastWillUserRegisteredConsumer
    implements ConsumerInterface
{
    private $commandBus;

    public function __construct($commandBus)
    {
        $this->commandBus = $commandBus;
    }

    public function execute(AMQPMessage $message)
    {
        $type = $message->get('type');

        if ('Lw\Domain\Model\User\UserRegistered' === $type) {
            $event = json_decode($message->body);
            $eventBody = json_decode($event->event_body);

            $this->commandBus->handle(
                new SignupCommand($eventBody->user_id->id)
            );
            return true;
        }
        return false;
    }
}
```

Note that in this case, we're only processing messages with the type of
`Lw\Domain\Model\User\UserRegistered`:

```
namespace AppBundle\Infrastructure\Messaging\PhpAmqpLib;

use Lw\Gamification\Command\RewardUserCommand;
use Lw\Gamification\Domain\Model\AggregateDoesNotExist;
use OldSound\RabbitMqBundle\RabbitMq\ConsumerInterface;
use PhpAmqpLib\Message\AMQPMessage;

class PhpAmqpLibLastWillWishWasMadeConsumer implements ConsumerInterface
{
    private $commandBus;
```

```
public function __construct($commandBus)
{
    $this->commandBus = $commandBus;
}

public function execute(AMQPMessage $message)
{
    $type = $message->get('type');

    if ('Lw\Domain\Model\Wish\WishWasMade' === $type) {
        $event = json_decode($message->body);
        $eventBody = json_decode($event->event_body);

        try {
            $points = 5;
            $this->commandBus->handle(
                new RewardUserCommand(
                    $eventBody->user_id->id,
                    $points
                )
            );
        } catch (AggregateDoesNotExist $e) {
            // Noop
        }

        return true;
    }

    return false;
}
}
```

Again, we're only interested in tracking `Lw\Domain\Model\Wish\WishWasMade events`.

In both cases, we use a Command Bus, which we discussed in the Chapter, Application. However, we can summarize it as a highway that decouples the Command and Receiver. The **when** and **how** a Command is executed is independent from **who** triggered it.

The Gamification Context uses `Tactician` (and `TacticianBundle`), a simple Command Bus that can be extended and adapted to your system. So now we're almost ready to start consuming Events from the Will Context.

The only thing we still need to do is define the RabbitMQBundle configuration in Symfony's `config.yml` file:

```
services:
    last_will_user_registered_consumer:
        class:
            AppBundle\Infrastructure\Messaging\
                PhpAmqpLib\PhpAmqpLibLastWillUserRegisteredConsumer
        arguments:
            - @tactician.commandbus

    last_will_wish_was_made_consumer:
        class:
            AppBundle\Infrastructure\Messaging\
                PhpAmqpLib\PhpAmqpLibLastWillWishWasMadeConsumer
        arguments:
            - @tactician.commandbus

old_sound_rabbit_mq:
    connections:
        default:
            host: " %rabbitmq_host%"
            port: " %rabbitmq_port%"
            user: " %rabbitmq_user%"
            password: " %rabbitmq_password%"
            vhost: " %rabbitmq_vhost%"
            lazy: true

    consumers:
        last_will_user_registered:
            connection: default
            callback: last_will_user_registered_consumer

            exchange_options:
                name: last-will
                type: fanout

            queue_options:
                name: last-will

        last_will_wish_was_made:
            connection: default
            callback: last_will_wish_was_made_consumer

            exchange_options:
                name: last-will
                type: fanout
```

```
queue_options:
    name: last-wil
```

The most convenient RabbitMQ configuration is probably the [`Publish / Subscribe`] pattern. All messages published by the Will Context will be delivered to all connected consumers. This is called **fanout** in the RabbitMQ exchange configuration.

The exchange consists of an agent being in charge of delivering messages to the corresponding queues:

```
> php app/console rabbitmq:consumer --messages=1000
last_will_user_registered
> php app/console rabbitmq:consumer --messages=1000 last_will_wish_was_made
```

With those two commands, Symfony will execute both consumers and they'll start listening for Domain Events. We've specified a limit of 1,000 messages to consume, as PHP isn't the best platform for executing long-running processes. It also might be a good idea to use something like `Supervisor` to monitor and restart processes periodically.

Wrap-Up

Although we've only seen a small part of it, strategical design is at the heart and soul of Domain-Driven Design. It's an essential part that aids in developing better and more semantic models. We recommend using messaging middleware to integrate Bounded Contexts, as this naturally leads to simpler, decoupled, and Event-driven architectures.

Hexagonal Architecture with PHP

The following article was posted in php|architect magazine in June 2014 by Carlos Buenosvinos.

Introduction

With the rise of **Domain-Driven Design (DDD)**, architectures promoting domain centric designs are becoming more popular. This is the case with **Hexagonal Architecture**, also known as **Ports and Adapters**, that seems to have being rediscovered just now by PHP developers. Invented in 2005 by Alistair Cockburn, one of the Agile Manifesto authors, the Hexagonal Architecture allows an application to be equally driven by users, programs, automated tests or batch scripts, and to be developed and tested in isolation from its eventual run-time devices and databases. This results into agnostic infrastructure web applications that are easier to test, write and maintain. Let's see how to apply it using real PHP examples.

Your company is building a brainstorming system called *Idy*. Users add and rate ideas so the most interesting ones can be implemented in a company. It is Monday morning, another sprint is starting and you are reviewing some user stories with your team and your Product Owner. **As a not logged in user, I want to rate an idea and the author should be notified by email**, that's a really important one, isn't it?

First Approach

As a good developer, you decide to divide and conquer the user story, so you'll start with the first part, *I want to rate an idea*. After that, you will face *the author should be notified by email*. That sounds like a plan.

In terms of business rules, rating an idea is as easy as finding the idea by its identifier in the ideas repository, where all the ideas live, add the rating, recalculate the average and save the idea back. If the idea does not exist or the repository is not available we should throw an exception so we can show an error message, redirect the user or do whatever the business asks us for.

In order to *execute* this *UseCase*, we just need the idea identifier and the rating from the user. Two integers that would come from the user request.

Your company web application is dealing with a Zend Framework 1 legacy application. As most of companies, probably some parts of your app may be newer, more SOLID, and others may just be a big ball of mud. However, you know that it does not matter at all which framework you are using, it is all about writing clean code that makes maintenance a low cost task for your company.

You're trying to apply some Agile principles you remember from your last conference, how it was, yeah, I remember "make it work, make it right, make it fast". After some time working you get something like Listing 1.

```
class IdeaController extends Zend_Controller_Action
{
    public function rateAction()
    {
        // Getting parameters from the request
        $ideaId = $this->request->getParam('id');
        $rating = $this->request->getParam('rating');

        // Building database connection
        $db = new Zend_Db_Adapter_Pdo_Mysql([
            'host'     => 'localhost',
            'username' => 'idy',
            'password' => '',
            'dbname'   => 'idy'
        ]);

        // Finding the idea in the database
        $sql = 'SELECT * FROM ideas WHERE idea_id = ?';
        $row = $db->fetchRow($sql, $ideaId);
        if (!$row) {
```

```
            throw new Exception('Idea does not exist');
        }

        // Building the idea from the database
        $idea = new Idea();
        $idea->setId($row['id']);
        $idea->setTitle($row['title']);
        $idea->setDescription($row['description']);
        $idea->setRating($row['rating']);
        $idea->setVotes($row['votes']);
        $idea->setAuthor($row['email']);

        // Add user rating
        $idea->addRating($rating);

        // Update the idea and save it to the database
        $data = [
            'votes' => $idea->getVotes(),
            'rating' => $idea->getRating()
        ];
        $where['idea_id = ?'] = $ideaId;
        $db->update('ideas', $data, $where);

        // Redirect to view idea page
        $this->redirect('/idea/' . $ideaId);
    }
}
```

I know what readers are thinking: *Who is going to access data directly from the controller? This is a 90's example!*, ok, ok, you're right. If you are already using a framework, it is likely that you are also using an ORM. Maybe done by yourself or any of the existing ones such as Doctrine, Eloquent, Zend, and so on. If this is the case, you are one step further from those who have some Database connection object but don't count your chickens before they're hatched.

For newbies, Listing 1 code just works. However, if you take a closer look at the Controller, you'll see more than business rules, you'll also see how your web framework routes a request into your business rules, references to the database or how to connect to it. So close, you see references to your **infrastructure**.

Infrastructure is the **detail that makes your business rules work**. Obviously, we need some way to get to them (API, web, console apps, and so on.) and effectively we need some physical place to store our ideas (memory, database, NoSQL, and so on.). However, we should be able to exchange any of these pieces with another that behaves in the same way but with different implementations. What about starting with the Database access?

All those `Zend_DB_Adapter` connections (or straight MySQL commands if that's your case) are asking to be promoted to some sort of object that encapsulates fetching and persisting Idea objects. They are begging for being a Repository.

Repositories and the Persistence Edge

Whether there is a change in the business rules or in the infrastructure, we must edit the same piece of code. Believe me, in CS, you don't want many people touching the same piece of code for different reasons. Try to make your functions do one and just one thing so it is less probable having people messing around with the same piece of code. You can learn more about this by having a look at the **Single Responsibility Principle (SRP)**. For more information about this principle: `http://www.objectmentor.com/resources/articles/sr p.pdf`

Listing 1 is clearly this case. If we want to move to Redis or add the author notification feature, you'll have to update the `rateAction` method. Chances to affect aspects of the `rateAction` not related with the one updating are high. Listing 1 code is fragile. If it is common in your team to hear *If it works, don't touch it*, SRP is missing.

So, we must decouple our code and encapsulate the responsibility for dealing with fetching and persisting ideas into another object. The best way, as explained before, is using a Repository. Challenged accepted! Let's see the results in Listing 2:

```
class IdeaController extends Zend_Controller_Action
{
    public function rateAction()
    {
        $ideaId = $this->request->getParam('id');
        $rating = $this->request->getParam('rating');

        $ideaRepository = new IdeaRepository();
        $idea = $ideaRepository->find($ideaId);
        if (!$idea) {
            throw new Exception('Idea does not exist');
        }

        $idea->addRating($rating);
        $ideaRepository->update($idea);

        $this->redirect('/idea/' . $ideaId);
    }
}
```

```
class IdeaRepository
{
    private $client;

    public function __construct()
    {
        $this->client = new Zend_Db_Adapter_Pdo_Mysql([
            'host' => 'localhost',
            'username' => 'idy',
            'password' => '',
            'dbname' => 'idy'
        ]);
    }

    public function find($id)
    {
        $sql = 'SELECT * FROM ideas WHERE idea_id = ?';
        $row = $this->client->fetchRow($sql, $id);
        if (!$row) {
            return null;
        }

        $idea = new Idea();
        $idea->setId($row['id']);
        $idea->setTitle($row['title']);
        $idea->setDescription($row['description']);
        $idea->setRating($row['rating']);
        $idea->setVotes($row['votes']);
        $idea->setAuthor($row['email']);

        return $idea;
    }

    public function update(Idea $idea)
    {
        $data = [
            'title' => $idea->getTitle(),
            'description' => $idea->getDescription(),
            'rating' => $idea->getRating(),
            'votes' => $idea->getVotes(),
            'email' => $idea->getAuthor(),
        ];

        $where = ['idea_id = ?' => $idea->getId()];
        $this->client->update('ideas', $data, $where);
    }
}
```

The result is nicer. The `rateAction` of the `IdeaController` is more understandable. When read, it talks about business rules. `IdeaRepository` is a **business concept**. When talking with business guys, they understand what an `IdeaRepository` is: A place where I put Ideas and get them.

A Repository *mediates between the domain and data mapping layers using a collection-like interface for accessing domain objects.* as found in Martin Fowler's pattern catalog.

If you are already using an ORM such as Doctrine, your current repositories extend from an `EntityRepository`. If you need to get one of those repositories, you ask Doctrine `EntityManager` to do the job. The resulting code would be almost the same, with an extra access to the `EntityManager` in the controller action to get the `IdeaRepository`.

At this point, we can see in the landscape one of the edges of our hexagon, the *persistence* edge. However, this side is not well drawn, there is still some relationship between what an `IdeaRepository` is and how it is implemented.

In order to make an effective separation between our *application boundary* and the *infrastructure boundary* we need an additional step. We need to explicitly decouple behavior from implementation using some sort of interface.

Decoupling Business and Persistence

Have you ever experienced the situation when you start talking to your Product Owner, Business Analyst or Project Manager about your issues with the Database? Can you remember their faces when explaining how to persist and fetch an object? They had no idea what you were talking about.

The truth is that they don't care, but that's ok. If you decide to store the ideas in a MySQL server, Redis or SQLite it is your problem, not theirs. Remember, from a business standpoint, **your infrastructure is a detail**. Business rules are not going to change whether you use Symfony or Zend Framework, MySQL or PostgreSQL, REST or SOAP, and so on.

That's why it is important to decouple our `IdeaRepository` from its implementation. The easiest way is to use a proper interface. How can we achieve that? Let's take a look at Listing 3.

```php
class IdeaController extends Zend_Controller_Action
{
    public function rateAction()
    {
        $ideaId = $this->request->getParam('id');
```

```
        $rating = $this->request->getParam('rating');

        $ideaRepository = new MySQLIdeaRepository();
        $idea = $ideaRepository->find($ideaId);
        if(!$idea) {
            throw new Exception('Idea does not exist');
        }

        $idea->addRating($rating);
        $ideaRepository->update($idea);

        $this->redirect('/idea/' . $ideaId);
    }
}

interface IdeaRepository
{
    /**
     * @param int $id
     * @return null|Idea
     */
    public function find($id);

    /**
     * @param Idea $idea
     */
    public function update(Idea $idea);
}

class MySQLIdeaRepository implements IdeaRepository
{
    // ...
}
```

Easy, isn't it? We have extracted the `IdeaRepository` behavior into an interface, renamed the `IdeaRepository` into `MySQLIdeaRepository` and updated the `rateAction` to use our `MySQLIdeaRepository`. But what's the benefit?

We can now exchange the repository used in the controller with any implementing the same interface. So, let's try a different implementation.

Migrating our Persistence to Redis

During the sprint and after talking to some mates, you realize that using a NoSQL strategy could improve the performance of your feature. Redis is one of your best friends. Go for it and show me your Listing 4:

```
class IdeaController extends Zend_Controller_Action
{
    public function rateAction()
    {
        $ideaId = $this->request->getParam('id');
        $rating = $this->request->getParam('rating');

        $ideaRepository = new RedisIdeaRepository();
        $idea = $ideaRepository->find($ideaId);
        if (!$idea) {
            throw new Exception('Idea does not exist');
        }

        $idea->addRating($rating);
        $ideaRepository->update($idea);

        $this->redirect('/idea/' . $ideaId);
    }
}

interface IdeaRepository
{
    // ...
}

class RedisIdeaRepository implements IdeaRepository
{
    private $client;

    public function __construct()
    {
        $this->client = new Predis\Client();
    }

    public function find($id)
    {
        $idea = $this->client->get($this->getKey($id));
        if (!$idea) {
            return null;
        }
        return unserialize($idea);
```

```
        }

        public function update(Idea $idea)
        {
            $this->client->set(
                $this->getKey($idea->getId()),
                serialize($idea)
            );
        }

        private function getKey($id)
        {
            return 'idea:' . $id;
        }
    }
```

Easy again. You've created a `RedisIdeaRepository` that implements `IdeaRepository`
interface and we have decided to use Predis as a connection manager. Code looks smaller,
easier and faster. But what about the controller? It remains the same, we have just changed
which repository to use, but it was just one line of code.

As an exercise for the reader, try to create the `IdeaRepository` for SQLite, a file or an in-
memory implementation using arrays. Extra points if you think about how ORM
Repositories fit with Domain Repositories and how ORM *@annotations* affect this
architecture.

Decouple Business and Web Framework

We have already seen how easy it can be to changing from one persistence strategy to
another. However, the persistence is not the only edge from our Hexagon. What about how
the user interacts with the application?

Your CTO has set up in the roadmap that your team is moving to Symfony2, so when
developing new features in you current ZF1 application, we would like to make the
incoming migration easier. That's tricky, show me your Listing 5:

```
    class IdeaController extends Zend_Controller_Action
    {
        public function rateAction()
        {
            $ideaId = $this->request->getParam('id');
            $rating = $this->request->getParam('rating');

            $ideaRepository = new RedisIdeaRepository();
```

```
        $useCase = new RateIdeaUseCase($ideaRepository);
        $response = $useCase->execute($ideaId, $rating);

        $this->redirect('/idea/' . $ideaId);
    }
}

interface IdeaRepository
{
    // ...
}

class RateIdeaUseCase
{
    private $ideaRepository;

    public function __construct(IdeaRepository $ideaRepository)
    {
        $this->ideaRepository = $ideaRepository;
    }

    public function execute($ideaId, $rating)
    {
        try {
            $idea = $this->ideaRepository->find($ideaId);
        } catch(Exception $e) {
            throw new RepositoryNotAvailableException();
        }

        if (!$idea) {
            throw new IdeaDoesNotExistException();
        }

        try {
            $idea->addRating($rating);
            $this->ideaRepository->update($idea);
        } catch(Exception $e) {
            throw new RepositoryNotAvailableException();
        }

        return $idea;
    }
}
```

Let's review the changes. Our controller is not having any business rules at all. We have pushed all the logic inside a new object called `RateIdeaUseCase` that encapsulates it. This object is also known as Controller, Interactor or Application Service.

The magic is done by the `execute` method. All the dependencies such as the `RedisIdeaRepository` are passed as an argument to the constructor. All the references to an `IdeaRepository` inside our UseCase are pointing to the interface instead of any concrete implementation.

That's really cool. If you take a look inside `RateIdeaUseCase`, there is nothing talking about MySQL or Zend Framework. No references, no instances, no annotations, nothing. It is like your infrastructure does not mind. It just talks about business logic.

Additionally, we have also tuned the Exceptions we throw. Business processes also have exceptions. `NotAvailableRepository` and `IdeaDoesNotExist` are two of them. Based on the one being thrown we can react in different ways in the framework boundary.

Sometimes, the number of parameters that a UseCase receives can be too many. In order to organize them, it is quite common to build a *UseCase request* using a **Data Transfer Object (DTO)** to pass them together. Let's see how you could solve this in Listing 6:

```
class IdeaController extends Zend_Controller_Action
{
    public function rateAction()
    {
        $ideaId = $this->request->getParam('id');
        $rating = $this->request->getParam('rating');

        $ideaRepository = new RedisIdeaRepository();
        $useCase = new RateIdeaUseCase($ideaRepository);
        $response = $useCase->execute(
            new RateIdeaRequest($ideaId, $rating)
        );

        $this->redirect('/idea/' . $response->idea->getId());
    }
}

class RateIdeaRequest
{
    public $ideaId;
    public $rating;

    public function __construct($ideaId, $rating)
    {
        $this->ideaId = $ideaId;
```

```
            $this->rating = $rating;
        }
    }

    class RateIdeaResponse
    {
        public $idea;

        public function __construct(Idea $idea)
        {
            $this->idea = $idea;
        }
    }

    class RateIdeaUseCase
    {
        // ...

        public function execute($request)
        {
            $ideaId = $request->ideaId;
            $rating = $request->rating;

            // ...

            return new RateIdeaResponse($idea);
        }
    }
```

The main changes here are introducing two new objects, a Request and a Response. They are not mandatory, maybe a UseCase has no request or response. Another important detail is how you build this request. In this case, we are building it getting the parameters from ZF request object.

Ok, but wait, what's the real benefit? it is easier to change from one framework to other, or execute our UseCase from another *delivery mechanism*. Let's see this point.

Rating an Idea Using the API

During the day, your Product Owner comes to you and says: *by the way, a user should be able to rate an idea using our mobile app. I think we will need to update the API, could you do it for this sprint?*. Here's the PO again. *No problem!*. Business is impressed with your commitment.

As Robert C. Martin says: *The Web is a delivery mechanism [...] Your system architecture should be as ignorant as possible about how it is to be delivered. You should be able to deliver it as a console app, a web app, or even a web service app, without undue complication or any change to the fundamental architecture.*

Your current API is built using Silex, the PHP micro-framework based on the Symfony2 Components. Let's go for it in Listing 7:

```
require_once __DIR__.'/../vendor/autoload.php';

$app = new Silex\Application();

// ... more routes

$app->get(
    '/api/rate/idea/{ideaId}/rating/{rating}',
    function ($ideaId, $rating) use ($app) {
        $ideaRepository = new RedisIdeaRepository();
        $useCase = new RateIdeaUseCase($ideaRepository);
        $response = $useCase->execute(
            new RateIdeaRequest($ideaId, $rating)
        );

        return $app->json($response->idea);
    }
);

$app->run();
```

Is there anything familiar to you? Can you identify some code that you have seen before? I'll give you a clue:

```
$ideaRepository = new RedisIdeaRepository();
$useCase = new RateIdeaUseCase($ideaRepository);
$response = $useCase->execute(
    new RateIdeaRequest($ideaId, $rating)
);
```

Man! I remember those 3 lines of code. They look exactly the same as the web application. That's right, because the UseCase encapsulates the business rules you need to prepare the request, get the response and act accordingly.

We are providing our users with another way for rating an idea; another *delivery mechanism*. The main difference is where we created the `RateIdeaRequest` from. In the first example, it was from a ZF request and now it is from a Silex request using the parameters matched in the route.

Console App Rating

Sometimes, a UseCase is going to be executed from a Cron job or the command line. As examples, batch processing or some testing command lines to accelerate the development. While testing this feature using the web or the API, you realize that it would be nice to have a command line to do it, so you don't have to go through the browser.

If you are using shell scripts files, I suggest you to check the Symfony Console component. What would the code look like:

```php
namespace Idy\Console\Command;

use Symfony\Component\Console\Command\Command;
use Symfony\Component\Console\Input\InputArgument;
use Symfony\Component\Console\Input\InputInterface;
use Symfony\Component\Console\Output\OutputInterface;

class VoteIdeaCommand extends Command
{
    protected function configure()
    {
        $this
            ->setName('idea:rate')
            ->setDescription('Rate an idea')
            ->addArgument('id', InputArgument::REQUIRED)
            ->addArgument('rating', InputArgument::REQUIRED);
    }

    protected function execute(
        InputInterface $input,
        OutputInterface $output
    ) {
        $ideaId = $input->getArgument('id');
        $rating = $input->getArgument('rating');

        $ideaRepository = new RedisIdeaRepository();
        $useCase = new RateIdeaUseCase($ideaRepository);
        $response = $useCase->execute(
            new RateIdeaRequest($ideaId, $rating)
        );

        $output->writeln('Done!');
    }
}
```

Again those 3 lines of code. As before, the UseCase and its business logic remain untouched, we are just providing a new *delivery mechanism*. Congratulations, you've discovered the *user side* hexagon edge.

There is still a lot to do. As you may have heard, a real craftsman does TDD. We have already started our story so we must be ok with just testing after.

Testing Rating an Idea UseCase

Michael Feathers introduced a definition of legacy code as *code without tests*. You don't want your code to be legacy just born, do you?

In order to unit test this UseCase object, you decide to start with the easiest part, what happens if the repository is not available? How can we generate such behavior? Do we stop our Redis server while running the unit tests? No. We need to have an object that has such behavior. Let's use a *mock* object in Listing 9:

```php
class RateIdeaUseCaseTest extends \PHPUnit_Framework_TestCase
{
    /**
     * @test
     */
    public function whenRepositoryNotAvailableAnExceptionIsThrown()
    {
        $this->setExpectedException('NotAvailableRepositoryException');
        $ideaRepository = new NotAvailableRepository();
        $useCase = new RateIdeaUseCase($ideaRepository);
        $useCase->execute(
            new RateIdeaRequest(1, 5)
        );
    }
}

class NotAvailableRepository implements IdeaRepository
{
    public function find($id)
    {
        throw new NotAvailableException();
    }

    public function update(Idea $idea)
    {
        throw new NotAvailableException();
    }
}
```

Nice. `NotAvailableRepository` has the behavior that we need and we can use it with `RateIdeaUseCase` because it implements `IdeaRepository` interface.

Next case to test is what happens if the idea is not in the repository. Listing 10 shows the code:

```php
class RateIdeaUseCaseTest extends \PHPUnit_Framework_TestCase
{
    // ...

    /**
     * @test
     */
    public function whenIdeaDoesNotExistAnExceptionShouldBeThrown()
    {
        $this->setExpectedException('IdeaDoesNotExistException');
        $ideaRepository = new EmptyIdeaRepository();
        $useCase = new RateIdeaUseCase($ideaRepository);
        $useCase->execute(
            new RateIdeaRequest(1, 5)
        );
    }
}

class EmptyIdeaRepository implements IdeaRepository
{
    public function find($id)
    {
        return null;
    }

    public function update(Idea $idea)
    {

    }
}
```

Here, we use the same strategy but with an `EmptyIdeaRepository`. It also implements the same interface but the implementation always returns null regardless which identifier the find method receives.

Why are we testing these cases?, remember Kent Beck's words: *Test everything that could possibly break.*

Let's carry on with the rest of the feature. We need to check a special case that is related with having a read available repository where we cannot write to. Solution can be found in Listing 11:

```php
class RateIdeaUseCaseTest extends \PHPUnit_Framework_TestCase
{
    // ...

    /**
     * @test
     */
    public function whenRatingAnIdeaNewRatingShouldBeAdded()
    {
        $ideaRepository = new OneIdeaRepository();
        $useCase = new RateIdeaUseCase($ideaRepository);
        $response = $useCase->execute(
            new RateIdeaRequest(1, 5)
        );

        $this->assertSame(5, $response->idea->getRating());
        $this->assertTrue($ideaRepository->updateCalled);
    }
}

class OneIdeaRepository implements IdeaRepository
{
    public $updateCalled = false;

    public function find($id)
    {
        $idea = new Idea();
        $idea->setId(1);
        $idea->setTitle('Subscribe to php[architect]');
        $idea->setDescription('Just buy it!');
        $idea->setRating(5);
        $idea->setVotes(10);
        $idea->setAuthor('john@example.com');

        return $idea;
    }

    public function update(Idea $idea)
    {
        $this->updateCalled = true;
    }
}
```

Ok, now the key part of the feature is still remaining. We have different ways of testing this, we can write our own mock or use a mocking framework such as Mockery or Prophecy. Let's choose the first one. Another interesting exercise would be to write this example and the previous ones using one of these frameworks:

```php
class RateIdeaUseCaseTest extends \PHPUnit_Framework_TestCase
{
    // ...

    /**
     * @test
     */
    public function whenRatingAnIdeaNewRatingShouldBeAdded()
    {
        $ideaRepository = new OneIdeaRepository();
        $useCase = new RateIdeaUseCase($ideaRepository);
        $response = $useCase->execute(
            new RateIdeaRequest(1, 5)
        );

        $this->assertSame(5, $response->idea->getRating());
        $this->assertTrue($ideaRepository->updateCalled);
    }
}

class OneIdeaRepository implements IdeaRepository
{
    public $updateCalled = false;

    public function find($id)
    {
        $idea = new Idea();
        $idea->setId(1);
        $idea->setTitle('Subscribe to php[architect]');
        $idea->setDescription('Just buy it!');
        $idea->setRating(5);
        $idea->setVotes(10);
        $idea->setAuthor('john@example.com');

        return $idea;
    }

    public function update(Idea $idea)
    {
        $this->updateCalled = true;
    }
}
```

Bam! 100% Coverage for the UseCase. Maybe, next time we can do it using TDD so the test will come first. However, testing this feature was really easy because of the way decoupling is promoted in this architecture.
Maybe you are wondering about this:

```
$this->updateCalled = true;
```

We need a way to guarantee that the update method has been called during the UseCase execution. This does the trick. This *test double* object is called a *spy, mocks* cousin.

When to use mocks? As a general rule, use mocks when crossing boundaries. In this case, we need mocks because we are crossing from the domain to the persistence boundary.

What about testing the infrastructure?

Testing Infrastructure

If you want to achieve 100% coverage for your whole application you will also have to test your infrastructure. Before doing that, you need to know that those unit tests will be more coupled to your implementation than the business ones. That means that the probability to be broken with implementation details changes is higher. So it is a trade-off you will have to consider.

So, if you want to continue, we need to do some modifications. We need to decouple even more. Let's see the code in Listing 13:

```
class IdeaController extends Zend_Controller_Action
{
    public function rateAction()
    {
        $ideaId = $this->request->getParam('id');
        $rating = $this->request->getParam('rating');

        $useCase = new RateIdeaUseCase(
            new RedisIdeaRepository(
                new Predis\Client()
            )
        );

        $response = $useCase->execute(
            new RateIdeaRequest($ideaId, $rating)
        );

        $this->redirect('/idea/' . $response->idea->getId());
```

```
        }
    }

    class RedisIdeaRepository implements IdeaRepository
    {
        private $client;

        public function __construct($client)
        {
            $this->client = $client;
        }

        // ...

        public function find($id)
        {
            $idea = $this->client->get($this->getKey($id));
            if (!$idea) {
                return null;
            }

            return $idea;
        }
    }
}
```

If we want to 100% unit test `RedisIdeaRepository` we need to be able to pass the `Predis\Client` as a parameter to the repository without specifying TypeHinting so we can pass a mock to force the code flow necessary to cover all the cases.

This forces us to update the Controller to build the Redis connection, pass it to the repository and pass the result to the UseCase.

Now, it is all about creating mocks, test cases and having fun doing asserts.

Arggg, So Many Dependencies!

Is it normal that I have to create so many dependencies by hand? No. It is common to use a Dependency Injection component or a Service Container with such capabilities. Again, Symfony comes to the rescue, however, you can also check `PHP-DI` 4.

Let's see the resulting code in Listing 14 after applying Symfony Service Container component to our application:

```php
class IdeaController extends ContainerAwareController
{
    public function rateAction()
    {
        $ideaId = $this->request->getParam('id');
        $rating = $this->request->getParam('rating');

        $useCase = $this->get('rate_idea_use_case');
        $response = $useCase->execute(
            new RateIdeaRequest($ideaId, $rating)
        );

        $this->redirect('/idea/' . $response->idea->getId());
    }
}
```

The controller has been modified to have access to the container, that's why it is inheriting from a new base controller `ContainerAwareController` that has a `get` method to retrieve each of the services contained:

```xml
<?xml version="1.0" ?>
<container xmlns="http://symfony.com/schema/dic/services"
    xmlns:xsi="http://www.w3.org/2001/XMLSchema-instance"
    xsi:schemaLocation="
        http://symfony.com/schema/dic/services
        http://symfony.com/schema/dic/services/services-1.0.xsd">
    <services>
        <service
            id="rate_idea_use_case"
            class="RateIdeaUseCase">
            <argument type="service" id="idea_repository" />
        </service>

        <service
            id="idea_repository"
            class="RedisIdeaRepository">
            <argument type="service">
                <service class="Predis\Client" />
            </argument>
        </service>
    </services>
</container>
```

In Listing 15, you can also find the XML file used to configure the Service Container. It is really easy to understand but if you need more information, take a look to the Symfony Service Container Component site in.

Domain Services and Notification Hexagon Edge

Are we forgetting something? *the author should be notified by email*, yeah! That's true. Let's see in Listing 16 how we have updated the UseCase for doing the job:

```
class RateIdeaUseCase
{
    private $ideaRepository;
    private $authorNotifier;

    public function __construct(
        IdeaRepository $ideaRepository,
        AuthorNotifier $authorNotifier
    ) {
        $this->ideaRepository = $ideaRepository;
        $this->authorNotifier = $authorNotifier;
    }

    public function execute(RateIdeaRequest $request)
    {
        $ideaId = $request->ideaId;
        $rating = $request->rating;

        try {
            $idea = $this->ideaRepository->find($ideaId);
        } catch(Exception $e) {
            throw new RepositoryNotAvailableException();
        }

        if (!$idea) {
            throw new IdeaDoesNotExistException();
        }

        try {
            $idea->addRating($rating);
            $this->ideaRepository->update($idea);
        } catch(Exception $e) {
            throw new RepositoryNotAvailableException();
        }
```

```
    try {
        $this->authorNotifier->notify(
            $idea->getAuthor()
        );
    } catch(Exception $e) {
        throw new NotificationNotSentException();
    }

    return $idea;
    }
}
```

As you realize, we have added a new parameter for passing `AuthorNotifier` Service that will send the email to the author. This is the *port* in the *Ports and Adapters* naming. We have also updated the business rules in the execute method.

Repositories are not the only objects that may access your infrastructure and should be decoupled using interfaces or abstract classes. Domain Services can too. When there is a behavior not clearly owned by just one Entity in your domain, you should create a Domain Service. A typical pattern is to write an abstract Domain Service that has some concrete implementation and some other abstract methods that the *adapter* will implement.

As an exercise, define the implementation details for the `AuthorNotifier` abstract service. Options are SwiftMailer or just plain `mail` calls. It is up to you.

Let's Recap

In order to have a *clean architecture* that helps you create easy to write and test applications, we can use Hexagonal Architecture. To achieve that, we encapsulate user story business rules inside a UseCase or Interactor object. We build the UseCase request from our framework request, instantiate the UseCase and all its dependencies and then execute it. We get the response and act accordingly based on it. If our framework has a Dependency Injection component you can use it to simplify the code.

The same UseCase objects can be used from different *delivery mechanisms* in order to allow users access the features from different clients (web, API, console, and so on.)

For testing, play with mocks that behave like all the interfaces defined so special cases or error flows can also be covered. Enjoy the good job done.

Hexagonal Architecture

In almost all the blogs and books you will find drawings about concentric circles representing different areas of software. As Robert C. Martin explains in his *Clean Architecture* post, the outer circle is where your infrastructure resides. The inner circle is where your Entities live. The overriding rule that makes this architecture work is **The Dependency Rule**. This rule says that source code dependencies can only point inwards. Nothing in an inner circle can know anything at all about something in an outer circle.

Key Points

Use this approach if 100% unit test code coverage is important to your application. Also, if you want to be able to switch your storage strategy, web framework or any other type of third-party code. The architecture is especially useful for long-lasting applications that need to keep up with changing requirements.

What's Next?

If you are interested in learning more about Hexagonal Architecture and other near concepts you should review the related URLs provided at the beginning of the article, take a look at CQRS and Event Sourcing. Also, don't forget to subscribe to google groups and RSS about DDD such as `http://dddinphp.org`and follow on Twitter people like `@VaughnVernon`, and `@ericevans0`.

Bibliography

Beck, Kent. Test-Driven Development: By Example. Addison-Wesley Professional, 2002.

Brandolini, Alberto. Introducing EventStorming. Leanpub, 2016.

Evans, Eric. Domain-Driven Design Reference: Definitions and Pattern Summaries. Dog Ear Publishing, 2014.

Evans, Eric. Domain-Driven Design: Tackling Complexity in the Heart of Software. Addison-Wesley Professional, 2003.

Fowler, Martin. Patterns of Enterprise Application Architecture. Addison-Wesley Professional, 2002.

Hohpe, Gregor, and Bobby Woolf. Enterprise Integration Patterns: Designing, Building, and Deploying Messaging Solutions. Addison-Wesley Professional, 2012.

Martin, Robert C. Agile Software Development, Principles, Patterns, and Practices. Pearson, 2002.

Martin, Robert C. Clean Code: A Handbook of Agile Software Craftsmanship. Prentice Hall, 2008.

Meszaros, Gerard. xUnit Test Patterns: Refactoring Test Code. Addison-Wesley Professional, 2007.

Newman, Sam. Building Microservices. O'Reilly Media, 2015.

Nilsson, Jimmy. `Applying Domain-Driven Design and Patterns: With Examples in C# and .NET`. Addison-Wesley Professional, 2006.

Sadalage, Pramod J., and Martin Fowler. `NoSQL Distilled: A Brief Guide to the Emerging World of Polyglot Persistence`. Addison-Wesley Professional, 2012.

Vernon, Vaughn. `Domain-Driven Design Distilled`. Addison-Wesley Professional, 2016.

Vernon, Vaughn. `Implementing Domain-Driven Design`. Addison-Wesley Professional, 2013.

The End

Congratulations, you've finished the book! We wanted to personally thank you, without your support and feedback this book would have never been possible. It has been an incredible journey, we feel very fortunate to count on you. We really hope you enjoyed the ride as much as we did.

We've been obsessed about delivering the best experience possible to our readers. We've iterated over and over the contents of the book based on your incredible feedback. If there is anything we can improve, please help us by `opening an issue in our Github project`.

If you liked it and was useful to you, it might be useful for others too! Feel free to `share your experience in Twitter` or `give us a review in Goodreads`.

Thanks again!

– Carlos, Christian and Keyvan

Index

W